BUILDING *with* STRUCTURAL INSULATED PANELS (SIPs)

BUILDING *with* STRUCTURAL INSULATED PANELS (SIPs)

Strength and Energy Efficiency through Structural Panel Construction

MICHAEL MORLEY

The Taunton Press

Cover photo courtesy Insulspan Inc.

Publisher: JIM CHILDS
Acquisitions Editor: STEVE CULPEPPER
Editors: ANDREW WORMER, PETER CHAPMAN
Copy Editor: DIANE SINITSKY
Indexer: HARRIET HODGES
Layout Artist: ROSALIE VACCARO
Photographer: MICHAEL MORLEY (EXCEPT WHERE NOTED)
Illustrator: RON CARBONI

Taunton
BOOKS & VIDEOS
for fellow enthusiasts

Printed in the United States of America
10 9 8 7 6 5 4 3 2 1

The Taunton Press, Inc., 63 South Main Street,
PO Box 5506, Newtown, CT 06470-5506
e-mail: tp@taunton.com

Distributed by Publishers Group West

Library of Congress Cataloging-in-Publication Data
Morley, Michael.
      Building with structural insulated panels (SIPs) / Michael Morley.
        p.   cm.
      Includes index.
      ISBN 1-56158-351-0
        1. Prefabricated houses. 2. Wall panels. 3. Exterior walls.
      4. Modular construction. 5. Dwellings—Insulation. I. Title.
      TH4819.P7 M63   2000
      693′.97—dc21   00-037394

Acknowledgments

I would like to thank some people without whose help this project would never have been completed: Steve Culpepper and Carol Kasper at The Taunton Press for sticking their necks out and believing in this project and editors Andrew Wormer and Peter Chapman for creating order and logic out of chaos and energy. Special thanks to Jim Tracy at SIPA for the professional reading and support and to Mic and Jim at Panel Built for opening up their bag of tricks for me. Thanks to all the manufacturers, suppliers, fabricators, architects, and Panelhead builders who contributed materials for this book and believe in the Power of Panels. And finally, thanks to my children, Amanda, Jackson, and Hazel, for picking up the slack around the house, and most of all to Angela, my wife and partner, for her love and support.

CONTENTS

(Photo courtesy SIPA.)

(Photo by Jon Blumb.)

INTRODUCTION

Every once in a while a new technology comes along that makes its predecessors obsolete. John Henry couldn't compete with the steam drill, power saws replaced handsaws, and drywall replaced plaster and lath. There is no going backward. Today, structural insulated panels (SIPs) are in the process of replacing the postwar norm of stick-framed, fiberglass-insulated houses and light commercial buildings. SIPs produce a structurally superior, better insulated, faster to erect, and more environmentally friendly house than before possible. This book will show you what a SIP is, how to decide if SIPs are for you, how to build with them, and where to find them. For homeowners as well as builders who want to build the best structure possible, this book is for you.

Since their introduction more than 60 years ago, SIPs have been used in many thousands of buildings and have been exhaustively tested, passing every barrier with flying colors. They are now a government- and industry-accepted material for residential and light commercial applications. Like most new materials, they have faced resistance from architects, builders, and home buyers because they are different and perceived of as limited in use and more expensive. However, with stable costs due to industry competition and manufacturing efficiencies, combined with the spiraling increase in lumber and labor costs, SIPs should be seriously considered by today's builders and conscientious home buyers.

I have been in the building business for more than 20 years, specializing in old-house restoration and remodeling. When I relocated my family and business from the West Coast back to the Midwest, I wanted to try my hand at new-home construction in addition to the bread-and-butter remodeling I had always done. I was surprised that the local builders were building basically the same old house they were building 26 years ago when I was a student at the University of Kansas. I was sure there had to be a better way to build a house than with 2xs and fiberglass insulation. That's when I found out about SIPs.

I read some articles and did some research on SIPs and

began to look for suppliers and to learn how to work with this new material. In 1995 my wife and I bought a lot and began plans for a SIP spec house. We didn't have anyone around here to ask questions of, so, with some help from the panel supplier, we jumped in with both feet. On that first project there were some bumps in the road and we did way too much manual lifting of the heavy panels, but we were hooked on the system. We found that SIPs are not difficult to work with and that there is a rapidly growing network of experienced builders to help with the learning curve.

You might ask what is so different about the SIP system. Here are a few of the advantages SIPs have over the standard stick-and-fiberglass approach to putting up buildings:

• From a material standpoint, SIPs take the place of a whole assembly. Instead of separate pieces of framing, insulation, and sheathing, a SIP panel incorporates all of these components and comes ready to install. Panels can be ordered from the factory with doors, windows, rakes, and blocking precut and assembled.

• The proven superiority in transverse- and axial-loading capabilities and increased racking resistance over conventional framing make SIPs a stronger, safer alternative.

• The insulation values for SIP panels are far superior to conventional framing and insulating methods. A SIP building is virtually airtight, giving the occupants more control over the interior environment. This energy efficiency will become increasingly important as the costs of heating fuels inevitably increase.

• A SIP shell can be erected much faster than a conventional shell. This increased speed enables builders to "close in" the job much faster. The enclosed space is more secure and provides a better environment for the other trades to begin their specialties.

• SIPs are environmentally friendly. Their facings are made from renewable, farm-grown trees, and none of their components contribute to environmental degradation. A SIP building helps reduce pollution by consuming much less heating and cooling energy. There is also much less waste

from a SIP-designed building than a conventional building, saving landfill space and reducing pollution from burning waste.

The SIP industry is poised to make a significant difference in the way people construct the buildings they live and work in. As a professional builder concerned about the sustainability of the building industry, I welcome the coming changes and want you, the reader, to understand how they will affect you. I'm keen to share what I have learned about this industry with my fellow builders and with potential homeowners who want the best home they can build. So let's take a close look at what's destined to become the preferred construction material of building professionals.

Chapter 1

STRUCTURAL INSULATED PANELS

The SIP Revolution

What Are SIPs?

Why Build with SIPs?

The SIP Industry Today

SIPs and the Building Community

Let's face it: The building business is changing. Labor costs continue to increase dramatically, and many builders are finding it hard to find young people who want to enter the construction trades. As current skilled journeymen carpenters end their careers, there just aren't enough skilled replacements coming along. Realizing that they need to build faster and with less-skilled help, builders are turning toward new building systems to maximize their labor resources.

An equally important factor in the changing building environment is that the availability of quality dimensional lumber is rapidly declining, while its price is fluctuating dramatically. The public's growing environmental awareness—in particular about the plight of our old-growth forests—has made the wholesale giveaways to the lumber companies a thing of the past. Engineered wood products are replacing structural lumber to meet builders' needs.

The result of these challenges is that many builders are cutting corners to meet demand. Based on my observations of the construction industry over the last 15 years, particularly of the residential sector, most houses are thrown up fast with little attention given to building a long-lasting, energy-efficient product. While this is due in part to increased labor and materials costs, builders say—with good reason—that the buying public cares more about having a two-story fake-

Structural insulated panels (SIPs) can be used to produce a structurally superior, better insulated, faster to erect, and more environmentally friendly house than before possible. (Photo courtesy Panel Built.)

stone-arched entry than about extra insulation in the walls and ceilings or a 90% efficient furnace because energy is now so cheap. A common complaint is that if more building dollars are spent on quality and energy efficiency, the added costs will drive a house out of a prospective buyer's price range. The construction roadside is littered with builders who have tried innovative technologies to resolve these dilemmas and who have not found a receptive market for their products.

The SIP Revolution

Structural insulated panels (SIPs) construction systems are rapidly revolutionizing the construction industry. Quite simply, SIPs are the proverbial better mousetrap whose time has finally come. My experience with these panels is that they are faster to erect, result in straighter, flatter walls, have excellent insulating properties,

and are significantly stronger than the antiquated stick-framing systems that are the norm in this country. The dimensional stability of SIPs means that there will be virtually no drywall callbacks caused by cracking seams, and the energy savings will result in significant savings in operational costs over the life of the building.

More and more people are talking about SIPs (at least, the mention of SIPs doesn't draw blank looks anymore among the builders I speak with). Over the past several years, the SIP industry has been experiencing a 35% annual growth rate. It is

SIPs can be fabricated into traditional forms, like the residence built above with Thermapan Industries panels, as well as more elaorate contemporary designs, like the one shown below. (Photos courtesy Thermapan Industries.)

an exciting time to be involved in this movement toward more sensible buildings. SIP manufacturers and builders who use SIPs feel as though the groundwork has been laid for a change in the way people look at the buildings they occupy. SIPs are a perfect fit with good passive solar design, energy-efficient windows and doors, high-efficiency heating and cooling systems, and small-is-beautiful thinking.

What Are SIPs?

SIPs, a "new" building material that has actually been in use since the 1940s, consist of two outer skins and an inner core of an insulating material to form a monolithic unit. Most structural panels use either plywood or oriented strand board (OSB) for their facings. OSB is the principal facing

material because it is available in large sizes (up to 12-ft. by 36-ft. sheets), and manufacturers have used OSB facings on structural panels used for the rigorous testing needed for code approvals. Structural panels can also have other materials, such as drywall, sheet metal, or finish lumber, laminated onto the OSB structural facings at the factory. This service eliminates one more step in the building process and speeds up assembly time.

The cores of SIPs can be made from a number of materials, including molded expanded polystyrene (EPS), extruded polystyrene (XPS), and urethane foam. Some SIP producers use isocyanurate foam as the core material, but since there is only a slight chemical difference between urethane and isocyanurate, I will refer to both of these core materials as urethane foam. Urethane foam panels comprise only about 5% of the panels produced.

The insulating core and the two skins of a SIP are nonstructural and insubstantial components in themselves, but when pressure-laminated together under strictly controlled conditions,

SIPs consist of an inner insulating core and two outer skins or facings. The author uses this corner and roof mock-up to demonstrate SIP connections.

Not All Building Panels Are SIPs

Building panels come in many configurations, known variously as foam-core panels, stress-skin panels, nail-base panels, sandwich panels, and curtain-wall panels, among others. Many of these building panels are nonstructural, while some have no insulation. And the term "panelized construction" can also include prefabricated stud walls and other configurations associated with the modular industry. But the focus of this book is on true structural insulated panels—panels that have self-supporting characteristics and that provide insulating properties to the exterior envelope of a building.

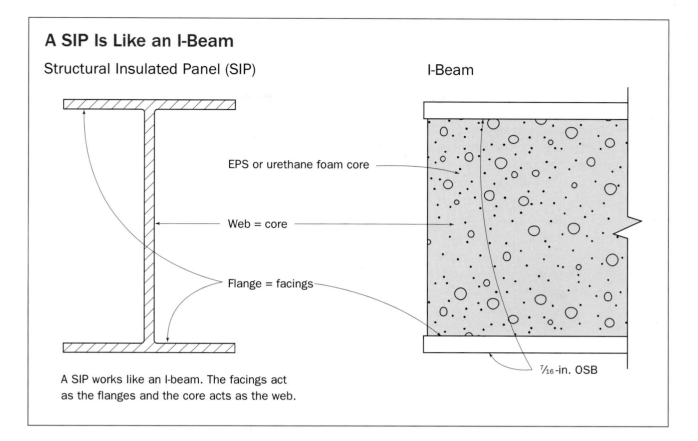

A SIP Is Like an I-Beam

Structural Insulated Panel (SIP)   I-Beam

EPS or urethane foam core

Web = core

Flange = facings

$^7/_{16}$-in. OSB

A SIP works like an I-beam. The facings act
as the flanges and the core acts as the web.

these materials act synergistically to form a
composite that is much stronger than the sum of
its parts. Panel manufacturers supply splines,
connectors, adhesives, and fasteners to erect their
systems. When engineered and assembled
properly, a structure built with these panels needs
no frame or skeleton to support it.

Structurally, a SIP can be compared to an
I-beam: The foam core acts as the web, while the
facings are analogous to the I-beam's flanges (see
the illustration above). All of the elements of a
SIP are stressed; the skins are in tension and
compression, while the core resists shear and
buckling. Under load, the facings of a SIP act as
slender columns, and the core stabilizes the
facings and resists forces trying to deflect the
columns. The thicker the core, the better the
panel resists buckling, so larger-core SIPs offer
more insulation and are stronger as well. (See

chapter 2 for a discussion of the chemistry and
structural properties of SIPs.)

Stock SIPs are produced in thicknesses from
4½ in. to 12¼ in. and in sizes from 4 ft. by 8 ft.
up to 9 ft. by 28 ft. Their R-values range from
about R-15 for a 4½-in. EPS or XPS panel to higher
than R-32 for a 6½-in. urethane panel. A 12¼-in.
EPS panel is rated at R-45. Custom sizes and
configurations are also available from some
manufacturers, and virtually any bondable
material can be applied as the facing material. The
flexibility of the manufacturing process means
that custom lengths and skins can be ordered for
nearly any application.

Currently, SIPs are used primarily in residential
and light commercial applications. While neither
EPS nor urethane foams (the main core materials)
are particularly flammable, they will burn when
exposed to flame, so their use in high-rise or

The Regulatory Environment

The manufacture and production of a material or an assembly of materials for sale in this country to use in structures that people live and work in is a highly regulated undertaking. In some areas, local building code enforcement authorities have been reluctant to accept SIPs because they are not familiar with the connection details and product testing results. But this situation is changing. The dominant code bodies—the Council of American Building Officials (CABO), the International Conference of Building Officials (ICBO), Building Officials and Code Administrators International (BOCA), and the Southern Building Code Congress International (SBCCI)—are being replaced by the International Residential Code (IRC), which went into effect in early 2000. The new IRC contains a section specifically establishing energy-related requirements for new construction.

There are also a number of signs that the U.S. government is taking steps to encourage greater awareness of energy issues and reward people who take this approach. Efforts by the Office of Science and Technology have led to the development of the Partnership for Advancing Technology in Housing (PATH). The PATH initiative seeks to reduce the environmental impact and energy use of new housing by 50% or more by 2010. SIPs are a featured technology in PATH's vision.

large public buildings without extensive fire suppression technology is limited. SIPs perform well under various flame and fire testing Most buildings higher than three stories are subject to a different set of building regulations due to the loads applied to the walls and floor systems. The current standard for this type of building is to construct the frame using structural steel members, then to infill the walls, floors, and partitions (see the sidebar at left). There is great potential for SIPs and curtain-wall panels to be used in these applications.

A brief history of SIPs

Some of the earliest examples of sandwich-panel technology can be found in the Usonian houses designed by Frank Lloyd Wright in the 1930s. These innovative structures were the result of Wright's attempt to incorporate beauty and simplicity into relatively low-cost houses. Some of the walls in these houses consisted of three layers of plywood and two layers of tar paper as structural elements. Unfortunately, these prototype wall designs lacked any insulation, so they were never produced on a large scale.

Alden B. Dow, an architecture student of Wright and brother of the founder of the Dow Chemical Co., experimented further with the concept. Concerned about energy efficiency and dwindling resources, Dow was dismayed by the lack of insulation in the Usonian projects. In 1950, he developed a structural panel with an insulating core, thus he is generally credited with producing the first structural insulated panels. His early houses were built in Midland, Michigan, using panels composed of 1⅝-in. Styrofoam cores and ⁵⁄₁₆-in. plywood facings for the load-bearing walls. The same panels were installed over roof framing on 42-in. centers. Some of these houses are still occupied today.

It wasn't long after this early experimentation with SIPs that some entrepreneurs tooled up to manufacture these new building materials. The

Alden B. Dow, a student of Frank Lloyd Wright, developed a structural panel with an insulating core and is considered the first practitioner of structural insulated panels. (Photos courtesy Alden B. Dow Archives.)

first significant manufacturing effort came in 1959 when the Koppers Company converted an auto production plant in Detroit into a SIP production facility. Koppers' production method involved blowing preexpanded Styrofoam beads between two sheets of plywood and bonding them with steam to the facings, which were already glued to a solid supporting framework.

Koppers' process was slow, and early SIP houses met unexpected resistance from carpenters' unions in the North. Fearing that SIP houses were constructed so rapidly that they would lose work, the unions deliberately slowed the erection process from the typical two days in the South to almost twice that in the northern states. In this period of inexpensive energy and labor, the panels weren't competitive in the marketplace, so Koppers left the residential business to build refrigeration components.

In the early 1960s, Alside Home Program made its entry into the SIP marketplace, introducing some significant improvements that drastically reduced the production time per panel from several hours to 20 minutes. But after several years of production and fewer than 100 SIP homes built, this company too was forced out of business due to lack of demand. It wasn't until the mid-1980s that a significant number of manufacturers began to produce SIPs and had the capability to meet the expected consumer demand.

Why now?

So what took SIPs so long to come of age? In industrial technology, there is invariably a lag between the invention and early development of a product and its acceptance into the mainstream of the industry, a delay that can last many years. There are many reasons for this delay. First, no one knows about the new product. Lack of performance data leaves doubt as to a product's safety and reliability. Second, users and potential consumers cannot easily access information about these new products.

General resistance to change can mean that even a much better mousetrap takes time to be accepted. This cycle of acceptability also allows for inherent problems associated with a new technology to be exposed and dealt with by the industry. The reliability of SIPs as a mainstream building material has been borne out by extensive industry testing and acceptance by all the model building codes. The American public is increasingly aware of widespread environmental problems, and green building materials and strategies have become an important consideration when designing sustainable buildings and communities. SIPs are the right material in the right place at the right time to be a cornerstone of this new approach to constructing the buildings we live and work in.

Why Build with SIPs?

The exterior envelope of a building creates a barrier from the elements for the comfort of the inhabitants. Many materials can be used to form that envelope, but none can do it as energy efficiently, as fast, as economically, and with as much design flexibility as SIPs. SIP system technology offers a number of advantages over

SIP walls go up quickly, which is a big part of the appeal of the SIP construction system.

conventional framing methods. Briefly, here is an overview of some of these advantages; they'll be discussed in greater depth in later chapters.

SIP structures are stronger

The structural integrity of a SIP building is significantly superior to a conventionally framed building in terms of shear resistance, flexural strength, compressive resistance, and uplift resistance. SIPs have undergone exhaustive testing by third-party testing firms. All of the major manufacturers are more than happy to provide National Evaluation Reports (NER) produced by the National Evaluation Service, Inc., for the BOCA, ICBO, and SBCCI code authorities.

Evidence of the superior performance of SIPs can be found in the real world, where SIP houses have survived earthquakes and hurricanes when the stick-built houses around them were destroyed. For example, a 1993 earthquake in Kobe, Japan, devastated a large section of that city, but SIP houses built with panels from Premier Industries (see Resources on p. 181) came through the earthquake virtually unscathed. SIP manufacturers have dramatically increased their sales to Japan over the last few years, in large part due to the structural integrity of the SIP system.

In another example, a SIP house was in the path of a tornado that struck Clermont, Georgia, in March 1998. The tornado destroyed 27 houses, including 7 homes near the SIP house. While the owner of the home lost 25 mature trees to the storm and half of its shingles, the house suffered

This SIP house suffered no structural damage when struck by falling trees. (Photo courtesy AFM Team Industries.)

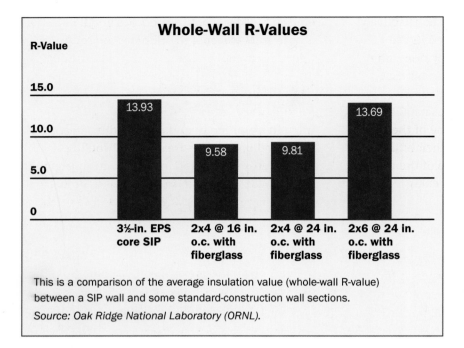

Whole-Wall R-Values

R-Value

13.93	9.58	9.81	13.69
3½-in. EPS core SIP	2x4 @ 16 in. o.c. with fiberglass	2x4 @ 24 in. o.c. with fiberglass	2x6 @ 24 in. o.c. with fiberglass

This is a comparison of the average insulation value (whole-wall R-value) between a SIP wall and some standard-construction wall sections.

Source: Oak Ridge National Laboratory (ORNL).

no structural damage. It's safe to assume that the neighbors will consider SIPs when they rebuild their homes.

SIP structures offer better thermal performance

Many side-by-side comparisons of stick-built versus SIP houses have been conducted over the years, with varying results depending on who conducted the tests and what methods were used. For example, in 1998 the Oak Ridge National Laboratory in Oak Ridge, Tennessee, completed thorough testing of various wall configurations. Results showed that a SIP wall with a 3½-in. EPS core had a 31% better insulation value than a conventional wall framed with 2x4s and insulated with fiberglass batts. The basic 3½-in.-core SIP wall also performed better than the 2x6 stick-built wall with fiberglass insulation (see the chart above). Even with recent spikes in fuel costs, energy prices will continue to climb, and the value of an energy-efficient building—a SIP building, for example—will increase.

SIP structures go up faster

The faster erection time of a SIP building can cut one to four weeks from the construction cycle. This can be a significant factor at a site with difficult access or when bad weather presents a constricted window of opportunity. The Energy Studies in Building Laboratory at the University of Oregon conducted extensive tests on stressed-skin insulated core (SSIC—their definition of a SIP) panels that closely monitored the labor required to erect one of these structures and its energy performance. They found that their SIP house was completed in 161 fewer hours compared with industry standards for stick-framed houses and that a SIP house required 34% less on-site construction time.

Builders across the country are finding that they can save time and money by erecting a ready-to-install wall assembly instead of having their carpenters construct the assembly on-site. In addition, SIP systems allow the use of less-skilled workers during erection. This factor will become increasingly important as the skilled labor force dwindles.

The fact that SIP structures can be effectively built by unskilled labor has resulted in the increased use of SIPs by Habitat for Humanity International, a nonprofit organization that produces affordable housing using mostly volunteer labor, which has more than 1,200 affiliates in the United States. Some of these affiliates are considering SIPs for their affordable housing projects not only because of the quick construction but also because the energy efficiency means that the occupants will be better able to heat and cool their homes in economically tight situations.

SIP buildings are more comfortable

Inhabitants of SIP homes and buildings report a high level of comfort. Heating and cooling is more evenly distributed in a SIP building, without the hot and cold spots found in conventional houses. The chart on p. 14, which shows interior

R-Values

An important consideration when specifying materials to be used in the envelope of a building is the material's thermal transmission qualities. The thermal resistance (R) is the unit of resistance to heat flow, expressed as the temperature difference required to cause heat to flow through a building material at the rate of one heat unit per hour (in U.S. practice, Btu/hour/ sq. ft.). The total thermal resistance (Rt) is the total resistance to heat flow through a complete building section expressed as the temperature difference in degrees Fahrenheit needed to cause heat to flow at the rate of 1 Btu/hour/sq. ft. of area. These values vary with different ambient temperatures and different moisture levels. From this formula, we can see that a higher R-value means that it takes longer for the material to allow the heat flow through the material.

The American Society of Heating, Refrigerating, and Air-Conditioning Engineers (ASHRAE) and the American Society for Testing and Materials (ASTM) have conducted comprehensive testing to establish technical standards for the thermal conductivity of various materials. These results are published in standard references such as the *ASHRAE Handbook of Fundamentals*. For more information, go to the websites www.ashrae.org and www.astm.org.

For a SIP panel, we are concerned with the R-values of expanded polystyrene (EPS), extruded polystyrene (XPS), and urethane and isocyanurate. The chart below offers a comparison of R-values for the cellular foam insulation materials only. For the total wall assembly R-values, you need to add the values of SIP facings as well as exterior and interior finishes.

Cellular Foam Insulation R-Values

Temperature	EPS	XPS	Urethane
75˚F	3.57	3.85	5.88
30˚F	3.85	4.17	5.88
0˚F	4.17	4.55	5.88

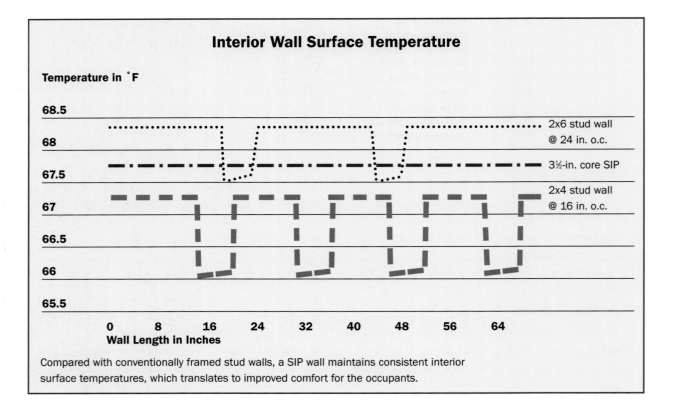

Interior Wall Surface Temperature

Temperature in °F

68.5
68 .... 2x6 stud wall @ 24 in. o.c.
67.5 — · — · — · — · — · — · — · — 3½-in. core SIP
67 ▬ ▬ ▬ ▬ 2x4 stud wall @ 16 in. o.c.
66.5
66
65.5

0   8   16   24   32   40   48   56   64
Wall Length in Inches

Compared with conventionally framed stud walls, a SIP wall maintains consistent interior surface temperatures, which translates to improved comfort for the occupants.

wall-surface temperatures, illustrates one of the main reasons a SIP building is more comfortable than a stick-framed building. The spikes in the 2x4 and 2x6 line graphs correspond to the drop in temperature at the stud locations as a result of thermal bridging. The continuous insulation of a SIP wall means even, comfortable interior temperatures.

SIP buildings are also much quieter inside, and the sound deadening offers respite from a noisy world. This is a difficult-to-measure quality of a home but one that has a significant effect on the occupants.

SIPs are the wave of the future

The SIP industry is in the midst of an expansion that many industry leaders predict will bring SIP technology to the forefront of residential and light commercial construction. The professional association that represents the industry is the Structural Insulated Panel Association (SIPA), formed in 1990 by SIP manufacturers. The mission of SIPA is to increase the use and

acceptance of SIPs by demonstrating to professionals and homeowners their technical superiority.

Besides promoting SIPs to designers, contractors, regulators, and homeowners, SIPA also helps develop industry standards for manufacturing and testing SIPs and promotes standards of ethics among industry members. While not all SIP manufacturers and suppliers are members of SIPA, the group represents most of the production capability of the industry. A recent SIPA study shows that the industry has experienced a 24% yearly growth rate between 1991 and 1994. Since then the growth rate has been more than 35% per year. SIPA estimates that 85 million sq. ft. of SIPs will be produced yearly over the next several years, a figure representing about 0.5% of the buildings built per year in this country. Although this is a very small percentage, it represents close to 100,000 SIP buildings.

Despite the steadily increasing volume, SIPA estimates that SIP production capabilities are operating well below capacity. As demand rises

The Structural Insulated Panel Association (SIPA) represents professional manufacturers, suppliers, architects, and builders. This logo appears on member literature.

www.sips.org

closer to capacity level, economies of scale will become a bigger factor and the costs to the consumer should come down, making SIPs even more attractive as a building material. And as the costs of dimensional lumber and skilled labor continue to increase at a rapid rate, SIP costs should become even more competitive.

The SIP Industry Today

In 2000, there were about 100 American manufacturers of SIPs. While SIP production is spread out over the country, the majority of manufacturers are located in the central and northeastern portions of the United States. There are also some manufacturing plants outside the United States. Quite a few domestic manufacturers are gaining footholds in international markets, particularly in countries with extreme climatic conditions or frequent earthquake activity, such as Japan. Countries that have limited wood resources or very high labor costs are also potential customers.

Manufacturers offer a wide range of services, which may include compatible foundation systems manufactured from foam-core panels or insulated concrete forms (ICFs). Engineering assistance for builders and homeowners is an important service, and on-site consulting and assistance are vital to help consumers get acquainted with this "new" technology. A number of the larger manufacturers offer precutting services and can send their own crews or subcontract out the erection work.

Large panel sizes mean fast site installation and fewer connections.

Another vital component in the industry are the custom fabricators/builders who typically shape the raw panels and install them for their customers. The customers here are likely to be high-end home buyers who demand a high level of service from the custom builder. These companies are the visible arm of the industry. Custom builders, along with architects and designers who specialize in SIP construction, are moving the industry forward, not with expensive ad campaigns but with customer satisfaction and solid word-of-mouth reputation. Finally, it will be

A SIP demonstration home was a popular attraction at the 1999 National Association of Home Builders (NAHB) show in Dallas.

The SIP industry is heading into high gear. There will likely be some fallout as larger companies absorb some of the smaller ones, while some companies will be forced out of business altogether by the competition. This is an inevitable part of growth and change, but right now the panel makers are enjoying this growth and its rewards. The companies that produce and fabricate panels with openings, rakes, and plumb cuts will likely get better at servicing their clients. At the same time, custom builders will be able to offer their customers more refined products and will keep that share of the market that needs its hand held tightly. And as with the construction industry in general, there will be the production builders who will build commercial buildings, tract homes, and the like.

There is an unfilled niche in the industry for companies that specialize in erecting SIP structures. In the near future, I expect to see a group of mobile erection companies for the SIP industry that would be similar to the custom grain harvesters that roam the midwestern plains like mechanized nomads. And there will always be a place for small contractors with nonmechanized crews; they will use SIPs because they want to offer a quality house to their customers. But what about the die-hard stick-framers? There will always be a special place in the museum of technology for these guys—maybe right next to John Henry.

SIPs and the Building Community

A growing number of smart builders are switching to the SIP system to satisfy the demands of an increasingly knowledgeable consumer base. SIP projects have been featured on the shows of popular home-improvement gurus Bob Vila and Norm Abram, generating considerable interest. All of these events hammer home the message that SIPs have finally arrived, offering more strength, more comfort, energy efficiency, and higher quality.

the consumers who "get it" who will drive this industry. An educated public aware of energy-efficient building possibilities will provide the biggest boost in production and sales.

Along with SIP manufacturers are the makers of the facings, cores, and adhesives used in the manufacture of SIPs. For example, the American Plywood Association (APA), now called the Engineered Wood Association, is the industry organization for engineered wood products. Its members produce the various skins for the SIP industry as well as the engineered products such as I-joists and laminated beams that are integral to a SIP house. There are also a number of manufacturers and suppliers of panel-related accessories and tools.

RJT Developers chose SIPS for the walls in this 330-home development shown above and right. (Photos courtesy Premier Industries.)

Large-volume builders

Until now, the small custom builder has been the leading force in spreading the word about SIPs. However, there are now some major homebuilding companies that are using SIPs for housing developments involving hundreds of houses. For example, RJT Development Co. recently built 330 homes in the Crown Hills housing development in Alpine, California, on a site originally designated for mobile homes. The builder wanted to offer a more substantial product than mobile homes but had to meet state requirements for factory-built components. Precut 6½-in. SIP walls helped meet these requirements, while the added volume given by vaulted ceilings and the homes' inherent energy efficiency helped attract buyers.

The development was begun in 1995, and by early 1998 all of the 1,200-sq.-ft. to 2,000-sq.-ft.

homes (which cost between $147,000 and $182,000) were sold. According to RJT, some of the rapid sales were due to the fact that the homes used only half of the energy of the stick-built competition, according to the local utility companies. In addition, the vaulted ceilings were easier to build and offered more curb appeal. The hard costs for the project were between $38 and $45 per sq. ft., which was only about $1 more per sq. ft. than conventional stick-built construction.

For large builders looking closely at the bottom line, changing to SIPs is not an easy decision. For the most part, potential home buyers are more interested in square footage and the bottom line than features that will save them thousands of dollars over the life of the building. However, the slight increase in production cost could easily be countered by energy savings and the power of "green" marketing. Success stories like the Crown Hills project always get attention from other builders, who do not want to miss any coming trends.

Small custom builders

The experience of my own company, Morley Inc. Builders, is probably fairly typical of a small contractor's first experience with the SIP system. In 1995, we built a spec house close to the Kansas City metropolitan area utilizing FischerSips panels (see Resources on p. 181). Architect Dan Hermreck designed a Prairie-style 4,000-sq.-ft. house for us that utilized 5½-in. SIP wall and roof panels. The house was designed on a 4-ft. grid to maximize panel coverage while generating very little waste, and the panels were extended over the eaves to give the house generous 3-ft. roof overhangs. This passive solar feature shields the home from the intense midwestern sun, while minimizing conventional stick-work framing around the exterior.

All of the walls and openings were fabricated in our shop from 4-ft.-wide panels and later erected manually on-site. When the roof package showed up, we had a crane sent to the site. With the

Architect Dan Hermreck collaborated with Morley Builders to design this 4,000-sq.-ft. Prairie-style SIP home in Baldwin City, Kansas.

FischerSips provided the 6½-in. panels for the walls and roof. The panels were extended over the eaves to give the house generous 3-ft. roof overhangs.

Building with SIPs allows for large, vaulted interior spaces. Here, a 52-ft.-long exposed glulam provides ridge support. (Photo courtesy Dan Hermreck.)

crane, we unloaded the stacks of panels from the semi and set one 52-ft.-long and one 40-ft.-long glulam beam and all eight of the full 8-ft. by 16-ft. gable-end roof panels in about six hours. We erected the remaining roof panels by hand.

With the help of some factory details, we developed a system that worked for us. FischerSips supplied us with a decent set of panel drawings and sent a complete package to work with, although we didn't like the idea of using the gutter spikes they sent to hold down the roof. We soon found out about Olympic panel screws (see Resources on p. 182) and substituted them for the gutter spikes. The shell went up in seven days and was "dried in" soon after, which let our subcontractors work in comfort as the Kansas winter set in.

Besides finding out about panel screws, we learned a lot of lessons on this first SIP

experience. For example, roof panels—even smaller cut sections—are too heavy to handle safely and efficiently, so we learned not to set any by hand after that first roof. We learned tricks to tighten the joints against air infiltration, and now we use a better insulated basement. All in all, this first house was a positive experience with a short learning curve and many tangible rewards, and it sold me on the SIP system. Our goal is now to build exclusively with SIPs.

As with any new system, there are lots of tricks and shortcuts to learn when working with SIPs. Fortunately, I've found a dedicated group of "panelheads" out there from all over the country eager to share experiences and move the industry forward one building at a time. Let's take a look now at what goes into a SIP and put the panels through their paces.

Chapter 2

ANATOMY OF A STRUCTURAL INSULATED PANEL

FACINGS

CORE MATERIALS

ADHESIVES

PUTTING THE PIECES
TOGETHER

TEST RESULTS

In the words of longtime SIP industry advocate Mic Carmichael of Panel Built Contractors, "We've come a long way from wood chips, glue, and old coffee cups." The reality is that the whole industry is based on an engineered application of these simple ingredients.

A structural insulated panel starts with some wood strands, phenol-formaldehyde glue, and polystyrene beads the size of sugar granules. In this chapter, I'll examine the materials that go into a structural insulated panel and the process that turns these ingredients into a SIP. Then I'll tell how the manufacturers try to crush, bend, rack, twist, and burn these panels, testing them to see if these products are good enough to build with.

The three main components of a SIP are the facings, the core material, and the adhesive agent that is used to bond the facings to the core. Pressure and setting time are also part of the equation and are used to help laminate these materials together.

According to the Forest Products Laboratory branch of the U.S. Department of Agriculture, a SIP is "a layered structural system composed of a low-density core material bonded to, and acting integrally with, relatively thin, high-strength facing materials. When used as a wall, roof, or floor system in housing, the sandwich panel provides exceptional strength for the amount of material used. In a load-bearing wall, the two

Most SIPs have a core of EPS sandwiched between two OSB facings. These panels, produced by Winter Panel, show the preferred wall connection: two thin splines with a center groove for a bead of expanding foam. (Photo courtesy Winter Panel.)

facings act as slender columns continuously supported by the core material to resist compression and buckling. In bending due to a live load or a wind load applied to a panel, the facings take most of the tensile and compressive forces and the core provides resistance to shear. The core and facings acting integrally provide exceptional stiffness to the member." I couldn't have said it better myself.

Most of the SIP panels (85% to 90%) produced in the United States are composed of two $\frac{7}{16}$-in.-thick OSB facings and a core of EPS. This OSB-EPS-OSB panel is the bread-and-butter panel of the SIP industry and will likely continue to be the standard panel for the foreseeable future.

Facings

Foam-core panels can be manufactured with any number of materials bonded to the core to make a building component, but OSB is the main material currently used for facings. The trend toward using different facings for specific applications is likely to continue to evolve.

OSB facings

There are two main reasons why OSB is the material of choice for SIP facings. First, it is an engineered wood product that has been extensively tested and found to be suitable for use as a load-bearing material. Second, it is readily available in the large sizes that are demanded by the SIP industry. OSB is not like any other glue-and-chip-based panels, such as particleboard, flakeboard, or waferboard. Since its invention in 1978, it has evolved into a high-tech panel that is changing to meet new demands.

Common thicknesses for OSB facings are $\frac{5}{16}$ in., $\frac{3}{8}$ in., $\frac{7}{16}$ in., $\frac{1}{2}$ in., $\frac{5}{8}$ in., and $\frac{3}{4}$ in. Theoretically, any of these thicknesses can be ordered for SIPs, but engineering test results aren't available for each panel thickness so the SIPs might not be covered under current code compliance reports. In addition, panels ordered in unusual thicknesses

About OSB

According to the APA-The Engineered Wood Association, OSB reached parity with plywood for structural use in residential construction by the early 1980s. Since then, the loss of old-growth timber has redefined the wood-products industry, and OSB's place in the market has grown even more. In 1990 OSB accounted for 20% of plywood production; now it accounts for almost 45%, an estimate of more than 10 billion sq. ft. in 1999. With more large-capacity plants coming on-line, the industry is poised to keep pace with the growing demand for this product, the availability of which affects SIP production more than any other element.

OSB begins with the harvesting of young, fast-growing trees, mainly aspen and southern yellow pine. After debarking, the logs are precision-cut into strands that are a maximum of 4 in. long and 0.0027 in. thick. These strands are graded and sent through dryers that can reach 1,400°F. Then the thin, rectangular-shaped wood strands are arranged in layers at right angles to one another, covered with liquid or powder resin waterproof glue, and laid up in mats that form a panel. For the face layers, the strands run along the panel, while for the core layers, the strands are oriented across the panel, giving OSB more strength along the length of the panel. These OSB mats are trimmed to size and bonded together under heat and pressure to create a structural panel.

Many new OSB mills are scaled for large production, and most can make panels up to

OSB has been accepted as a structural panel equivalent to plywood by the major code authorities. OSB facings on all certified SIPs should have a mill stamp, which assures the end user of code compliance.

8 ft. by 28 ft. For example, Dieffenbacher has four plants on-line capable of producing 12-ft. by 24-ft. panels. These large-size panels help to distribute the loads uniformly across the surface of the panel, which adds to the tensile strength of a SIP. With both OSB and SIPs, the limitations are not in the production but in the transportation and placement of the products.

aren't as readily available as those ordered in standard thicknesses.

OSB panels used by the SIP industry have a fully waterproof bond and carry the Exposure 1 rating of the APA, meaning that they are designed for applications where long construction delays could result in significant exposure to weather. Because of the tendency to absorb moisture on the edges and swell, many panels are treated with an edge sealant.

Other facings

The technology is available to laminate many materials, such as aluminum and steel sheet metal, fiber-reinforced plastic (FRP), various types of cement board, and many plywoods and finish wood products, to foam cores. Some manufacturers produce a panel that has drywall as the interior facing. None of these are rated as a structural panel nor do they have code listing, but they can be used as curtain wall panels and partitions when used with timber frames or structural-steel frames.

More and more, secondary laminations of materials onto one or both of the structural facings are becoming available. The main impediment to a larger variety of facings becoming rated for structural use is that each different configuration of panel has to undergo extensive testing required for CABO and ICBO code acceptance. Manufacturers are not willing to put forth this expenditure without some real volume demand for a particular configuration.

Once the SIP industry becomes a major player in the building materials supply chain, I anticipate that the panel buyer will be able to fill out an order form that specifies the type and thickness of exterior facing material with options for added laminations. The same selection of structural and finish elements will likely be available for the interior facings, and there's no reason why the buyer won't also be able to select the type and thickness of the core material. So, for example, a buyer might be able to specify a cement tile backerboard for the exterior facing (for direct application of stucco), a 5½-in. urethane core (for an R-33 wall insulation), and a fire-retarding finish over the OSB interior facing (to speed interior finishing).

Core Materials

There are three main categories of foam cores: EPS, XPS, and urethane foam. Each has unique properties, but all provide the structural and fire-resistance characteristics required by the various

Premier Building Systems produces panels with fiber-reinforced plastic (FRP) facings for an easy-to-maintain surface or with a cementitious plank bonded to the foam core. (Photo courtesy Premier Industries.)

building codes while offering the dramatic energy efficiency associated with the SIP construction system. Additionally, compressed straw cores have some potential in the industry.

EPS

The BASF Corporation patented the first expandable polystyrene in 1950. Today, 85% of SIPs have an EPS core. EPS foam has a closed-cell, moisture-resistant structure composed of millions of tiny air-filled pockets; it is manufactured from beads that are formed by the polymerization of a styrene monomer along with an expansion agent.

EPS foam is produced using a multistage process. During the preexpansion phase, polystyrene beads are heated beyond the glass transition temperature of polystyrene (194°F to 212°F), while the addition of the expansion or blowing agent causes a very fine cellular structure to develop within the polymer. Because the blowing agent in EPS is pentane, a hydrocarbon gas found naturally in the environment, the EPS manufacturing process uses no chlorofluoro-carbon (CFC) or hydrochloro-fluorocarbon (HCFC) products that can deplete the ozone layer.

During the second intermediate stage of production, the beads expand, which forms a closed-cell foam structure. As the foam cools, the blowing agent dissipates and some condensation occurs, causing negative pressure in the cells. Air diffuses through the cells, stabilizing the beads and dissipating moisture into the atmosphere. These stabilized, expanded beads are then blown into a mold, where more heat and steam are applied and the beads expand further into large blocks up to 4 ft. by 4 ft. by 24 ft. The blocks are set aside to stabilize and release the moisture injected by the steam process. Some newer "block plants" use vacuum-assisted molds that are more energy efficient and reduce the overall production time.

Next, hot-wire cutters are used to slice the blocks to the thickness of the SIP core. The hot-wire cutting method is ideal for making panels because the hot wire leaves a flat, melted surface that gives an increased surface area for the glue to bond to.

Most of the EPS foam used for SIPs has a density of 1 pound per cubic foot (pcf), giving it an R-value of 3.85 per inch of thickness. Extensive third-party testing has shown that EPS and the chemically similar XPS are not susceptible to thermal drift, the tendency of an insulating material to lose insulating values over time.

XPS

Extruded polystyrene has been used as a core material in SIPs, but it costs more than EPS and is currently not being used by the major SIP

EPS molded blocks are sliced down to the required core thickness using a hot-wire cutter. (Photo courtesy Premier Industries.)

manufacturers. XPS has greater compressive strength, slightly higher R-values per inch of insulation, and more resistance to water vapor than EPS. The material is used extensively in the manufacture of refrigeration walls and as a surface-attached insulating material.

XPS is formed from polystyrene pellets that are heated and extruded into sheets, typically with a density of 1.5 pcf. After XPS has aged for several months, the outgassing of the blowing agent levels off and a consistent R-value of 5.0 per inch is achieved.

When comparisons are made regarding compressive strength, flexural strength, and shear resistance, XPS performs almost twice as well as EPS. Given these properties, panels that use XPS as a core material should have increased spanning and load-carrying capabilities. Some of this may be attributable to the higher density of the XPS material.

Relative Weight of SIP Panels

Panel thickness	Core material	Weight (lb./sq. ft.)
4½ in.	EPS	3.35
6½ in.	EPS	3.52
8¾ in.	EPS	3.67
4½ in.	Urethane	3.64
6½ in.	Urethane	4.00
6½ in.	Straw	6.86

Calculations are for panels faced with ⅞₆-in. OSB on both sides.

Structural Properties of Foam Cores

	EPS	XPS	Urethane
Density	1 lb./ft.^{3}	1.5 lb./ft.^{3}	2.2 lb./ft.^{3}
R-value per inch (at 30°F)	3.85	4.17	5.88
H_2O permeability (per inch of thickness)	3.0	1.1	1.0
Compressive strength (to 10% distortion)	15 psi	25 psi	25 psi
Shear strength	20 psi	35 psi	16 psi
Shear modulus	300 psi	500 psi	750 psi
Flexural strength	30 psi	50 psi	65 psi

One of the limitations of XPS (besides the cost) is that the extrusion equipment can produce only 4-in.-thick sheets of the material. In addition, XPS isn't as dimensionally stable as the wire-cut EPS cores and does not provide as flat a gluing surface as EPS. This can create some irregularities and perhaps interfere with the bond between the facings and the core. This in itself is a major drawback for use in structural panels and is one of the main reasons so little XPS is currently used in SIPs.

Polyurethane and polyisocyanurate

Polyurethane and polyisocyanurate—generally referred to as urethane and isocyanurate—foams are chemically similar, but their manufacturing processes differ, as do some of their properties. They are both closed-cell foams containing a low-conductivity gas in the cells. Isocyanurates are produced using the polymerization method with isocyanurate molecules, whereas urethanes are polymerized with equal parts of isocyanurate and polyol molecules. The 100% isocyanurate foam is expensive to produce and has a low thermal conductivity but tends to break down over time. The urethane foam is less costly to produce and less susceptible to breakdown but does not produce as high an R-value per inch as does isocyanurate.

One problem with these foams is that the blowing agents were originally CFC-based gases with ozone-depleting potential (ODP) in the range of 1.0. As awareness of the ozone problem increased in the 1990s, urethane manufacturers switched to HCFC gases, which have an ODP in the range of 0.05 to 0.1. But this is a stopgap measure, and production of HCFC-141b—the most widely used HCFC blowing agent—will cease by 2003. Pentane gas (used in EPS manufacturing) is the likely replacement and is already on-line in some plants.

These foams produce a higher R-value per inch of material than EPS foam but how much higher depends on whom you talk to. This is partly due to thermal drift, a drop in R-value over time caused mainly by the infusion of air into the cell structure, which displaces the low-conductive gas in the cells. "Fresh" urethanes have an R-value of 6.0 to 7.0 per inch, but "aged" foams should be figured to have an R-value of 5.88 per inch of material. Testing on cores that have been in service for seven or eight years shows that with low-perm facings, such as FRP or metal, very little thermal drifting took place. Still the R-value of these urethanes is almost 50% higher than the equivalent thickness of EPS.

Straw cores

Another material that is being used for insulating cores in the manufacture of SIPs is compressed straw. Straw is an agricultural waste product that is both plentiful and inexpensive. The first successful compression of straw as a structural material was made by Theodor Dieden in Sweden in 1935. The technology to produce compressed agricultural fiber (CAF) panels was developed and patented under the commercial name of Stramit by Torsten Mossesson in England in the late 1940s. The original patents have expired, so Stramit technology has been adapted by others to produce cores for SIPs and other interior dividers and acoustical panels.

The process is based on the fact that straw fibers bond together without any adhesives when compressed at a high temperature (about 400°F). These compressed cores are then bonded with urethane glues to OSB like their petrochemical cousins to form SIPs.

There has been a great deal of controversy regarding the insulating value of these panels, with some manufacturers claiming almost twice the R-value that independent tests show. According to the *Environmental Building News*, a realistic range is from R-1.4 to R-2 per inch of compressed product. This relatively low insulation value, combined with its high weight (8.4 pcf versus 1 pcf for EPS), suggests that the industry has an uphill battle to produce a viable, competitive product.

Adhesives

The final key ingredient in a SIP is the adhesive that bonds the facings to the core. This glue has to resist the forces of buckling and racking, resist moisture penetration, and keep the panel from delaminating. Two of the major suppliers of adhesives to the SIP industry are Rohm and Haas (formerly Morton International) and Ashland Chemical Co. (see Resources on pp. 182-183).

Rohm and Haas claims that the adhesives it supplies to the SIP industry are water based, solvent free, and don't have a negative impact on the environment. The company is working closely with panel manufacturers to keep up with the rapidly changing production environment. For example, some new high-speed production facilities can produce a completed panel in minutes, where it once took several hours. Adhesive manufacturers can now formulate different setup times into the adhesives to either accelerate or retard the pot life of these sophisticated products. Urethane adhesives can bond metal and various types of plastic skins to foam cores or, in the case of a structural panel, bond these different facings to the OSB structural skins.

Winter Panel has a state-of-the-art SIP production line for manufacturing EPS core panels. (Photo courtesy Winter Panel.)

Rohm and Haas's Morad M-600 series of adhesives is a general-purpose product that is a moisture-cure, one-part urethane glue applied with roller or spray technology. Different versions of this adhesive have different curing speeds depending on the production process and how long the pressure is applied to the panels.

Rohm and Haas also produces the Morad 700 series of adhesives, which is an emulsion polymer isocyanurate glue, called an EPI crosslink adhesive. This is a two-part water-borne adhesive, where the A-part emulsion is mixed with a crosslinker to form the product, which is typically roll-coated to the foam cores. The facings are then positioned before moving the entire assembly into the press. The Morad 700 series is the glue of choice for OSB, plywood, and other wood-based facings.

Along with the rest of the ingredients in a SIP, the adhesives are tested and monitored for code compliance.

Putting the Pieces Together

Now that we have taken a look at the components of a SIP, let's see how they are assembled. The vast majority of SIPs consist of two OSB facings pressure-laminated with adhesives to an EPS foam core. Various-size presses are used to apply this pressure to allow the panels to cure properly.

Currently, the industry standard is an 8-ft. by 24-ft. panel. But now there are machines that can produce 9-ft. by 24-ft., 10-ft. by 28-ft., and even 10-ft. by 36-ft. panels. In addition, there are designs for a new generation of roller presses that will utilize fast-set reactive hot-melt urethane glues that will essentially be able to produce a continuous panel. Of course, new fabrication technologies are moderated by the realities and limitations of material shipping, handling, and placement.

A typical sequence for producing a group of SIP panels isn't complicated. First, the bottom facing

Do-It-Yourself SIPs

Many fabricators and builders express a desire to manufacture their own panels to increase the custom possibilities for their clients. I spoke with Jean T. Simpkins of Black Brothers Co. (see Resources on p. 183) to find out if it's something worth doing. Black Brothers manufactures presses, glue-spreading machines, and material-handling equipment. The company gets calls almost daily from as far away as Scotland and Germany from builders and others who want to know how to get started making panels. Here's the basic machinery that you'd need to manufacture a SIP with a maximum size of 4 ft. by 16 ft.:
- two infeed transfer carts to stage stock prior to the glue spreader
- a top and bottom glue spreader
- a 4-ft. by 16-ft. scissors lift for layup of panels
- an end-loading air-pod laminating press
- a 16-ft. offloading transfer cart

The total cost for this machinery would be about $100,000. Of course, once you've manufactured your custom panels, you'd have to spend upwards of $1 million to have your panels tested and certified by a third-party testing agency and to obtain BOCA and ICBO approvals. This time-consuming, expensive, and red-tape-filled prospect ought to convince you to decide to work with one of the existing SIP suppliers, who can absorb these costs as part of doing business. There are a number of small SIP manufacturers, but their lack of code acceptance limits their sales and appeal.

Black Brothers' air-pod press uses low pneumatic pressure to press up to a 60-in.-high stack of panels. (Photo courtesy Black Brothers.)

is laid out in the assembly area. The desired core thickness pieces are run through the glue-spreading machine, where the adhesive is applied to both sides of the core pieces. These core sections are placed on the bottom facing, then the top facing is positioned. The assembly is aligned before being moved into the press, which can typically accept up to a 60-in.-high stack of panels. The assembly sequence is repeated until the specified stack is in place in the press.

Most presses in use today are pneumatic, with the air pressure applied evenly to the top or

This stack of EPS core panels has been fabricated and is ready for shipping to the job site. The foam has been relieved at the corners to accommodate the thin spline connectors, and electrical chases have been cut.

the facings are separated by spacers and the mixed components of the foam core are injected in between the facings. As the foam expands and fills the void, the foam bonds the two facings together. No other adhesive is needed. As the injected foam expands, it can cause differential pressures within the panel, resulting in some surface unevenness or distortion. Urethane panels can also be produced by forming the cores in a mold, then laminating the cores to the facings with adhesive spread onto the core.

Test Results

When builders construct a building, they don't just guarantee the structure for the length of its one- or two-year warranty; their liability trails behind like a string of tin cans behind a couple of newlyweds. The idea is to keep the clanking to a minimum. I am convinced that using SIPs in structures will enhance a builder's reputation for quality work and significantly lessen the number of callbacks.

One concern about a relatively new product like SIPs is reliability. Has this product been thoroughly tested? Will it stand up over time? The rest of this chapter will deal with the extensive testing that has been undertaken by SIP manufacturers and explain how to interpret the results. These tests are all designed to see how these panels perform when subjected to forces found in the real world.

Transverse load test

The transverse load is the applied load on a floor or a roof; it is the combination of the dead load (the weight of the assembly) plus the live load (people, objects, and snow, which will vary, and a calculation of the wind load). The allowable load is determined by setting up the span to be tested, then uniformly loading the assembly to the point of failure. That figure, which is measured in pounds per square foot (psf), is divided by a safety factor of 3 to establish the allowable load for the assembly at that span.

bottom platens until the required pressure is applied to the stack of panels. Different adhesives have different setting times, which will determine how long the pressure is applied. Curing times are determined by temperature and humidity. After removal from the press, the stack of panels needs to cure in place for 24 hours before being moved to the storage or shipping areas or to the fabrication section of the plant where doors, windows, rakes, and other openings are machined into the panels and prepared for final installation. While there is some equipment that uses a vacuum approach to applying pressure to the panels, this method is not yet widespread.

The procedure for producing a urethane or isocyanurate panel is much different. In this case,

The allowable deflection of the panel is measured by taking the length of the span and dividing by a deflection factor (L/480, L/360, L/240, or L/180, where L is the span). The larger the denominator in this equation, the stiffer the assembly. Typically, L/360 is used to calculate floor loads and L/240 to calculate roof loads. The test criteria is ASTM E-72, "Acceptance Criteria for Sandwich Panels," section 11.

When designing for load spans in different parts of the country, span charts that are representative of results for the EPS panel industry can be very useful. SIPs are engineered products, and it's important to work with the panel manufacturer or an engineer when calculating the actual loads of your building (see the chart on the facing page).

For example, here in the Midwest we have a moderate snow-load factor, so we should design for 50 psf of total load. If I have a span of 10 ft. from ridge to eave and I want an R-value of R-30, then I look at the roof-load chart for a 7¼-in. core (R-30) panel at L/240 and follow the 10-ft. span row to see that this assembly will give me an allowable load of 68 psf. I could even extend the span to 12 ft. and still have an allowable load of 56 psf.

Axial loads

The compressive force that puts load on a wall is called the axial load, which is measured in pounds per lineal foot (plf). The standard test that panel manufacturers have to comply with is ASTM E-72, section 9, amended by ICBO "Acceptance Criteria for Sandwich Panels," section 4.4. Loads are measured by situating four "compressometers"—two on each side—to

Transverse Load Design

Roof and wall panel span		EPS core thickness														
		3½-in. core			5½-in. core			7¼-in. core			9¼-in. core			11¼-in. core		
		⁷⁄₁₆-in. OSB thickness			⁷⁄₁₆-in. OSB thickness			⁷⁄₁₆-in. OSB thickness			⁷⁄₁₆-in. OSB thickness			⁷⁄₁₆-in. OSB thickness		
Deflection		L/360	L/240	L/180	L/360	L/240	L/180	L/360	L/240	L/180	L/360	L/240	L/180	L/360	L/240	L/180
Trans-verse load (psf)	8 ft.	25	39	46[1]	40	61[1]	61[1]	55	76[1]	76[1]	76[1]	76[1]	76[1]	76[1]	76[1]	76[1]
	10 ft.	19	29	38	30	44	46	56	68[1]	68[1]	68[1]	68[1]	68[1]	68[1]	68[1]	68[1]
	12 ft.	NA	NA	NA	33	44[1]	44[1]	42[1]	56[1]	56[1]	56[1]	56[1]	56[1]	56[1]	56[1]	56[1]

[1] = Limited to ultimate failure load divided by a safety factor of 3.
NA = not advised.
Source: AFM Corp.

Creep

The transverse loading values for SIPs presented in the chart above seem to be on the conservative side. In part, I attribute this to the necessarily conservative nature of the engineers of the world. The safety factor of 3 makes up for a lot of seat-of-the-pants types who make bad guesses. But another contributing factor is the phenomenon called creep. Under load, the top facing of a SIP is under compression, while the bottom facing is under tension. This leaves the foam core trying to equalize, and its tendency is to shear away from the facings. Any organic material will creep under load, but in the case of a SIP, delamination is potentially serious.

Studies indicate that creep is most noticeable when a panel is designed for a light load over a long span. In other words, the greater the deflection, the more creep becomes a factor. This creep factor—or long-term deflection—needs to be considered when planning spans for roofs and floors using SIPs. Staying on the conservative side of the charts will ensure straight assemblies over the long haul. Still, with engineered splines, it is quite possible to design a roof that spans 20 ft. or more horizontally, and 8-ft.-wide panels—a natural fit for timber frames and some of the red-iron steel systems—offer a large grid to work with.

SIP walls spread loads evenly over the entire facings. Their ability to withstand axial loading is superior to stick-frame construction. (Photo courtesy Panel Built.)

measure deformation in a vertically oriented panel. The load is applied uniformly in 100-lb. increments along the top of the panel being tested until either the panel deflects ¾ in. or the panel fails.

In one example that is representative of SIP performance, PFS Corporation testing service conducted a series of tests on a 4-ft. by 20-ft. by 4⁹⁄₁₆-in.-thick panel with a urethane foam core manufactured by Winter Panel (see Resources on p. 182). The average load to ¾-in. deflection was 10,300 lb. The average maximum load (to fracture point) was 23,000 lb. Dividing this figure by the 4 ft. of panel width gives a figure of 5,750 plf. Dividing that number by the safety factor of 3 gives us a working allowable load of 1,917 plf.

When conducted on panels from different manufacturers with different core thicknesses and core materials, this same axial loading test resulted in similar allowable loads in the range of 2,000 plf. That load rating would be the equivalent of a typical bearing-wall loading for a three-story building (see the chart on the facing page).

Racking resistance

Racking—or shear—resistance is the ability of an assembly to withstand horizontal forces applied to a structure by earthquakes and high winds. This is where the most important difference between SIP construction and conventional framing methods shows up. The standard ICBO and BOCA approved test is ASTM E-72-80, "Conducting Strength Tests of Panels for Building Construction," section 14. In this test, two 4-ft. by 8-ft. by 4½-in. SIPs are assembled as shown in the illustration on p. 34. Note that this test panel assembly has no studs and is connected by OSB surface splines.

After the assembly is locked into place, force is applied to the top corner. In a series of tests

Allowable Axial Loads for SIPs

Height (ft.)	Wind pressure (psf)				
	12.5	16.5	20.5	31	65.5
	Maximum wind speed (mph)				
	70	80.5	89.5	110	160
	Allowable axial load (plf)				
4	5,637	5,590	5,542	5,420	5,032
5	5,551	5,477	5,404	5,216	4,630
6	5,445	5,339	5,235	4,969	4,160
7	5,319	5,179	5,036	4,683	3,631
8	5,172	4,987	4,808	4,361	951
9	5,004	4,774	4,553	4,006	
10	4,816	4,538	4,273	3,625	
11	4,609	4,281	3,971	3,223	
12	4,383	4,006	3,651	2,562	
13	4,142	3,714	3,317	896	
14	3,886	3,411	2,973		
15	3,620	3,100	2,410		
16	3,345	2,783	1,140		
17	3,066	1,969			
18	2,784	884			
19	2,145				
20	1,247				
21	379				

Calculations are for 5⅝-in. EPS core panel with ⅜-in. facings on both sides.
Source: FischerSips

conducted in 1995 by PFS Corporation on panels manufactured by W. H. Porter Inc., assembly failure occurred at an average load of 10,700 lb. Here, failure is defined as the point where the fasteners pulled out of the bottom edge of the panel and along the center seam. Dividing this figure by the safety factor of 3 gives 3,566 lb. This figure is again divided by 8 (the length of the assembly) to arrive at an allowable load of 446 plf before failure. The average allowable racking resistance for the tested panels was about 400 plf.

As a comparison, the APA-Engineered Wood Association offers test results for the following assembly, which is the standard wall construction currently used. It consists of an 8-ft. by 8-ft. wall composed of 2x4 bottom and top plates, double end studs, and studs 16-in. o.c. along the assembly. Using 8d nails, ½-in. plywood was applied at 6-in. spacing around the perimeter and at 12-in. spacing throughout the field. This assembly reached the failure point at 4,744 lb. of applied pressure. When this figure is divided by the safety factor of 3 and the length of 8 ft., an allowable load for this type of wall is calculated to be 197 plf.

Panel Setup for Racking Test

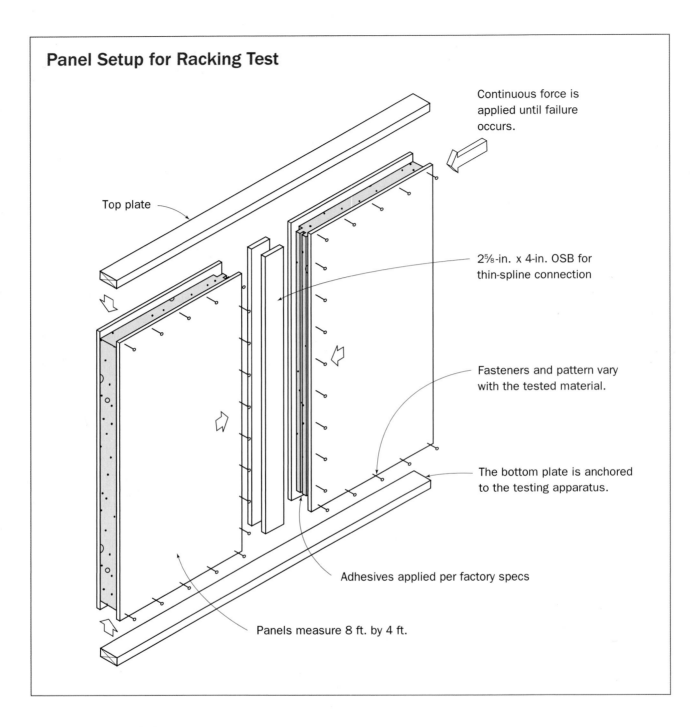

Continuous force is applied until failure occurs.

Top plate

2⅝-in. x 4-in. OSB for thin-spline connection

Fasteners and pattern vary with the tested material.

The bottom plate is anchored to the testing apparatus.

Adhesives applied per factory specs

Panels measure 8 ft. by 4 ft.

So right off the truck and installed in the basic configuration, a SIP has an allowable load factor of 446 plf compared with the standard wall value of 197 plf. This difference is clearly evident in a SIP structure that is exposed to high winds: The absence of creaks and groans is very noticeable. This is also why a SIP building has few or no drywall callbacks due to cracking or fasteners backing out. The failure locations along the bottom edge of the panel assembly also point out that the addition of steel strapping or other hold-down methods will add significantly to the lateral resistance to shear forces in the structure (see chapter 7 for more information on hold-downs).

Tests show that SIP buildings are better able to withstand horizontal forces applied to a structure by earthquakes and high winds. This house is in an area exposed to high winds in Idaho. (Photo courtesy Ronnee McGee.)

Tensile strength

SIP manufacturers subject their products to another test to determine the strength of the lamination and of the core material itself. The accepted ASTM C-297 test for dry tension determines how much force it takes to pull the SIP apart in the cross section. Selected 2-in. by 2-in. cross sections are carefully removed from various parts of a test panel. These samples are then surface-attached to the testing equipment and pulled until either the core shears or the facings delaminate.

The dry tension result on a Winter Panel Corporation SIP with a 3⁵⁄₁₆-in. urethane core was an average of 87 lb. In all of the 10 tests performed on these samples, the core sheared before the skins delaminated, clearly demonstrating the structural integrity of these panels.

Fire hazard

The issue of how a material performs in the presence of fire is a primary concern to the code authorities as well as to the manufacturers of products that are used in the construction of

SIPs and Pests

One area of debate connected with SIPs is their susceptibility to insect and rodent infestation, particularly termites and carpenter ants. There are reported cases where these pests gained access to the interior of SIP structures and in a short time made extensive pathways into the foam cores for nesting areas. Although the foam is not nutritive for the insects, it is easily excavated—and that can compromise the integrity of the structure if the infestation is severe enough. It will also compromise thermal performance of the panels. These pests can be particularly active in some southern states and where wood and moisture are prevalent.

One SIP manufacturing group, AFM (see Resources on p. 182), has developed and patented an EPS foam with an added borate that it markets under the name Perform Guard. AFM has conducted extensive testing that indicates that the product resists some termites and carpenter ants. AFM points out that Perform Guard is not a barrier system and that insects may enter through other areas. There is also some question as to the strength of this foam compared with nonborate foam. There is evidence that the borate salts weaken the bond between the polystyrene beads and reduce the tensile strength of the foam, although a careful review of testing results from many SIP makers doesn't show lower tested strengths.

Although Perform Guard foam does resist intrusion by some pests, that should not be the only factor when selecting SIPs. Like all houses made from wood products, a SIP house is susceptible to insect attack. Builders should have a thorough plan and details for preventing the intrusion of pests, regardless of how a house is built. Further, homeowners need to have a regular maintenance schedule to guard against infestation.

Rodents can present a problem if access to the interior of the walls is gained. In the Midwest, gray squirrels are known to attack houses and can chew into an eave or crawl space in a short period of time. While there are various high-pitched sonic devices and voodoo approaches, none have a reliable track record of repelling squirrels. These critters simply like to chew through boards and get inside. But I doubt that they are that interested in chewing a whole lot of foam when they can get into the neighbor's stick-framed house a lot easier.

homes and other buildings. There are a number of ways to test both the cores themselves and the panels as wall and roof assemblies.

Before considering any SIP panels for your project, contact the manufacturer for fire safety test results. Reputable companies will be happy to provide you with an extensive array of information about testing procedures and results.

Test results indicate that a SIP system can be designed to meet current codes for fire-resistant wall assemblies. A SIP wall with ½-in. drywall on the interior surface will meet the mandated 15-minute resistance requirement for residential structures. A $\frac{1}{10}$-in.-thick, factory-applied "fire finish" coating will also meet the 15-minute fire requirement. A two-layer surface of $\frac{5}{8}$-in. type X drywall or one layer of type C drywall will meet the requirements for a one-hour-rated wall assembly. Tests indicate that a SIP structure performs safely in a fire situation because the walls have no air cavity to spread the fire and the airtight construction will quickly starve a fire of oxygen. (For further discussion, see pp. 175-176.)

Another concern in a fire situation is the toxicity of the burning material. Current BOCA codes have deleted requirements for combustion

Combustion Toxicity

Material	Toxicity factors due to:					Maximum sum of toxicity factors
	CO	CO^2	HCl	HCN	Others	
Polystyrene	19	2				20
Polyethylene	21	1				20
Polyester	24	2				30
Phenolic resin	5	1			22	30
Wood (white pine)	47	3				50
Cotton	59	2				60
PVC	12	1	343			360
Wool	14	1		375		390
ABS	10	1		367		280
Urethane (rigid)	14	1		273		290
Nylon-6	17	1		931		950
Polyacrylonitrile	7	1		1,201		1,200

Note: The National Research Council of Canada supplied this information to determine health risks associated with various combustible materials. The United States currently does not have a standard because there is no acceptable test protocol.

toxicity because there is no acceptable test protocol simulating actual fire conditions. But some studies that have been done on combustion toxicity suggest that most SIP core materials are no more hazardous than other common building materials (see the chart above).

In all testing categories, SIPs performed above the standards set by the governing code bodies. Of course, there is more testing to be done, which will result, as it has already, in a better-performing product as adjustments are made. But it is clear that manufacturers and others involved in the SIP industry strongly believe in their product and are dedicated to making SIPs the building material for the 21st century.

Chapter 3

DESIGN CONSIDERATIONS

SIPs: An Integrated System

Design Advantages of SIPs

Designing and Building with SIPs

Many people unfamiliar with new building technologies confuse SIP building systems with prefab or modular construction methods. This confusion can lead to the mistaken impression that the SIP system is "cheap" construction and that the type and style of buildings constructed with SIPs are limited. Actually, modular production and SIPs are two very different approaches. In this chapter, I will compare approaches to factory-built components, take a look at the advantages for designers using SIPs, and show how SIPs can be used in various types of buildings.

SIPs: An Integrated System

Modular buildings are mass produced to take advantage of the cost savings realized by producing a great number of the same thing. Modular building sections are prefabricated in a controlled factory setting, then transported to the job site and erected. This approach shortens the erection time, but any savings realized here are offset by the difficulty of making a tight building because there is no way to wrap a building/vapor membrane around corners that have completed trim and siding.

In fact, modular buildings are virtually identical to stick-built structures constructed on-site, having the same problems of making them straight, level, and airtight during construction and with the additional problem of transportation

Complicated shapes can be produced economically with SIPs. Designed by Stephen N. Nemtin of Taliesin Architects, Windintide is built around a giant sequoia tree overlooking Puget Sound in Washington. The project was built by Shirey Contracting using Enercept SIPs on a steel frame. Enercept precut the panels, and the shell was erected in five days. (Photos courtesy Shirey Contracting.)

to the site that can result in loosened joints and out-of-square conditions. This cookie-cutter, mass-production approach limits the design choices available to potential homeowners and all too often results in the repetitive houses commonly seen in suburban America.

SIP design and construction, on the other hand, take advantage of the modern approach to production, where communication between the design people, sales people, and the production people are all linked horizontally. When an order comes into the design department of a SIP manufacturer/fabricator, the time line starts. If the plans have been drawn with SIPs in mind, then the job goes directly to the production department for scheduling. If the plans need to be

modified to work with the SIP system, the design department takes the job and works with the engineering department to make the job compatible. This usually won't affect the look of the project, although some details may need to be modified to work with the SIP system. When a project is designed with SIP components from the start, the size and spanning capabilities of SIPs can be fully utilized. The flexibility of the CAD design process and the speed of SIP production techniques mean that a project can be conceived, designed, modified, delivered, and built in significantly less time than a conventional structure.

This rapid communication means that each SIP project can be uniquely designed and custom-built to architect- or designer-provided specifications. At the other end of the scale, production speed and fabrication capabilities mean that high-quality, energy-efficient components are available with which to build affordable housing. Design flexibility and production capabilities inherent in the SIP system make it attractive for both custom buyers and those interested in affordable housing. And as the SIP industry gains strength and volume, the lead time between design, sale, and production should be reduced even further.

Selling SIPs to the design community

Given the benefits of building with SIPs, you may well ask why the design community has been slow to utilize them in the design of residential and light commercial buildings. Many architects simply don't know about this class of products and their capabilities. Some share a misconception with the general public that the use of SIPs is limited to simple shapes and that they aren't flexible enough to be used for innovative or unusual designs. Many architects want to see a product establish a track record in the working world before incorporating that product into their design work.

The original design for this 43,000-sq.-ft. ski lodge called for stick-built construction using hard-to-harvest large timbers. Changing to glulam trusses and SIPs resulted in considerable material savings and an extremely energy-efficient building capable of withstanding a severe climate. Reclaimed heat from the restaurant kitchen is the only source of heat. (Design: Smith-Koenka Architects, Montreal; panels and photos courtesy Thermapan Industries.)

Located near Park City, Utah, this architect's home takes advantage of 24-ft. SIP wall panels to eliminate "hinge" connections. The roof is conventionally framed, an economical alternative to a SIP roof when snow loads are less than 70 psf. (Architect: Max Anderson; builder: Mike Hoth/Seneca Design and Development; panels and photos courtesy AFP, Gainesville, Georgia.)

But the number of architect-designed residences nationwide is relatively small—only about 5% of all houses built. Why haven't builders themselves embraced SIPs, considering the inherent advantages of building with this system? For one, innovations in construction practices traditionally come into the industry from the top down. That is, architects and designers—rather than contractors and home buyers—incorporate the new ideas that result from new technologies, which then filter down and are adapted by the general public.

In addition, many builders won't work with architects, feeling that money spent on design fees is money out of their pockets. They see no added value in having an architect involved when they have built the same house over and over and can still sell those houses as fast as they can build them. But that situation is changing as designers and builders alike are learning about SIPs and incorporating them into projects that are successful and profitable.

The question is how to educate architects about SIP technology. One step in that direction is a requirement for continuing education for practicing architects adapted by the American

Institute of Architects (AIA) in 1993, which is intended to encourage them to embrace new technologies that come into the marketplace. Some SIP suppliers are tapping into this program as a way to get their messages out to professionals. For example, the Associated Foam Manufacturers (AFM) recently subsidized the development of a CD-ROM about the history and use of SIPs, using this as a part of presentations for architects and other professionals in the design community. While programs like this help keep architects abreast of current materials and practices, the real key is for builders and suppliers to establish relationships with architects and help them to incorporate SIPs into their work, simply because it is a better way to build buildings.

An example of how this cooperative approach could work occurred in 1998 at Van Der Ryn Architects of Sausalito, California. Specializing in sustainable, environmentally sound building practices, VDR was interested in learning more about SIP technology, so they enlisted Mic Carmichael of Panel Built (see Resources on p. 180) and architect Fred Stoenner to make a presentation on SIPs to the firm. After reviewing an actual panel take-off and pricing schedule, the

This 2,200-sq.-ft. Nevada City, California, residence was built with 6½-in. SIP wall panels and 8¼-in. SIP roof panels. The passive solar orientation and simple geometry are enhanced by Japanese-influenced detailing on the exterior. Exposed on the interior, 4-in. by 8-in. timbers were used for the roof splines and act as the main element of the 4-ft. roof overhang. (Design: David Wright; fabrication and photos courtesy Ed Stahl/ Sunworks Co.)

project architects were able to refine the design to take advantage of the unique capabilities of the material and cost the job. This kind of approach can be a big help in making architects and designers aware of the possibilities of working with SIPs.

Design Advantages of SIPs

In preparing this book, I asked several architects and builders experienced in SIP construction about the advantages of working with SIPs. For the most part, they agreed with my assessment of SIPs being an integrated building system that offers numerous advantages to clients. Some mentioned that building with SIPs is a resource-efficient process that results in very energy-efficient buildings. Others liked the speed of SIP erection. But almost all these professionals pointed out that SIPs are only *one* component in

the overall design of a building. To fully utilize the benefits offered by these panels, they must work in conjunction with siting, HVAC requirements, windows, and the other components used in the making of a building.

SIPs are an engineered system

A SIP house is a tighter, more energy-efficient house than a stick-built one because it is engineered more precisely. While straight walls and roofs are taken for granted by home buyers, they are more and more difficult to produce with today's erratic lumber supply and conventional framing systems. But CAD drafting systems help detail the SIP fabrication process, allowing precise instructions to be sent to the SIP manufacturer for foam relief and spline setup. The result is a SIP package that is built to ⅛-in. tolerances. This precision makes for well-built houses, a refreshing approach when the industry standard today for

SIPs and Energy Efficiency

A 1993 study prepared for the U.S. Department of Energy through a joint effort by the University of Oregon's Center for Housing Innovation, the Florida Solar Energy Center, and the Department of Industrial Engineering of the University of Central Florida provides a graphic example of how a SIP house outperforms a comparable stick-built house. In this side-by-side evaluation, two 1,200-sq.-ft. two-story houses were built adjacent to each other in Louisville, Kentucky. Although one house was stick-framed and the other was built with SIPs, the houses were designed to have the same thermal conductive transmittance and they were built by the same builder, who had experience with both types of construction.

Both houses were built to be more airtight than the average house in Louisville, but the SIP house proved to have 22% less air infiltration than the stick-framed house. Exhaustive testing utilizing both gas and electric heat sources indicated a 15% to 17% energy savings over a typical 24-hour period. Predicted annual heating-season savings for the SIP house were 14% to 20%.

Exterior Materials Used in Two Study Houses

Component	House type	Construction type	Insulation
Foundation	Both	Block stem wall and slab	R-10 to 2-ft. depth
Walls	Frame	2x4 stud	R-13 fiberglass batt, partial R-3.5 sheathing
	SIP	3⅝-in. EPS core panel	R-14 EPS core
Windows	Both	Double glazed, wood frame, aluminum cladding	R-2.0
Second-floor ceilings	Frame	2x4 truss	R-30 loose-fill cellulose
	SIP	Flat, 7⅜-in. EPS core panel	R-29 EPS core

Source: Florida Solar Energy Center

framing tolerances is 1 in. A straight and true building shell gives every other trade a better chance to do their best work, too.

SIPs can be used to form an excellent structural and thermal envelope that allows other aspects of energy-efficient design to be utilized. SIPs should be considered the core material for building a home, while all the technology and components in the marketplace are worthwhile add-ons. If clients are interested in an energy-efficient building, they will likely want better windows, more efficient heating and cooling systems, an insulated concrete form basement, and good passive solar design.

In addition to the relatively high insulating values per inch of EPS and urethane cores (see pp. 23–26), there is another thermally related advantage of SIPs that translates into energy efficiency. The moisture permeability of a SIP panel is very low, which changes a number of design aspects, especially for roofs. For example, the old question of cold roof versus hot roof doesn't need to have a definitive answer in a SIP system. Here's why: Buildings—especially residences—produce a large amount of moisture daily from cooking, from showers, and from the breathing of their inhabitants. As that moisture migrates through the wall and roof of a conventional structure, it gets trapped by the exterior vapor barrier, condensing when it contacts any surface with a much different temperature. This, in turn, causes mildew, dry rot, and premature failure of building components. This is a big problem that is often ignored in conventional construction, with predictable, disastrous results.

One answer to moisture control has been elaborately designed, expensive ways to vent this moisture to the outside. The difficulty of venting is compounded in a roof with hips and valleys because there is no straight, open channel from eave to ridge to create an airflow path. A SIP roof system eliminates these problems.

Even though the SIPs themselves have a low moisture permeability, the differential pressure generated within a building tries to force moisture through joints in the panels. This accelerated moisture concentration can cause deterioration of the exterior facings of the panels and has led to some replacement of roof panels. For this reason, it is strongly advised to install a complete vapor barrier under the roof panels. This approach to keeping moisture away from the roof is very different than typical venting of a stick-built roof. It simplifies both the construction and the detailing because no vents are necessary at the eaves or ridge.

Of course, the moisture is still inside a SIP building. A well-built SIP house can have air change per hour (ach) rates of less than 1.0. So what do you do about this moisture? The best way to control moisture is to use an air-to-air heat exchanger that allows a constant air change to take place in the house, removing stale and humid air while retaining some of the inside air temperature before it exhausts. I'll cover this device more thoroughly in chapter 8.

SIPs are resource efficient

There is little doubt that there is much less wood used in the construction of the shell of a SIP house than in a conventional one. Plus, the OSB that is the wood component of a SIP comes from younger farm-grown trees that are a renewable resource. In addition to the wood savings, the thermal performance of a SIP building further reduces resource consumption because it costs far less to heat and cool due to the building's higher energy efficiency.

There is also much less waste when a project has been designed to use the SIP system. This not only saves the customer money but also is an environmentally sound idea. As waste-disposal fees rise, designers and builders of SIP buildings like the fact that there is very little job-site waste at the end of construction. Many manufacturers have factory recycling programs to reclaim cutouts and put scrap foam to other uses. This recycled EPS foam—called regrind in the trade—is useful for aerated soil amendments, furniture

Comparison of Wood Products Used in a Framed Wall vs. a SIP Wall

Wall configuration	Whole-wall R-value	Dimensional lumber (in board feet)	OSB (in board feet)	Total board feet
8-ft. x 8-ft. 2x6 wall	13.69	105	32	137
8-ft. x 8-ft. 4½-in. SIP wall with EPS core	13.93	20	64	84

Both walls have a 3-ft. x 4-ft. rough opening for a window. The 2x6 wall uses a double top plate and 16-in. o.c. frame spacing. The SIP wall has a solid top and bottom plate and a solid window frame.

insulation, and other uses, although it can't be reduced to the polystyrene beads that the expanded foam starts out as.

SIPs offer speed and security

Builders love the fact that a SIP building can be erected in up to one-third less time than a conventional building. Estimating labor—particularly for a complicated custom project—has always been the area where contractors sweat the most. After building a few SIP structures, a contractor will be able to accurately predict the labor involved in erecting a SIP shell and to benefit from the resulting labor savings. This is especially true if the panel fabrication is done by the supplier or an outside fabricator (see p. 76). This, in turn, means that a much tighter construction schedule can be drawn. Subs will know exactly when they are expected to be on-site. All these points add up to a faster production schedule and a more profitable job for the builder.

According to the Natural Resources Defense Council, "Using stressed-skin panels (SIPs) can reduce the time to frame the building envelope by more than a third. This time savings can improve a builder's productivity and profitability by 16%. In addition, the end product is energy and wood efficient, generating operating savings for the owner and minimizing negative forest impacts."

Finally, SIP construction sites are less susceptible to job-site theft, an increasingly large problem, especially in exurban building projects. For one thing, the large size of the panels themselves is a deterrent because it is nearly impossible to walk off with them. In addition, it is a big advantage to be able to close in and secure a building in a short window of time. Often a SIP building will have the windows, doors, and roof on before it makes it onto the easy-pickings list of local thieves.

This 28,000-sq.-ft. medium-volume light commercial building was originally scheduled for a tilt-up concrete panel wall system. But the concrete curing delay time, as opposed to the quick delivery of prepared SIP wall panels, made the choice of SIPs for this project a logical one. (Design: Fred Stoenner; builder: Chuck Slavonic; photo courtesy Better Building Systems.)

Long roof panels make it possible to incorporate wide eave overhangs into the roof design of a SIP building.

Designing and Building with SIPs

When 4-ft. by 8-ft. materials such as plywood and gypsum drywall first came onto the market, designers and builders still designed buildings that looked like their predecessors. They didn't design around the new module or take advantage of the cost savings offered by it but continued to build the way they always had. For example, before gypsum drywall you would find 8½-ft., 9-ft., 10-ft., and higher ceilings—the height didn't really matter because it was all custom work anyway. Now, almost all ceiling heights in rooms other than entries and living rooms are 8-ft. high. Not 7 ft. 10 in. or 8 ft. 4 in. but an even 8 ft. Why? Because drywall is most commonly available in 4-ft. widths and 8-ft. lengths, and designing nonstandard ceiling heights would add a premium to construction costs: more seams, more material, and more time.

Significant savings can be realized by using SIPs from the beginning in a design project, although professionals are just scratching the surface when it comes to optimizing the use of SIPs in design work. But it is starting to happen. Probably the biggest change is getting used to working in an 8-ft. module instead of a 4-ft. module, which in itself offers tremendous potential savings in support-related structure.

SIPs simplify roof and wall construction

Except in the cases of extreme snow loads, 8¼-in. and 10¼-in. roof panels can span 16 ft. and longer with a large safety factor for transverse loads. Long lengths mean that generally one panel can reach from the ridge to the eave with some material left overhanging to implement an eave, soffit, and fascia design that fits the building. Dramatic visual effects and energy-saving passive solar details can easily be incorporated into a

Expanding Design Possibilities with SIPs

According to architect Colin M. Cathcart, a self-confessed "panel zealot," good value in a home doesn't come from cutting corners from the beginning. It comes from making wise use of materials and technologies that pay for themselves as you live with them, a hallmark of environmentally friendly construction.

SIP panels fit perfectly into this equation. Cathcart believes that passive environmental strategies are suited to the home: Thoughtfully implemented, they increase value and comfort without adding cost. Earth sheltering, superinsulation, solar orientation, and cross ventilation are simple but effective ways to reduce energy consumption and enhance light, comfort, and air circulation. Active measures, such as

building with SIP panels and using appropriate technologies such as mechanical ventilation systems and solar electric systems, provide opportunities for further energy savings as well as engaging architectural expression.

For example, a recent Cathcart project incorporates a barrel-vault roof system built with SIP panels that offers both dramatic architecture and functional performance. While the house didn't start as a SIP project, the high insulation values and the open ceiling desired by the clients made SIPs a perfect fit. The roof starts close to the ground on the north and deflects the wind as well as provides shading for three stories of glass on the south.

This house in Woodstock, New York, uses curved panels for the roof. (Design and photos courtesy Kiss + Cathcart Architects.)

Many custom builders use 4-ft.-wide panels because they produce less waste and can be erected by a small crew without heavy equipment. (Photo courtesy Jim Crowley Builders.)

Using a crane makes placing jumbo panels fast and safe. (Photo courtesy SIPA.)

home's design with these cantilevered pieces. And some panel manufacturers offer curved panels, which can make beautiful vaulted roofs (see the sidebar on the facing page).

One design approach to wall construction is to incorporate 8-ft. by 24-ft. panels so that the wall is basically one piece. The doors and window openings are then cut into the wall, leaving the panel with its structural stability intact. This approach enables the factory to recycle the cutouts and leftover materials to some extent. A more common approach is to fabricate walls from 4-ft.-wide stock. Header and sill pieces are fabricated for window and door openings so that there are no cutouts to dispose of. Also, these smaller pieces are easy to handle on site and to erect without mechanical assistance until the larger roof panels need to be installed.

SIPs are adaptable to different types of construction

It may seem paradoxical to talk about how appropriate SIP construction is for high-end projects, yet on the other hand talk about how well suited SIPs are for fast-track, light commercial, and affordable housing projects. Yet different aspects and benefits of SIPs suit each of these branches of the construction business. All can share the features of very high strength-to-weight ratios, super energy efficiency, and rapid erection. Let's look at some of the specific benefits and see how they apply to the different construction niches.

High-end projects SIPs is a precision system, making it particularly well suited to high-end, custom projects. In this niche, owners want the best materials money can buy. These buyers are educated consumers and look for and understand the various product benefits that are touted by manufacturers and installers. And once the program for a high-quality building has been

Winter Panel SIPs were used for the walls and roof of this custom home in the Northeast. (Photo courtesy Winter Panel Corp.)

Fast-food franchise buildings are increasingly being built using SIPs. Shown here is a Taco Bell restaurant under construction. (Photo courtesy AFM.)

established with the owners, it is a logical step to upgrade the various systems in the house, such as windows and doors, heating and cooling, and even roofing material.

Upgrading the building shell by using SIPs has the same logic for this group of buyers, who can best be served by the custom builder who can produce a building tighter, straighter, and quieter than anything on the market. The ability to produce a very square and level building means that all of the custom finishes that go into this type of project can be installed with a high degree of accuracy. Simply put, there will be less fudging and fewer headaches to make all the details work out.

For many high-end homebuyers, unfortunately, energy efficiency isn't very high on the list of important features (although it should be). But resistance to high winds and/or earth movement is. Like a well-made automobile, a SIP house has the solid sound of quality when you slam the door that a high-end home buyer will appreciate. And because these projects almost invariably have an architect involved, this is an opportunity for

both the builder and the architect to raise the bar for building performance excellence.

Commercial buildings Another area where architects are generally involved is light commercial buildings, including franchise outlets for everything from fast food to shoes, as well as schools, churches, banks, and office buildings. Some time ago, a panel supplier told me about a fast-food chain that decided to build some new units with SIPs. When I asked if it was because the operating costs of a SIP building versus a stick building penciled out much better over the life of

A massive steel framework composed of I-beams set on a 24-ft. grid supports the 10½-in.-thick R-Control SIP walls and roof of this 36,000-sq.-ft. equestrian center in eastern Maryland. The long spans of the steel framework necessitated ripping the SIPs to a width of 2 ft. and using doubled 2x10s as spline connectors. (Architect: Mahdad Saniee; builder: Mike Williams/ Cottage Craftsman Inc.; panels and photos courtesy Pacemaker Plastics.)

the building, he laughed and said that the only reason the chain opted for SIPs was that it could start selling hamburgers faster.

Speed, of course, is an important concern in commercial construction, but it isn't the only one. For example, new school buildings need to enclose quality space, be comfortable to learn in, and be safe. They also need to have reasonable building and operating costs and an effective life span that are acceptable to the school board and ultimately the taxpayers.

Buildings larger than residences can take full advantage of jumbo panels to enclose space quickly with less structural material. In some ways, the SIP industry is in competition with the light steel-framing industry for many of these medium-sized buildings. A big problem with steel frames is the tremendous thermal transference of heat or cold via the frame to the inside, causing severe condensation problems and attendant callbacks, but these problems can be addressed by incorporating SIPs into the design and construction.

This 20,000-sq.-ft. dining hall near Winter Park, Colorado, incorporates SIPs over a red iron frame set on an 8-ft. grid. Because of the building's mountain location, the roof system is designed to support a 170 psf snow load. Interior finish details include wrapping the steel frame with ripped log sections. (Builder: Bob Boxwell Construction; panels and photo courtesy Advanced Foam Plastics.)

The marriage between the SIPs and steel-framing industries is still in the courtship stage, although they both have a lot to offer each other. Steel framework (particularly the 12- to 14-gauge red-iron systems) can be economically erected and when designed with the great spanning capabilities of SIPs in mind can provide a strong, tight shell that is suitable for many uses. In the next few years, I expect to see more and more hybrid systems come into the marketplace.

Timber frames The timber-framing industry has been around for several hundred years and is now, once again, a popular choice for structural framework. The large spans and open spaces of a timber frame lend themselves to the use of foam panels for infill and insulation. Technically, most of the panels used by timber framers are known as curtain wall panels, and they are typically made with OSB as an outer skin and drywall as an inner skin. Timber-frame structures can either be sheathed with SIPs or nonload-bearing curtain-wall panels because the timber frame is the structure. Timber framers gave a great deal of the initial impetus to the SIP industry, and they still purchase a large quantity of foam-core panels.

Affordable and innovative housing Besides earning a reputation as a precision framing system for the upscale market, SIPs are making inroads into the affordable housing industry (see the sidebar on p. 54). In this area, energy efficiency and rapid construction are the keys to success, and a repeatable, functional design program can mean a very cost-effective structure. Another big plus for SIPs in the affordable housing field is the ability to utilize unskilled labor for much of the shell erection. In programs such as Habitat for Humanity, which rely on volunteer labor, SIPs are a perfect fit, allowing people without construction skills to make a real difference.

Innovative approaches to design and construction can also benefit from SIPs. For example, geodesic domes have been around since Buckminster Fuller introduced them in the 1950s. They are one of the strongest structures possible, but as originally conceived they weren't a particularly resource-efficient system. The odd-shaped triangles and different-length struts meant lots of waste. Geodesic domes have always had

This traditional timber-frame residence in Wisconsin incorporates SIPs to enclose the frame. With greater spans between frame bents, SIPs can meet the load demands better than nonstructural cladding panels. (Timber frame: Glenville Timberwrights; panels and photos courtesy Enercept.)

the reputation of being complicated to build because of their difficult math and the need for fabricated hubs. They also have a well-deserved reputation for leaking.

All these drawbacks have prevented geodesic domes from being readily accepted into the mainstream. But the perception of domes as an architectural dark horse may be about to change. The introduction of SIPs into geodesic architecture has the potential to revitalize the industry. As energy efficiency becomes more of the norm for builders, designers will begin to turn away from out-of-date, copycat traditional European styles and design buildings for the 21st century that utilize 21st-century materials. Domes should become a part of this landscape, and the combination of dome architecture and panel efficiency could claim a part of this business. Look for more designs that incorporate triacon-based, right-angle triangles to eliminate waste and increase material efficiency.

Off-the-grid buildings When a site for a building has difficult or very remote access, SIPs may well be the only practical approach to putting up a building. SIP technology gives a builder the ability to precut roof rakes, door and

Affordable Housing: A SIP Case Study

The Samson Homes division of FischerSips has provided much-needed affordable housing in Louisville, Kentucky. (Photo courtesy FisherSips.)

Fred Fischer of FischerSips Inc., one of the founders of SIPA and the organization's first president, has been a leader in the industry for many years. In the mid-1980s, Fischer learned that high winter energy bills were one of the leading causes of eviction and foreclosure for low-income families. Since then, FischerSips has dedicated considerable effort to filling the need for quality affordable housing. FischerSips puts its money behind this philosophy and has recently opened a state-of-the-art modular plant that uses the company's SIPs for wall and roof components (its leadership and innovation in the affordable housing market earned FischerSips an award from the U.S. Department of Housing and Urban Development in 1997).

FischerSips recently built 850 houses in a subdivision outside of Louisville, Kentucky. One of the principal builders in this subdivision, Fischer charges a premium of $500 per home, reflecting their Energy Star rating and the fact that his SIP homes are a quality upgrade that is better than the competition. His focus on this market has quadrupled FischerSips' sales since 1997, while at the same time serving the community with a much-needed quality product.

Buildings for the National Science Foundation in the Antarctic have to be durable, energy efficient, and quick to construct. SIPs are the perfect match for these demanding conditions. (Photo courtesy Steve Meredith.)

SIPs Work in Hostile Environments

Eric Bonnyman of Scanada Consultants worked with SIP manufacturer Thermapan Industries (see Resources on p. 182) to prefabricate a laboratory for the Otto Svendrup Centennial Expedition to be erected 200 miles from the magnetic North Pole. The panels have special coatings to resist the abrasive effects of wind-blown ice crystals. Researchers will alternate between the 12-ft. by 24-ft. structure and the main expedition headquarters located on the expedition's ship, which is locked into the ice offshore until spring. Emil Taraba of Thermapan claims that the building is so tightly constructed that the body heat of the occupants will be sufficient to heat the lab.

The laboratory under construction. (Photo courtesy Eric Bonnyman, Scanada Consultants.)

window openings, and complete walls. Of course, the panels for this type of building would necessarily be small, easily handled ones (probably 4 ft. wide). An erection crew could put this type of building together in a very short time, taking advantage of a narrow weather window or other restrictions.

SIP building packages have been carried by helicopter into sites as remote as the South Pole because the durable panels can withstand the rough handling that can happen when getting a package to an out-of-the-way site. Steve Meredith, architect for Antarctic Support Associates, has designed and constructed a number of two-story buildings at research stations in the Antarctic using panels from Winter Panel, Advance Foam Plastics, Enercept, and Premier Industries (see Resources on pp. 180-182). These buildings, which use SIPs for floors, walls, and roofs, are constructed for the National Science Foundation, which has specified that only SIPs be used in this hostile environment.

An insulated concrete form (ICF) first level ties into the existing house.

SIP additions

A question I'm often asked is whether you can build a SIP addition onto an existing house. The answer is yes, but there are some things to bear in mind. While the assembly techniques involved to build additions are basically the same as for new construction, it's important to have a square and level slab or subfloor when building with SIPs. A high percentage of existing buildings are out of square as a result of settling over time; tying into a crooked building with SIPs can be done, but you'll need to bring the addition plumb and level at the first panel.

Another factor to consider before choosing SIPs for an addition is the accessibility of the site. Space limitations around the existing building may make it difficult to get panels to the back of the house or up onto the addition roof. You should also consider the practicality of putting a highly energy-efficient addition that is, say, 20% of the floor area onto a home that is built to outdated standards of air leakage.

In spite of these limitations, for additions that have their own foundations and minimal contact with the existing structure, SIPs offer the same benefits as they do for new construction. For example, the addition shown in the photos above and on the facing page was a perfect fit for SIPs.

The second floor under construction. Siding and windows are installed on the panels before the SIP walls are raised.

The addition awaits its roof.

The finished addition, with stucco on the first-floor exterior and cedar siding on the second floor.

Chapter 4

TOOLING UP FOR THE JOB

POWER TOOLS

SPECIALTY FASTENERS,
ADHESIVES, AND
CAULKS

JIGS, TEMPLATES, AND
CONVEYING SYSTEMS

Although SIPs is a new technology, for the most part you'll be able to put up a SIP building with the tools and equipment already in your job boxes. There are a few specialized tools and equipment that you'll need to erect a SIP structure, as well as a number of templates, jigs, and conveyers that will make the project faster and more accurate. What you need depends to a large extent on whether you decide to use prefabricated panels or cut your own. But even if you take advantage of the precut services offered by many manufacturers, you'll still need to be able to cut and scoop panels on-site to adjust them to fit.

Power Tools

Besides being a necessity for work, good tools are a pleasure to use. Most contractors may grumble about the high cost of workers' compensation insurance and taxes but really don't mind spending money on the latest and greatest tools to come down the pike. So to most builders it isn't difficult justifying the investment in a few new tools for working with SIPs. The tools you'll need to build a SIP structure include beam saws and cutting tools, foam scoops, and caulk guns.

Cutting tools

Cutting panels to shape and cutting out the openings for doors and windows are the first tasks that require special SIP tools. Unfortunately, a

The author lets the foam fly as he trims a wall panel to fit using the Linear Link saw from Muskegon Power Tool Co. (Photo by Jon Blumb.)

The Linear Link, a worm-drive saw with a 12-in. bar and chain, is well suited for heavy-duty cutting of SIPs.

standard 7¼-in. or 8¼-in. circular saw won't cut through even the thinnest 4½-in.-thick panels. If you had to make only a few cuts, a reciprocating saw could do a reasonable—although slow—job. But even if you'll only be building your own SIP house or a one-time project, it would be worthwhile to invest in a saw designed to cut through these thick panels accurately.

Used extensively in the timber-frame industry, beam saws do a good job of cutting SIP wall panels as well. One of the most popular oversize circular beam saws on the market is the 16⁵⁄₁₆-in. Makita 5402A. This monster is designed for cutting beams, packs 12 amps of power, and sells for about $680. This saw is heavy (weighing just more than 30 lb.) and has a maximum depth of cut at 90 degrees of 6³⁄₁₆ in. When fitted with a carbide blade, it will cut through 4½-in. and 6½-in. SIPs like butter. The narrow kerf does not displace much of the foam core as the saw cuts, and the

foam does not offer enough heat friction to worry about melting the foam on the blade.

This saw does have some serious drawbacks, however. The major drawback is that the saw won't cut through 8¼-in. or thicker panels in one pass. This 8¼-in. panel thickness is the mainstay of roof panels in moderate climates of the United States because of its R-30 rating, while many builders prefer even thicker 10¼-in. and 12¼-in. panels that can bring a roof up to R-45 and higher. Another drawback of the Makita 5402A beam saw is that when cutting out openings, the circular blade cannot cut flush into an inside corner. You can backcut these with a reciprocating saw, but that takes two tools to do one job. A final drawback is that the saw's weight makes it unwieldy to cut wall openings in place.

The big guys in the SIP industry use a worm-drive saw called the Linear Link, made by Muskegon Power Tool Co., to cut panels (see

Both the Linear Link (left) and the Prazi PR-7000 (right) have the depth of blade necessary to cut through jumbo panels quickly. (Photo by Jon Blumb.)

Making a plunge cut with the Prazi beam cutter is safe and fast.

Resources on p. 183). I tried the model VCS-12, which lists for $620. This unit will cut 12 in. at 90 degrees and 8¾ in. at 45 degrees. The Linear Link features a manually operated oiler with a large translucent reservoir, making it easy to quickly check the oil level. The company urges the use of a low kickback, ANSI-standard blue label chain, and the saw uses a standard Oregon Manufacturing 12-in. bar, so it should be able to handle a larger 16-in. bar for cutting through monster panels at an angle.

Although this saw is heavy, the balance is good and the saw has a solid feel while cutting. Debris from the cuts is a nuisance, but the Linear Link's speed and durability make up for that drawback.

Saw attachments Instead of buying a complete saw, you can add an attachment to your present saw. One light, versatile, and inexpensive (about $100) saw attachment that's extremely useful for cutting SIPs is the Prazi USA model PR-7000 beam cutter (see Resources on p. 183). An attachment that's designed to fit onto the frame of many of

the top-selling worm-drive circular saws, the Prazi comes with a variety of bushings and bolts that will adapt the device to fit Skil 77, 77M, and 5860, Craftsman 2761, Black & Decker 3051, Milwaukee 6377, and Makita 5077B saws. This device devours SIPs, and I use it as my main cutting and shaping tool.

It takes only a few minutes to convert a worm-drive saw into a panel-cutting workhorse with the Prazi beam cutter. Once the saw is set up, it can make a variety of cuts. The attachment is an adapter that substitutes a $\frac{5}{32}$-in. chainsaw chain for the regular circular saw blade, and it runs the chain vertically. No modifications to the shoe of the saw are necessary to get the unit up and running, and the adapter unit includes a tensioner lever, geared sprocket tip with oil hole, and an antikickback guard. I have my Prazi PR 7000 attached to my Skil 5860 8¼-in. worm-drive saw, which allows me to cut up to 60-degree bevels, a useful feature for cutting complex hips and valleys.

The original versions of this tool used a standard 12-in. chain with offset teeth every 1½ in. that was available from chainsaw supply outlets. In 1998, Prazi introduced its own design of a thin-kerf chain that makes a cleaner cut and throws off less debris. The saw can be used to freehand-cut a straight line, but the flying foam debris makes it a good idea to darken your snap line with a blue or red keel for visibility. Making plunge cuts with the Prazi is easy, even through thick panels. It will cut to a depth of 12 in., which will handle all but the largest SIPs. The whole setup is light enough to cut window openings in place if necessary.

There are some drawbacks to this tool. Although the resistance of the panels to the chain is low, not having an automatic oiler will likely become a problem for heavy-duty production cutting. According to some of the fabricators I spoke with, the Prazi isn't suited to all-day, day-in, day-out panel cutting. Chainsaw-based tools produce quite a bit of annoying debris. I rigged up a collector made from cardboard and duct tape to funnel debris through a 3-in. dryer vent line into a shop vac. This crude setup eliminates about 35% of the stuff, but since the cut is made on the downstroke, not all the sawdust comes back up through the kerf. Prazi makes a dust-collection attachment, which can be purchased for about $150.

While these beam saws, worm-drive saws, and beam-cutter attachments are heavy-duty tools that offer a stable platform to machine SIPs, many builders get by using an electric chainsaw for the job. Premier Building Systems offers an aluminum shoe fabricated to fit on a Poulan electric chainsaw. This stable, lightweight unit is excellent for cutting window openings in place (see p. 115).

Foam scoops

Once the panels are cut to size and the door and window rough openings are made, the foam needs to be cut away, or relieved, at the edges to accommodate plates, studs, trimmers, and other dimensional members to prepare the panels for installation. There are a number of tools on the market to accomplish this task, including several types of foam scoops. Many manufacturers of SIPs provide scoops as part of the panel package. As with most tools, there are the sport utility beasts and then there are the homely sedans.

There are a number of scoop options for cutting back the foam from panels to accommodate studs, plates, and connecting splines. (Photo by Jon Blumb.)

The basic hot scoop is reliable, tough, and can withstand job-site abuse. The adjustable bar can be set to different depths to remove more or less foam depending on the application. (Photo by Jon Blumb.)

Hot scoops The most basic of these foam scoops uses what I refer to as the BBQ starter or branding iron approach, which consists of a heavy resistance wire that burns its way through the foam. The foam scoops I use are manufactured by L & H Manufacturing Co. (see Resources on p. 183). It makes models that will cut 3½ in., 5½ in., 7¼ in., 9¼ in., and 11¼ in. of foam. Unfortunately, a separate tool is needed to scoop each different thickness of foam. L & H's scoops have an adjustable bar that can be set to different depths depending on whether you are prepping for a spline connector or for a header or other structural element.

These hot scoops are durable and very reliable, but they do have some drawbacks. Because the hot resistance element is radiused about ½ in. at the corners, they don't cut a square corner, so you have to make a separate pass down both sides of the cut to clean back to a crisp corner. In addition, the resistance element is a ⁵⁄₁₆-in.-dia. tube, which displaces the foam by burning it out of the way. This takes some time, and an 8-ft. pass takes a while. Hot scoops also produce clouds of noxious fumes that require the operator to wear

The hot scoop can also be used to open up panels for plumbing chases.

The Hot Rod tool by Demand Products cuts fast and clean. The NiChrome cutting wire can be adjusted to change the cutting depth.

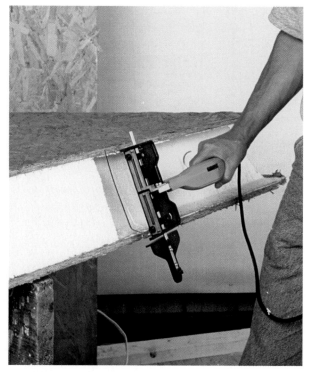

The QC Hot Knife comes with handy preformed shapes, and the flat NiChrome wire can be custom-bent. Here a custom-shaped tool is used to relieve a valley cut. (Photo by Jon Blumb.)

breathing protection. The industry assures that the smoke produced is no more toxic than burning Douglas fir, but this stuff smells bad! There is no adjustment for the heat either, so when the tool's not being used, it can accidentally start a fire quickly.

Hot-wire systems A more sophisticated approach to removing foam also utilizes electrical resistance—in this case, nickel-chrome wire (NiChrome). I've used three different NiChrome systems. The Hot Rod, manufactured by Demand Products, Inc. (see Resources on p. 183), has a remote transformer with an adjustable-range heat setting. A 10-ft. insulated cord hooks to a sled that will accept up to an 11½-in.-wide profile. The flat NiChrome cutting wire is available in various stock shapes and lengths, and the wire can also be bent into almost any shape for custom applications. This tool costs almost $1,100 and is well suited for production cutting of most profiles in EPS.

Windlock Corporation manufactures another version of a NiChrome resistance device. Its QC Hot Knife system (see Resources on p. 183) has no transformer but instead sends AC current directly to a handle with an on/off trigger and a heat-adjustment wheel. This handle can be connected to either flat NiChrome wire or to a sled that will accept up to a 5-in.-wide profile. The Hot Knife kit costs about $300 and has a number of available accessories for the foam industry, some of which are helpful in shaping SIP foam.

A standard accessory that comes with the Hot Knife is a shape for cutting 1½-in.-dia. electrical chases, which comes in handy at the ends or at the top or bottom of a SIP. The Hot Knife's handle and sled are made of molded plastic, and the handle has a flex protector on the end of the cord. This tool is light and durable and has the flexibility to perform many tasks, although a wider sled would be useful for working with the thick roof panels.

This hot-wire system, which requires two people to operate, uses electrical resistance through a piano-string-thin wire to cut foam quickly and accurately. (Photo by Jon Blumb.)

In another resistance tool approach, a piano-string-thin NiChrome wire is stretched between two independent handles at whatever length panel you are working on. The wire is attached to the handles with thumbscrew-type terminals, and two people must move the handles in a coordinated fashion to cut shapes in the foam. The circuit is completed through a transformer with adjustable heat ranges. This tool cuts clean, accurate shapes very quickly with almost no smoke or odor. Some versions have the transformer miniaturized on one of the handles, but field reports on the small portable transformer indicate that it can be prone to fatal overheating and is expensive to replace. Care must also be taken not to trip over the wire if it is left lying around. Although this tool requires two operators, it does such a fast, clean job that I think many fabricators would find it extremely worthwhile.

Putting the various hot-wire tools to side-by-side tests for speed, accuracy, and durability brings me to the following conclusions: The Hot Rod and the QC Hot Knife both cut through foam faster than the branding irons, but both of the NiChrome wire tools noticeably distorted the cut foam, especially along the flat bottom of the cut. This distortion was dependent on the speed of travel. When we slowed the travel rate down, the cuts were cleaner and more accurate. (Incidentally, the cuts made by these two tools were almost smokeless.) But once the speed was reduced to make more accurate cuts, the Hot Rod and the QC Hot Knife were only marginally faster than my L & H branding iron. And I can attest to the durability of L & H's product—mine has literally been kicked around my job sites for years, yet it keeps melting foam when asked. I like the simplicity of the branding iron approach for everyday use and the QC Hot Knife for custom chases and details.

One other method of removing the foam from panels is to use a grinder attachment that removes foam with a router-like bit. Urethane foam has a much higher melting point than EPS, so it needs to be removed using a mechanical process. Although I haven't had the chance to use one of these units, it seems that having foam bits flying around is an undesirable by-product. If, on the other hand, its speed makes up for some of its drawbacks, I would try it out. As more people use urethane panels, tools to shape and install them will likely become available.

Caulk guns

In a SIP building, a tremendous amount of caulk and adhesives is used at the panel connections. Because some adhesives and caulks will react with the cores of the panels in a negative way, the SIP supplier will either provide or recommend an adhesive caulk. A typical 8-ft. wall spline joint uses 32 ft. of an adhesive bead, so over the course of a typical project many hundreds of feet of caulk beads are necessary. This is a lot of caulk to be pumped by hand, so it's a good idea to consider one of the powered alternatives.

I use a PG 151 professional Caulk Master manufactured by Kahnetics LLC (see Resources on p. 183) that's powered by compressed air. Because this tool operates at a maximum air pressure of 70 psi, which is less than the 100 psi that most air tools operate on, it requires a separate regulator or another compressor setup. It will accept ⅒-gal. or 1-qt. tubes with an interchangeable adapter. I've found that this tool really speeds up the application of caulks and adhesives.

The tool has no moving parts because the air itself provides the piston action to push the end plug up the tube, so it should last longer than a regular caulk gun. The impact-resistant plastic housing is durable, and the $75 price tag seems reasonable. Just be sure to remove the caulk tubes at the end of the day. Because of the closed housing, if glue gets in between the tube and the case, it will be a big problem to get the tube out. Removing the tubes prevents that from happening.

There are also cordless powered caulk guns that look promising. For example, Windlock Corporation makes Power Caulkers that can be adapted to cordless drills. Their 10-oz. version costs $50 and the 1-qt. size costs $57. You can also use self-contained cordless caulk applicators.

The pneumatic Caulk Master has no moving parts and pumps caulks and adhesives effortlessly. Here the author is applying a bead of glue to both facings before positioning the stud for a corner panel. (Photo courtesy Jon Blumb.)

Specialty Fasteners, Adhesives, and Caulks

What holds all the parts and pieces of a SIP house together? In addition to various types of mechanical fasteners, all manufacturers require systematic application of adhesives and caulks to the connections of a SIP structure. These products take time to apply, but in the construction of a SIP structure, they will ensure the most airtight and structurally sound building possible.

Nails, staples, and screws

To construct a SIP shell requires thousands of fasteners, including nails, staples, and screws, depending on the connection. My rule of thumb is that a nail or a staple needs to penetrate at least 1 in. into wood. I increase that to a penetration depth of 1½ in. for the panel screws.

OSB spline wall joints can be either nailed or stapled.

For panel corners and panel roof to plate or beam connections, I use long panel screws. But when a SIP to plate, SIP to door/window trimmer or stud, or SIP to solid spline or rafter connection is needed, I use collated 8d nails. I have used ringshank nails in these situations in the past, but since the OSB is glued to the wood member, the chance of any fastener working loose is remote at best. And as in other situations where plywood or OSB is nailed off, it is important not to break the outer skin of the material with the nail head. If this happens, reduce the air pressure until the head sets flush with the surface.

The nailing schedule is part of the SIP system's engineering and should be specified by the panel manufacturer. When I am fastening OSB to OSB with no solid wood behind the connection (such as with an OSB spline for wall panels), I use ½-in. by 1½-in.-long crown staples that are installed every 4 in. The staples hold very well in this application, whereas a nail loses some of its holding power after it penetrates the two OSB layers and continues into the nonstructural foam. Staples are also less expensive than nails for these standard connections. In all cases, be sure to check the requirements of the panel manufacturer whose panel you are using for fastening schedules.

Nails and staples are not interchangeable because they are connecting different materials. I have a staple gun and a nail gun hooked up in the same area on the job site so I can make either connection without having to change tools on the air hoses. During the assembly process, panels are going together at such a rate that one worker will have difficulty keeping up with the joints that have to be fastened.

Heavy-duty connectors

A SIP building is much stronger structurally than a conventionally framed building, so it's even more important to detail how it is connected to the ground to take full advantage of the SIPs' qualities. In some areas of the country (California, for example), seismic activity has prompted building codes to require a series of hold-down connections for any floor system—regardless of construction method—before the walls and roof are even ready for installation. The Midwest (where I work) is in the middle of tornado country, so uplift resistance is a real concern in the structures I build.

In addition to the steel connectors that are used to anchor the building to the foundation and the straps that make the floor to floor connections strong, a SIP building can take advantage of the long panel screws to hold corners solid and keep the roof panels secured to the wall. When all these steel connectors are incorporated into the SIP system, the buildings have shear and uplift resistance unattainable by using conventional stick-framing techniques. For

Panel Screws Are Not Drywall Screws

About 10 years ago, engineers came up with an improved panel screw design that enables the screws to be quickly driven through even thick SIPs yet has tremendous shear and pullout resistance. These screws come in lengths to fit any panel application and can be installed with standard screw guns.

I like to use Olympic Fasteners #3 square-drive, pancake-head panel screws. These screws drive flush into OSB, so they won't telegraph through the roofing. Their heat-treated, coated-steel shank is $\frac{3}{16}$ in. dia. and has a $\frac{1}{4}$-in. major diameter at the threads. The spade point is designed to self-tap into wood and easily installs with a couple of blows with a framing hammer to penetrate the skins and foam, while a cordless screw gun quickly anchors the screw to the solid framing member below. These screws are typically placed every 12 in. around the eaves, ridge, and rakes of a roof and at corners in the walls. Each panel screw has a pullout resistance of 840 lb. When these screws were tested to failure for shear, the OSB skins failed before the screw would break.

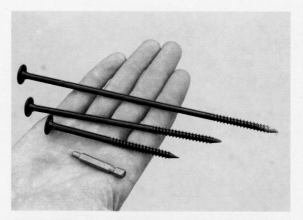

Panel screws are self-tapping, quick to install, and are rated at more than 800 lb. of pullout resistance. (Photo by Jon Blumb.)

me as a builder, this extra margin of safety and strength of construction is one of the most impressive features of the system. I'll show how to incorporate these connectors into the building in chapter 6.

Adhesive caulk

The EPS-core SIPs that most builders work with require multiple beads of adhesive caulk at every connection between panels. As is typical in the industry, my SIP supplier has its own particular adhesive, which it supplies in 1-qt. tubes. Any glue used with EPS must not be a solvent-based product or it will melt the foam, causing voids in the envelope and possibly voiding the panel manufacturer's warranty. In most cases, adhesives that are specifically designed to be used with SIPs are included with the initial panel order, with the required quantity calculated by the supplier.

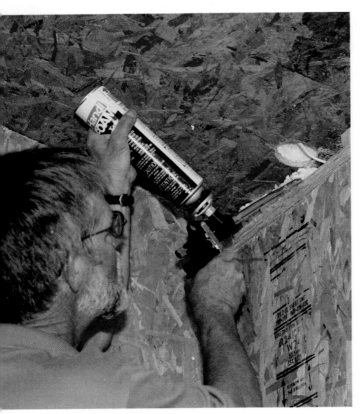

An applicator gun adjusts the amount of expanding foam that can be applied to fill gaps at connections between panels (here, between a wall panel and a roof panel).

Foam-dispensing system

During the fabrication and erection stage, one of the key components to a tight building is the application of expanding foam to all connections and assemblies. Besides being used at panel-to-panel connections and behind studs and plates, foam should also be applied to gaps between window and door frames. You can buy disposable 12-oz. and 16-oz. cans of expanding foam from hardware stores and lumberyards, but these always seem to get as much on the person dispensing the foam as on the joint being foamed.

A much more professional and economical way to apply foam is to use a polyurethane sealant kit. Fomo Products, Inc. (see Resources on p. 182) produces Handi-Foam moisture-cure one-component kits and a Handi-Foam two-part kit. The one-component product is a low-expansion foam that tacks up in 10 minutes and cures in about an hour. This easy-to-use system has three application nozzles available and comes with a solvent to keep the guns clean. Kit sizes range from a 24-oz. screw-on can to a 16-lb. jug for the big jobs. Fomo also makes construction adhesives that are compatible with the applicator gun.

The two-part Handi-Foam self-contained system features nozzles that adjust to three fan patterns and kits that contain up to 605 bd. ft. of foam. The foam expands to a ratio of 8:1 and cures in seconds. Both of these foam products meet or exceed BOCA, ICBO, and SBCCI building codes. This type of foam application system is a must for a really tight building.

Jigs, Templates, and Conveying Systems

The task of moving SIPs around the shop or job site, especially when the panels can be up to 8 ft. wide and 20 ft. or more long, can be daunting. These panels are expensive, so cuts need to be accurate and error-free. I use jigs and templates to make my cuts easier and a number of types of

A simple rolling cart made from a panel scrap makes moving large panels around the shop a one-person job. (Photo by Jon Blumb.)

A straightedge guide attached to the panel helps ensure a straight, accurate cut.

conveying systems—ranging from carts to cranes—to help move the panels around.

Jigs and templates

Fabrication of SIP panels can be made faster and easier by using templates and straightedges. For my guides, I use ½-in. MDF strips because this material won't warp like plywood and the ½-in. thickness makes it easy to lift up the base of the saw to cut into the corners.

These jigs and templates can be used again and again. I countersink holes every 16 in. and use 1½-in. screws to quickly attach and remove these guides. Once the cut lines are snapped onto the panel, I offset the guides the distance from the edge of the shoe of the saw to the cut line. For long straight cuts, I use a series of these straightedges.

Equipment for moving panels

Job-site handling of SIPs and their placement present logistical problems that are different from those encountered with conventional building systems. The size and weight of the panels necessitate that the sequence of site storage and assembly be set up so that the panels are not moved more than necessary. Of course, every site is different and every contractor has a slightly different sequencing system, so there isn't any one best way to do this.

For example, the first few SIP jobs I took on were mainly handled manually. A 4-ft. by 8-ft. by 6½-in. panel weighs about 115 lb., and one person can walk it around. But an 8-ft. by 24-ft. panel that weighs more than 600 lb. is a different story. I moved these large panels around the shop with four men, which is an inefficient use of scarce manpower. It isn't realistic to think you can move these big SIPs onto a roof manually, so some sort of mechanical assistance is necessary.

To facilitate moving panels, I fabricated a wheeled cart from a panel scrap that makes moving parts around the shop floor or the deck of a job site a one-man job (see the photo at right on p. 69). This is an important point because layout and fabrication of a panel is a one-person job, but if it takes two people to move the panel, it's inefficient. My cart is a convenient height for layout, and with its large open center, windows can often be cut out without much shifting around of the panel. The cart has heavy-duty 4-in.-dia. casters with one pair fixed and one pair able to swivel and lock.

The first powered moving unit you might want to consider is a pallet jack, which is helpful for moving panels from station to station. But it's of limited use for vertical stacking. For this, a forklift is a better option. If you're fabricating the panels in your shop, a forklift is an essential tool for unloading the units and moving them onto the fabrication tables. An even more versatile unit is a gas-powered lift with pneumatic tires that would be able to navigate gravel to unload truckloads of panels at the job site. I prefer to use forks that are 5 ft. long because I can load 8-ft. panels past their balance point. Used units are available at around $3,000 and up.

The greatest way to gain mechanical advantage in moving and placing SIPs is by buying a reticulated forklift. These large, rubber-wheeled workhorses can unload the panels at the site, move them up to the roof, and position them with great accuracy, even the monster panels that are often used in roof sections. These forklifts are a standard tool for modern framing contractors and are seen on job sites throughout the country. They can extend their forks to a distance of 40 ft., which can reach to almost any point on any roof, and they can operate on hilly, uneven ground even when it's muddy. Some have a hinged frame that allows them to "crab" along and get into

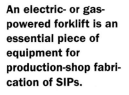

An electric- or gas-powered forklift is an essential piece of equipment for production-shop fabrication of SIPs.

A reticulated forklift with a boom attachment can accurately place a large roof panel up to 40 ft. from the ground.

Most builders working with SIPs quickly find that a crane is an essential piece of equipment for installing roof panels. (Photo courtesy Panel Built.)

places that would otherwise be inaccessible to a wheeled vehicle.

Forklifts equipped with a boom offer a greater degree of control than is available with a crane. Because of the forklift's shorter distance between the boom and the panel, a roof can be set with a fork when a crane may have to stay off the job for safety's sake on a windy day.

Of course, there are many sites where limited access means that the only way to move large panels into place is with a crane. In most cases, a crane to assist in the placing of roof panels or groups of panels is essential and should be considered part of the budgeting for job labor. Cranes can typically be set in just one or two positions on a job site, moving all of the panels for a job from those locations. Occasionally, I've found that in lots with difficult access, there may be only one spot to set up a crane. Crane time can run to $100/hr., so it's a good idea to have everything set for a quick erection once the meter is running on the crane. (See chapter 7 for more information on cranes and how they are used to set roof panels.)

Modular Cranes

The idea of a small construction company owning its own crane seemed far-fetched until I came across a company that makes a series of modular cranes that can be mounted to a pickup truck bed or trailer. This setup gives a smaller operation much more control of the timing for a job. Little Samson, Inc. manufactures a series of small cranes that can add to the flexibility and profits of any small construction company. Their LS 30-ft. crane can lift 2,000 lb. at 65 degrees up to 31 ft. and operates on 12-volt DC, 220-volt AC, or gasoline power. It costs about $18,000.

A simple welded lifting plate installs through a 1-in.-dia. hole in the panel and can be quickly detached.

Lifting plates and devices

On my first SIP project, I coordinated my schedule so that a tractor-trailer load of roof panels arrived on the same day that I'd hired a crane. We used 4-in. nylon straps wrapped around the panels to lift them. Everything was going smoothly until it came time to remove the nylon straps from the first heavy 8-ft. by 16-ft. roof panel that had just been lifted up. The problem was that when the panel was lowered into place, the straps were pinched between the panel and the top plate. I had the crane pull the straps back out, but when the knot of the strap hit the plate it still needed to be levered over the hump, an awkward procedure.

Another widely used (although crude) method is to whack a pair of hay hooks into the top skin of a panel, screw a 2x4 into the panel to hold them in place, then hook the whole assembly to the crane with a lifting strap. While both the strap method and the hay hook method are used often, I've come to appreciate that this is an area where you shouldn't take any chances of accidents and that some sort of safe, easily attached and detached device to assist in lifting the panels into place by crane or forklift is essential.

This spring-loaded lifting pin fabricated by Little Samson, Inc. can be released from the top.

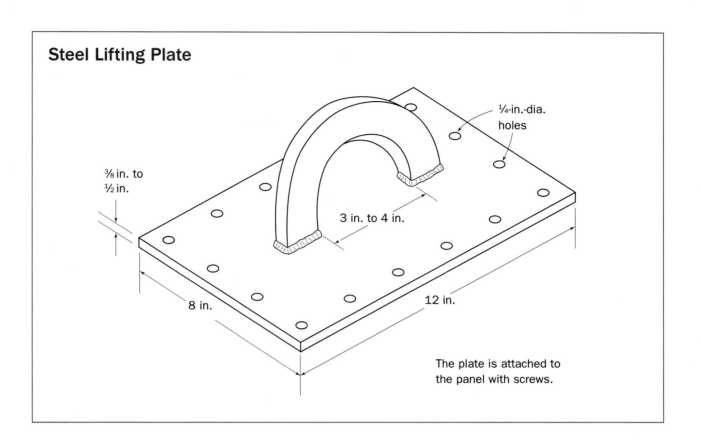

Steel Lifting Plate

¼-in.-dia. holes

⅜ in. to ½ in.

3 in. to 4 in.

8 in.

12 in.

The plate is attached to the panel with screws.

These devices are called lifting plates, and it is a simple and inexpensive task to draw up a design for a lifting plate and have it fabricated at your local welding shop (see the top photo on the facing page). To use a lifting plate, I first find the horizontal centerline of the panel and set the plates just above it. This way, when lifted the panel is tilted close to the pitch of the roof, which makes the positioning and setting of the roof panels an easy task. When the position is located, a 1-in.-dia. hole is drilled through the panel, the threaded rod is inserted, and the nut is tightened over the stiffening plate.

Another innovative lifting device is a spring-loaded rod with a welded eye and a swivel bar (see the bottom photo on the facing page). When stuck through a hole and over a stiffening plate, the rod springs out to lock in the panel. Made by Little Samson, Inc. (see Resources on p. 183), this device can be removed by one person from the top of the panel. It is rated at 1,000 lb. per pin by the manufacturer.

More and more of the current generation of panels come with a finished surface on the interior. In this situation, I don't like to drill a hole all the way through the panel, so a device that secures the panel from the top skin is needed. I use a rectangular steel plate with a welded eye and a series of screw holes drilled through the plate for attaching it to the panel (see the drawing above). Panel screws can be drilled through the panel into blocks underneath or just from the top with drywall screws. The number of screws needed to attach the plate to the panel depends on the weight of the panel and the pullout resistance of each screw.

In the case of gable walls and rake walls, it may make sense to assemble the panels into a whole wall on the ground and raise the wall as a unit. I install windows and siding where possible, then raise the wall using wall jacks. Wall jacks are a standard part of any framing crew's job tools: They make lifting these heavy walls safe and sure.

Chapter 5

FABRICATING PANELS AND COMPONENTS

FABRICATION OPTIONS

PLANNING AND LAYOUT

FABRICATING WALL PANELS

FABRICATING ROOF PANELS

PACKING AND SHIPPING

Now that you know all about SIPs, the benefits of the SIP construction system, and the tools you'll need to work with them, it's time to start thinking about putting up a SIP building. Before you start to build, you will have to make sure each panel is prepared for its location in the building. A blank panel comes from the factory with the manufacturer's standard details prefabricated, but most of the panels will need some additional modifications before they are ready for installation.

A typical "off-the-shelf" panel comes from the factory with the top and bottom relieved for the plates (typically 1½ in.). The factory provides the detail to connect adjacent panels side by side as part of their basic setup along with their spline material. Panels usually come with two electrical chases run horizontally at receptacle height and at switch height. There will also be a vertical electrical chase in the middle of the panel (see the illustration on the facing page).

These are the basic prefabrication features of a panel; any additional cuts, such as for windows, doors, rakes, and roof-panel plumb cuts, are all considered extra fabrication. Think of it as ordering add-on options for a car. For example, you might want to order gable-wall panels with the rakes precut and the foam relieved 1½ in.; you might want panel #22 to have a 3-in. relief on the right side for a structural post to support a ridge

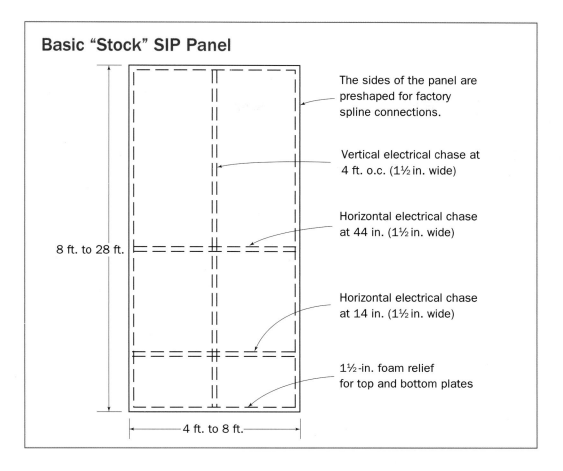

Basic "Stock" SIP Panel

8 ft. to 28 ft.

4 ft. to 8 ft.

The sides of the panel are preshaped for factory spline connections.

Vertical electrical chase at 4 ft. o.c. (1½ in. wide)

Horizontal electrical chase at 44 in. (1½ in. wide)

Horizontal electrical chase at 14 in. (1½ in. wide)

1½-in. foam relief for top and bottom plates

beam; or you might specify the electrical chases at 16 in. and 52 in. instead of at the standard height. You can have all the panels custom-built for your job, but there are also some other fabrication options.

Fabrication Options

Early in a panel project, you need to decide who is going to fabricate the panels. There are four options: have the panels prefabricated by the manufacturer; have them fabricated by an independent contractor; fabricate them on-site; or fabricate them in your own shop. As a builder, your choice will depend on a number of factors: how comfortable you are taking on new responsibilities; the number of panels involved in the project; how complicated the panels are to machine; your ability to fit the fabrication into your schedule; the availability of suitable shop

Panels come from the factory with the foam relieved for plates, splines, and electrical chases.

space; and, to some degree, the weather conditions during the panel fabrication. After the first couple of SIP projects, you'll be able to decide if SIP fabrication can make you money, keep you in control of the schedule, and add a positive dimension to your business.

Prefabrication by the manufacturer

If you decide to have the manufacturer prefabricate the panels for you, it can simplify your part of the process quite a bit. You let go of the responsibility of producing the shop drawings and preparing the panels and continue with the task of running the overall job. Reputable manufacturers will send an experienced representative to work with you if necessary. The rep's job is to make sure the parts will fit together, show the crew how to work with the panels, and answer questions about procedures and details. Many industry people I have spoken with say that if the first SIP experience is a positive one, the builder gets comfortable with the system and wants to use SIPs again. If building with SIPs is a hassle the first time, there likely won't be a second time.

Fabrication by an independent contractor

For a "briefcase" builder who subs out all of the work on a job, a second option is to find an independent fabricator to shape the panels, deliver the panels to the site, and install them. The demand for crews that specialize in fabrication and erection of panel systems is growing rapidly. If the builder decides to purchase a precut package, he will have to organize heavy equipment and staging locations and coordinate the installation crew. Many builders think that it's usually cost-effective to subcontract areas of the work that can be done faster, better, and cheaper than "in house." The tradeoff is to let go of some responsibility and some control and incur some additional expenses in terms of profit and overhead for these providers. For this type of

builder, it's just another sub to deal with but one that will be a key part of the success of a project.

On-site fabrication

The builder who chooses to purchase blank panels and fabricate them on-site will have the advantages of being able to take instant measurements for critical details, being able to adjust panel dimensions to meet actual requirements, and not having to move the panels twice. On the downside, he will also have to have a full complement of fabricating tools that will have to be rolled out each day and secured at the end of the day, be subject to weather delays, and have to worry about weather protection of the panels.

Many pioneer SIP builders started out this way because houses were built on-site. Period. The panels showed up on the job, and the crew put the building together. But experienced builders normally move away from this approach to gain the efficiency and all-weather capabilities of a shop setting. Not all builders will be able to find or justify the expense of a larger shop, however, but they can still be competitive by fabricating and installing panels on-site. Given the resourcefulness of builders, most will come up with a suitable arrangement—a custom van or trailer setup, perhaps—with all the equipment needed to fabricate and install SIPs on-site.

Shop fabrication

For a custom builder used to handling framing work with his own crew, working with SIPs has a short learning curve, and the new skill will add another dimension to his business. Sooner or later, a shop large enough to handle the fabrication of large panels will become a necessity. A systematic approach to labeling, layout, and fabrication will pay big dividends in efficiency. In most parts of the country, it is a big advantage to have the majority of the construction work take place in a controlled environment and not subject to the hazards of weather. By having a shop, the work goes on rain or shine, the tools are safe at night and can be easily maintained, and you can

On-site fabrication of panels allows you to adjust panel dimensions to meet actual requirements, but you'll need a full complement of fabricating tools for the job.

In-house fabrication keeps the builder in control of the job schedule.

wait for the right window in the weather patterns to deliver and install the package in a very short period of time.

This chapter focuses primarily on the builder who wants to have control of the project from the beginning and to have the SIPs delivered as a blank material ready for fabrication, either to his shop or to the building site. The fabrication techniques are the same in either situation, but the custom SIP builder will need a fabrication shop to do his best work most efficiently.

Planning and Layout

Once the basic floor plans and elevations for a project have been developed, it's time to produce a set of shop drawings. These panel drawings are necessary in order to do an accurate takeoff, either for the manufacturer to generate costs and incorporate your particular panels into its production schedule or for the builder planning on fabricating his own panels. These drawings will help the builder visualize each of the panels as a unit so that all the openings, connection details, rakes, and angles can be accurately and efficiently fabricated into the individual panels.

During planning and layout, it can be determined where cutoffs from one panel can be utilized to serve as headers or filler panels elsewhere, thus eliminating waste and saving money. At this point, it may be that a slight change in design can help your material and labor savings by more efficiently using the panels. With shop drawings in hand, the dimensional lumber and headers that are required in each panel can all be precut, labeled, and installed. Accurate shop drawings are your roadmap for ordering, fabrication, and erection.

Shop drawings

Start with the main floor plan and pick a point that's a convenient place to begin (typically a corner). It's also a good idea to make this the point from which you start to build. Denote each separate wall with a letter, then add the panels in a numerical sequence, that is, A-1, A-2, A-3, A-4,

These precut studs, trimmers, and blocks are labeled to correspond with their matching panels. The studs are predrilled with holes to line up with the electrical chases in the panels.

The lumber stream

As part of working out all the details of each panel on the elevations, you need to mark on the plan the lengths of each stud, trimmer, cripple, and block as well as the panel these pieces are connected to. (Bottom and top plates are part of the job-site material package, so they are not precut in the shop.) A cut list is produced, and as each piece is cut it is checked off the list. When cutting these pieces, aim for a tolerance of $\frac{1}{16}$ in. to ensure a close, accurate fit. Drill $1\frac{3}{4}$-in.-dia. holes in the studs and trimmers to correspond with the electrical chases precut into the factory panels.

Once all the pieces are measured and cut, use a magic marker to label all the studs, trimmers, and cripples with the code for the panel that they are installed in. Each piece gets a letter and number. When a two-piece assembly, such as a door or window trimmer next to a full stud, is needed, it's a good idea to nail these two parts together before installing the assembly into the panel because it is easy to line up the bottoms on the bench and nail the assembly together and label it only once.

It's possible to have a much more precise structure by carefully detailing these crucial lengths and connections beforehand, rather than scrambling around the job site trying to put it all together and hoping it comes out right. Once you have all the lumber cut to length and a large stack of raw panels, it's time to label and prep some panels.

Again, detailed shop drawings showing all the details that happen to the individual panels are essential at this point. Careful review of these shop drawings before ordering the SIPs can maximize what the factory provides in the way of electrical chases and edge detail and reduce or eliminate a lot of headaches later on.

and so on. I don't clutter the floor plan with all this information, but I do indicate the wall letter and show the panel breaks on the floor plan to work out panel relationships with openings and which walls will run through to the corners and which will butt into the walls. The last panel to complete the perimeter should be one that runs through to the corner. Otherwise, the installers will be trying to fit the last panel down from the top, a very difficult undertaking. (If you have to do this, make the last panel a 2-ft. section so it can be handled more easily.)

Once you have the floor plan worked out to make efficient use of the panels, it's time to transfer this information to the elevations. I make an extra set of elevations before all the standard notes are drawn so that the only information on these sheets is panel related. There's a lot of information on these sheets, and you'll want to cover all the details so that studs, trimmers, headers, chases, and all pertinent information can be drawn and transferred easily to full scale. At this point, you may not know who is going to install the package, so it pays to be thorough.

Fabricating Wall Panels

Once the wall panels have arrived from the factory with the foam relieved for the plates and splines and the electrical chases in place, you're

SIP Shop Layout

A large, open floor space and roll-up doors are assets for SIP-production shops. This well-organized shop is used by Panel Built Contractors in Nevada City, California.

A production shop is a big asset for a SIP builder. Its floor plan will have a lot to do with the speed and efficiency in which a job can be turned out. Because of the size of the materials, a functional SIP fabrication shop will need more room than most woodworking shops, and large roll-up doors that can be cleared by a forklift with a group of panels are a real asset.

Designing a shop is something like designing a kitchen for a customer. There's a basic work triangle between materials, tools, and fabrication area that's somewhat flexible according to available space and a builder's particular way of doing things. In an ideal setup, raw SIPs and lumber will come in one end, be machined in the middle of the shop, and be packed and staged for shipping at the other end.

This is not to say that you need a shiny new shop to work with SIPs, and most of us have to make do with the space we have. At the current growth rate of the industry, some contractors will be making SIPs a big, if not the only, part of their future business and will need to expand their facility to accommodate these bigger pieces.

Shop Drawing of a Wall Section

This shop drawing provides all the information needed for fabricating this wall: individual panel numbers and panel dimensions; all plate lengths and sizes; and lengths for studs, trimmers, headers, sills, and cripples.

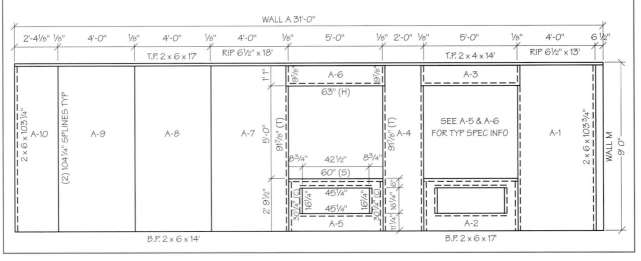

Depending on the manufacturer, you may need to cut an eave-wall panel to the measured height.

After cutting the panel to length, scoop the foam back to the depth of the top plate.

ready to label and fabricate each panel to get it ready for installation. There are a number of things you may have to do, depending on the application. These include cutting the panels to length; installing studs in the ends of corner panels; predrilling for the long panel screws that tie corners together; cutting door and window openings, scooping out the foam, and nailing in studs, trimmers, and blocking; fabricating the header and sill sections; cutting plumbing chases; and cutting beam pockets.

In any group of panels used for one wall, it's very helpful to machine the panel that will be used last first so that when the stack of SIPs on the job site is ready for installation the first panel is on top. Once a panel is positioned for fabrication on some sturdy sawhorses, the first task is to use a thick marker to label the outside and top of the panel with an arrow and the panel code. When that panel is lying flat on the deck, the outside will be up and easy to read. It's also a good idea to mark all sides of the foam of a panel so it can be determined which panel it is from any view—a 30-second procedure that can eliminate a lot of confusion later on.

Cutting panels to length

Whether you'll need to machine the top of a wall panel depends on whether it's for an eave wall or a gable/rake wall. Many factories cut the eave wall panels to the exact height as part of their basic service. Because the foam core will be relieved 1½ in. for the top plate, there is little to do except check that the heights of the panels are correct. Some manufacturers, however, supply panels only in 1-ft. increments. In this case, you'll have to cut the panel to length and scoop the foam to the desired depth.

The standard wall configuration with a single 2x top plate has been extensively tested and has an axial load rating of about 2,000 lb./linear foot, depending on the height of the wall and wind-load factors. The plates are cut and installed at the

The double top plate detail almost doubles the bearing capacity of the wall.

site, but if the walls have to carry more load or if point loads will bear on the wall, you might want to add a second plate (known as a "cap" plate). This cap plate can be 1⅛-in. particleboard or plywood or ripped 2x material. The plate should be ripped to the width of the overall panel so that it bears fully on both of the panel facings. This inexpensive addition to the wall has been shown to nearly double the load-bearing capacity of the wall below. (For more on top-plate details for roof to wall connections, see chapter 7.)

Whereas on an eave wall you're dealing with square-cut panels, on a gable or rake wall the top panels are cut at an angle. The factory will charge extra for laying out and cutting these panels; here, I'll explain how to do the work yourself. The first thing you need to do is to order the panels so that each section is long enough to accommodate the high point. Lay out a rake wall by first marking the low point of the wall on the outside panel; establish this point by measuring to the top outside corner of the adjacent eave wall. Next, lay out the roof pitch on the first panel of the

rake wall, and mark the high point on the panel. Transfer this same measured point to the next panel as the low point and continue the procedure all the way up the rake.

Once you've marked the high and low points on the panels, snap a chalkline between the points and then make the cut at 90 degrees. The foam core needs to be relieved 1½ in. for the top plate, but the plate isn't installed until the walls are erected.

When fabricating a rake wall, I'm often able to save material by using the triangular offcut from a fabricated rake panel. I flip it over to use with the flat top of another gable-end panel that has been calculated to accept this piece (see the illustration on p. 82). The offcut panel triangle will already have a 1½-in. setback in the foam core on the top edge, but it will need a double 2x spline along the base of this triangle to anchor the two pieces together (see "Wall Spline Connections" on p. 82).

I don't use these offcut triangles when I am supporting a purlin or a ridge beam because I want the point load to be continuous to the

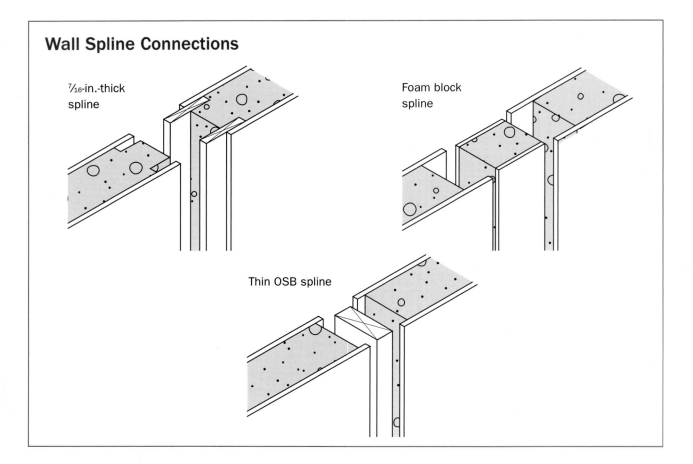

Wall Spline Connections

⁷⁄₁₆-in.-thick spline

Foam block spline

Thin OSB spline

ground. It's better structurally to stagger a full-height panel next to a spliced-together panel. It seems to work out in regular gable-end walls that the offcut panels will work on the opposite side of the ridge. This efficient use of the panels can be worked out in the shop-drawing phase.

Spline connections

Panel to panel connections are a very important part of a SIP system. Besides being a structural joint critical to the integrity of the building, there are more linear feet of potential air leakage at the panel joints than at any other part of the system. Splines are used at panel joints to securely hold panels together and stop air infiltration.

Configurations for wall splines vary from manufacturer to manufacturer, with close to 20 different types of connections. The three most common wall connections are shown in the illustration above (roof panel splines are discussed later). The thin OSB spline method has become the standard in the industry because it is inexpensive and has no thermal bridge. Next most common are the single or double 2x spline connection and the foam block spline.

All panels come from the factory precut to fit their spline system; the factory provides the splines, except for the 2x type. There isn't any fabrication to be done with factory splines, but I do test-fit all spline connections before erection. I don't glue or fasten them at this stage because the splines can sustain considerable damage during shipping, which makes it difficult to fit panels together during erection.

Outside corners

The two end panels on any wall have a solid stud at the outside corner for nailing and stiffness (see the illustration on the facing page). These full-height studs in an 8-ft. wall actually measure

Test the fit of the factory-supplied OSB splines in your shop, but don't glue them in until you assemble the panels on-site.

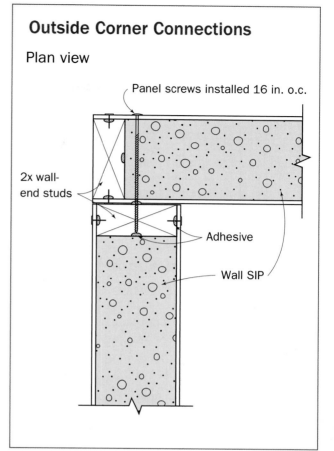

Outside Corner Connections

Plan view

Panel screws installed 16 in. o.c.

2x wall-end studs

Adhesive

Wall SIP

92⅞ in. long, allowing them to fit inside the top and bottom plates.

To install the corner stud, first scoop the foam back 1½ in., then apply a bead of glue to both facings and to the center of the core, and position the stud. Nail the stud off through both facings with 8d nails 6 in. o.c. If this is the panel that runs through to the corner, you'll need to screw through this one into the adjacent corner panel to hold the corner together tight. In a standard corner, the screws will fasten through the outside panel and into the 2x end stud of the adjacent panel during erection. This corner detail is suitable for exterior finishes such as stucco, shingles, and stone and brick veneers.

If wood or other lap siding is to be used, a cap corner detail can provide extra insurance for nailing the corners. A cap corner adds another 2x at the corner to provide additional nailing for siding or corner trim pieces. A hot-wire setup will make short work of relieving the foam for this piece (see pp. 63-64). In the case of a cap corner or any other solid wood corner, it's a good idea to

Install a corner stud after applying glue to both facings of the panel and to the foam core.

One-Piece Walls

A trend in the SIP industry is to take advantage of the large panel sizes available by working with as large a panel as possible. If heavy lifting equipment is going to have to be on the job anyway (and it will be needed at least to install large roof panels), then it stands to reason to use the equipment as much as possible. In many situations, an entire 8-ft.-high wall can be made out of one panel.

There are a number of advantages to using single-panel walls. Besides offering greater strength, one-piece walls simplify the fabrication process so that only windows and doors need to be cut. (Because of site-handling difficulties, these large panels are best fabricated by the factory.) Also, a large one-piece wall won't grow in length due to less-than-tight-fitting joints. And in the case of a two-story building, craning the wall section into place avoids having to move materials and workers to a second-floor deck to perform the assembly.

Of course, the drawback of these larger panels is that moving them into position takes a coordinated effort and heavy equipment to tilt or lift them up. And because window and door openings take up much of the vertical space of a wall section, the cutouts are waste. If a long wall has two 3-ft. by 4-ft. windows in it, then the cost of those discard pieces at $3.30/sq. ft. is about $80 you've thrown away. Many builders find it makes sense to fabricate headers for doors and windows and piece a wall together out of multiple SIPs. Wall sections that are 4 ft. are very material efficient and can be handled easily by two workers.

One-piece wall panels are very rigid and go up fast. (Photo courtesy Thermacore.)

If a cap corner is installed, you'll need to predrill for the corner panel screws. Here, the screw locations are marked with a permanent marker so they won't be overlooked in the field.

predrill a row of ¼-in.-dia. holes for the installation of panel screws into the adjacent corner panel during erection. These holes, spaced 16 in. o.c., should be positioned one-half the thickness of the walls in from the corner.

Cutting windows and doors into SIPs

Rough openings for windows and doors can easily be cut into the middle of a panel using one of the chainsaw-type cutting tools described in chapter 4. I use guides to ensure a straight line when cutting panels to length or width, but rough openings for windows and doors don't require that degree of accuracy. To cut an opening, mark the rough opening on the panel, then darken the layout lines with crayon or marker for easy visibility when the foam flies. Carefully plunge the saw into the panel close to a corner, back the saw into the corner, then make the cut to the opposite corner.

Once the opening is cut, use a foam scoop (see pp. 61-64) to relieve the foam from the rough opening for the header, trimmers, and sill, which are cut from lengths of 2x framing lumber ripped to the thickness of the foam core. I relieve the foam for the trimmers and sill 1½ in., but I relieve the header only 1¼ in. Glue and nail the sill first with 8d nails 6 in. o.c., then glue and tack the top header just enough to hold it in position. Cut the trimmers to the rough opening height, glue them, then drive them vertically into each side pocket, which pushes the header up the last ¼ in. into the header pocket, making a nice, tight fit. You should apply a bead of caulk to the foam core before the 2x blocks are installed. This procedure sounds time-consuming, but a complete window can actually be fabricated in a few minutes.

Headers and sills

The type of header required in a SIP structure depends on the span of the opening and the loads imposed on the header from above. If the rough opening of the window is 4 ft. or less and there is

Plunge cuts with a chainsaw-type tool for a window opening are a snap, and there is no risk of kickback because the chain is traveling vertically.

The rough opening for a window is trimmed out with 2x stock. (Photo courtesy Jon Blumb.)

FABRICATING PANELS AND COMPONENTS **85**

Headers

For a typical 3,000-sq.-ft. house, the total header length may add up to more than 100 ft. Many manufacturers offer factory-produced, insulated header stock for these tasks. The advantage of this approach is that manufacturer-supplied load tables can be easily and quickly consulted to determine what size header to use in a given situation. There is also the speed factor: Header stock can simply be cut to length and it's ready to go.

On the other hand, fabricating your own header stock doesn't take very long, and it is a good way to use some of the panel offcuts effectively. A 12-in.-deep section of 5½-in. core panel with a double bottom plate glued and nailed 3 in. o.c. can take some serious weight. The problem is, how *much* weight will it hold? The cost of testing the assembly is prohibitive, and that puts the builder in the position of being a seat-of-the-pants engineer. That said, I build my own headers for windows and doors with spans of 5 ft. or less without specific point loads over the headers.

Shown in the illustrations at right are three types of headers. The first is a shop-built unit that can be made from offcut scrap pieces as little as 12 in. in depth. Simple to make and adaptable to special situations, its major drawback is that it cannot be load-tested economically. To prepare this header, cut the header section to the height specified and 3 in. longer than the rough opening. Scoop out the foam 1½ in. on all sides of the header. (Scooping 3 in. at the bottom and installing two 2x blocks will increase the load-bearing ability of this piece.) Glue and nail in bottom and trimmer sides for the header and label it for field installation. Do not install a piece in the top—this is where the top plate is installed in the field.

The second type of header is a factory-built, insulated unit made by Premier Building Systems.

The manufacturer claims that it can be used in spans up to 16 ft. The third type is another insulated header manufactured by Superior Wood Systems. These headers are tested and third-party verified and are available through several SIP manufacturers in addition to Superior Wood Systems.

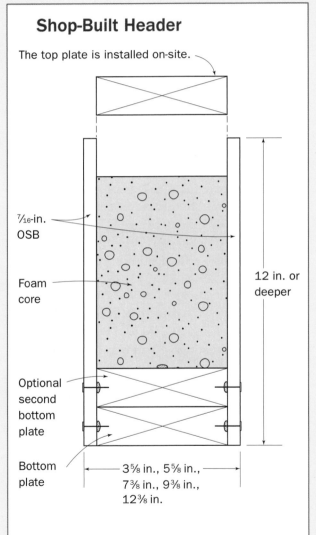

Shop-Built Header

The top plate is installed on-site.

7/16-in. OSB

Foam core

12 in. or deeper

Optional second bottom plate

Bottom plate

3⅝ in., 5⅝ in., 7⅜ in., 9⅜ in., 12⅜ in.

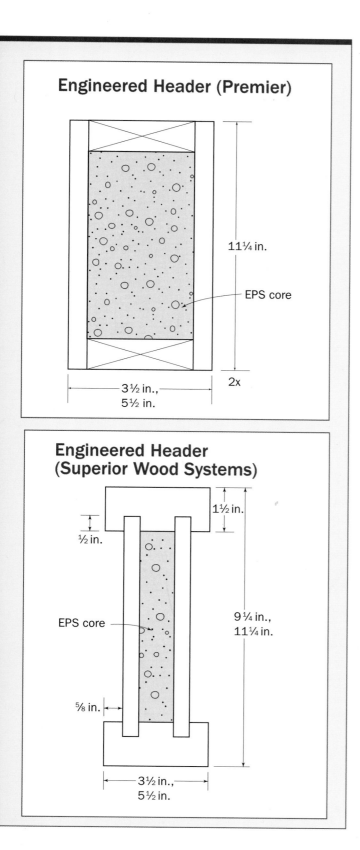

Engineered Header (Premier)

11¼ in.

EPS core

3½ in.,
5½ in.

2x

**Engineered Header
(Superior Wood Systems)**

1½ in.

½ in.

EPS core

9¼ in.,
11¼ in.

⅝ in.

3½ in.,
5½ in.

at least 12 in. of panel above the opening, the header can be integrated with the panel or span two panels. In this case, the window is cut out of the panel, the foam relieved, and 2x material installed as described on p. 85.

For walls with window and door openings wider than 4 ft., you need to install a separate header. The header can be made in house from panel offcuts or you can buy header stock from the factory (see the sidebar at left). The advantage of the factory-supplied units is that they are fully engineered for specific spans and loads. The shop-built units are quick to build and use up potential waste, but they are not engineered. Adding a cap plate as described on pp. 83-85 will help the header support more load, but as a rule of thumb it's a good idea to use an engineered header when the span is more than 6 ft.

To prepare the panels on either side of the header that will support the header, first measure the height of the header and mark the side panels. Next, cut a notch 1½ in. wide and the height of the header in each side. Scoop the foam back 1½ in. in the panel, and glue and nail a 2x block into the notch to complete the solid blocking around the panel. Don't forget to make (or order) the headers 3 in. wider than the rough opening.

The sill panels have the job of infilling the area under a window; this is a good place to use up window and door cutouts and scrap pieces. Fabricate the sill panels to the same width as the rough opening for the window minus ⅛ in. and make sure all four sides are relieved 1½ in. After the sill is labeled, it is ready to ship to the job. The 2x cripples or sill blocks for this piece are installed during the erection process.

Structural connections and hold-downs

In California and other states where specific seismic connections are required, it will be necessary to install hold-downs to lock the SIP into the foundation or to the wall below. A

Fabricating a Panel for Use with Hold-Downs

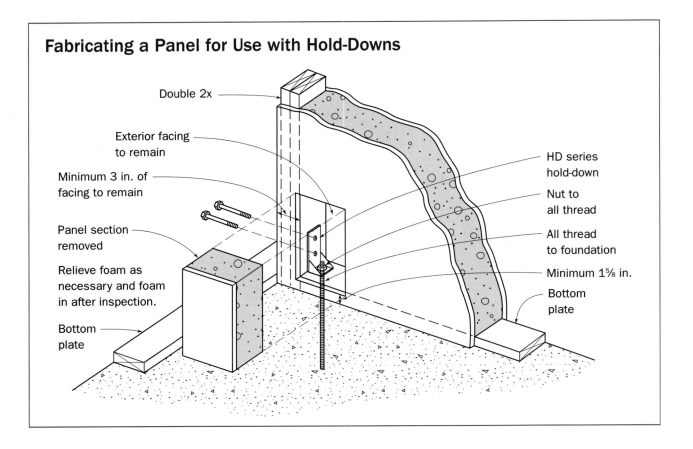

Double 2x

Exterior facing
to remain

Minimum 3 in. of
facing to remain

Panel section
removed

Relieve foam as
necessary and foam
in after inspection.

Bottom
plate

HD series
hold-down

Nut to
all thread

All thread
to foundation

Minimum 1⅝ in.

Bottom
plate

typical foundation hold-down incorporates a steel plate bolted to the framing. This plate is connected to the foundation by heavy all-thread material.

A small access opening needs to be cut out of a SIP panel in preparation for installing one of these hold-downs. When preparing the panel, it is important not to cut through the perimeter of either of the skins so that the tensile strength of the SIP isn't compromised. A minimum of 1⅝ in. needs to be left around the perimeter of any panel, except of course where a door is located. Careful coordination with the project engineer at this point is necessary to ensure that the hold-downs are positioned in the proper locations at the edges of the panels.

Once the location of the all-thread is determined, the offset of the hold-down mounting plate can be calculated in relation to the panel. A minimum of two studs are necessary

to anchor a typical hold-down, with the second 2x serving as the spline for the next panel. Cut out the access panel skin from the inside, being careful not to cut the outer skin, then use a long reciprocating sawblade or handsaw to cut the foam away from the outer skin. After the framing inspection, remove some foam from the plug to fit around the hold-down, then glue the foam back in place.

Because a SIP wall behaves more like a structural unit than a stick-built wall, fewer hold-downs are typically needed to ensure the connection to the foundation. If the whole wall is fabricated in one piece, a larger hold-down at each end may suffice. It's important to work out these details with the inspection officials and the engineer before proceeding with the installation. (See chapter 6 for more about structural metal connectors in a SIP building.)

Cutting custom plumbing chases

Another cut you may need to make in a SIP wall panel is a chase for a plumbing vent. The two-handled, hot-resistance wire tool described on p. 64 works well for making this cut, although you'll need a helper to hold the other end of the tool.

Begin by marking the top and bottom of the panel for the chase. Try to keep the chase within 1 ft. of the edge of the panel to maintain the structural integrity of the panel. Make a horizontal cut from the side of the panel to the edge of the chase location (see the photo at right). Then, with tension on the wire, move the wire around the circular layout line to cut out the core as shown in the photo below (make sure to coordinate the direction of cut with your helper before you start). Finish by taking the wire back through the entry slit. Push out the core (see the bottom right photo), then glue and nail in a solid spline to the side of the panel to return integrity to the SIP.

Mark the top and bottom of the panel for the plumbing chase, and slowly move the hot wire from the edge of the panel to the edge of the hole.

Working with another operator at the opposite end of the panel, carefully move the wire around the circumference of the hole. Keep steady tension on the wire.

Once the cut is made, push out the foam plug and the plumbing chase is ready. All that remains is to glue and nail a stud along the side edge of the panel for reinforcement.

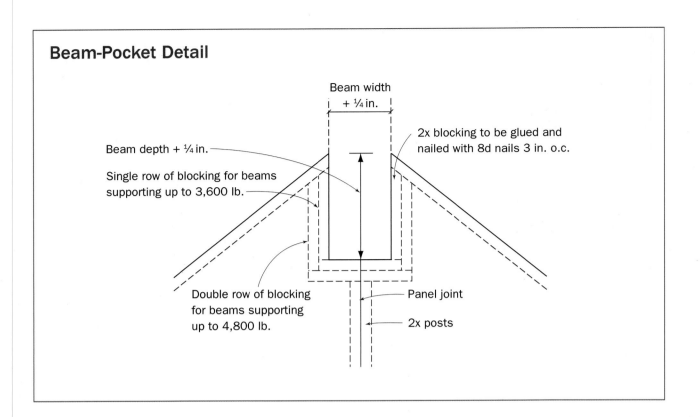

Beam-Pocket Detail

Beam width + ¼ in.

Beam depth + ¼ in.

Single row of blocking for beams supporting up to 3,600 lb.

2x blocking to be glued and nailed with 8d nails 3 in. o.c.

Double row of blocking for beams supporting up to 4,800 lb.

Panel joint

2x posts

Beam pockets

When a roof system is supported by a structural ridge beam and/or purlins, these members will have to be let into the end walls. Beam and purlin pockets should be built into the walls during the fabrication phase.

Lay out the outline of the framing member on the wall panel, adding ¼ in. to the cutout in both directions to allow room for adjustment and shimming. After making the cutout through the interior skin, cut back the foam core, being careful to leave the exterior facing intact.

The load of the beam is spread out over the facings. For a beam that will have to support up to 3,600 lb., FischerSips Corporation specifies a single row of 2x blocking glued to both faces and nailed with 8d nails 3 in. o.c. on both sides. For beams that will have to support up to 4,800 lb., it specifies two rows of 2x material glued and nailed 3 in. o.c. all around the pocket and on both sides. This is a typical beam pocket detail for SIPs (see the illustration above).

In some situations, the facings of the panel can support the load, but it is more typical of SIP construction to have one or more solid studs under this pocket if it occurs at a panel joint. I always try to design the SIP layout so that the main bearing points happen at panel joints. This engineered connection is supporting a significant load, so your panel supplier or your engineer should be consulted as to particular details for your specific application.

Fabricating Roof Panels

Roof layout and panel fabrication are the areas where true "panelheads" can really separate themselves from their stick-building brethren. While the relationship between pitch angles and hip and valley angles remains the same as in conventional framing, the ability to work on these complicated planes while the panels are lying flat on sawhorses in the shop will save many hours of scrambling up and down ladders later on. When a complex roof package shows up

Prefabricating large roof panels will tax a builder's skill but pay off with a strong, tight roof that goes up fast.

on the job, fits together like a jigsaw puzzle, and is erected quickly and efficiently, the customer is thoroughly on board. It should set the tone for a good working relationship during the project.

Another significant advantage of SIP roofs is that they don't have the same ventilation requirements as a stick-built roof. A critical and expensive step in the planning of a stick-built roof is how to ventilate it, and these details can be expensive, time-consuming to build, and questionable in their performance. But because of the consistent density of the foam core of a SIP and its low moisture permeability, ventilation issues become simpler, whether or not a cathedral ceiling is planned.

As discussed in chapter 3, the key is keeping the moisture away from the interior of the panels and ventilating the interior space of excess moisture. Whether EPS or urethane panels are used, it's important to include a vapor barrier on the interior of the roof panels. With some manufacturers, the presence of a vapor barrier can affect the warranty, so be sure to ask the sales rep

questions. (See chapter 9 for more information on hot roofs, cold roofs, and vapor barriers.)

Planning and layout

I'm one of those cautious builders who always has to visualize events a number of times to be comfortable with them. That is why I spend time building scale models to help me see how a particular roof will go together (see the sidebar on p. 92). It's also why my Construction Trig Plus II calculator is my most valuable tool at this stage of the game. Here I'll briefly run through the math that I use to lay out a couple of different roof types, showing the basic relationships of the cuts and angles.

There are some excellent books available on the science of cutting roofs, and this book does not address all of the complexities of this part of building construction. With a sound under-standing of the principles of roof construction and the availability of handheld calculators with right-triangle functions, a good carpenter should be able to design and fabricate the most complex roofs.

Miniature Roofing

Most good books on calculating roofs recommend building a scale model of a roof to help visualize and understand the relationships between sections. It is even more important to do this when working with SIPs because a cutting mistake on a monster panel can be an expensive mistake, especially if the mistake is discovered while the panel is dangling from a crane while the meter is running.

I use foam core for my model-making material. With its paper facings and foam core, it makes an almost exact replica of a SIP. To see how the bevel cuts will align, I make a small hardwood guide ripped to the bevel angle. I use this guide when cutting with my X-Acto knife to make my model cuts more accurate. Of course, the larger the scale used the more accurate the model will be. I generally use my typical scale for working drawings, which is ¼ in. = 1 ft.

Pocket calculators such as Calculated Industries' Trig Plus II model make short work of complicated roof math. (Photo courtesy Jon Blumb.)

Building a scale model helps a builder to be efficient with the SIP roof layout. The model also helps the client visualize the building.

A lot of time and effort has been spent explaining how to compensate for the thickness of the ridge board in a conventionally framed roof, and a lot of heads have been scratched trying to figure out jack rafters for irregular hips and valleys. But in many ways, a SIP roof is simpler to calculate. For example, measurements for roof panels are taken from the actual outside edge of the top of the wall panel facing to the point of the actual ridge. Not only does this cut down on confusion because you won't have to subtract one-half of the width of a ridge board and so on, but also with fewer pieces SIP roofs tend to fit together better.

Measurements taken for roof cuts are transferred to the bottom of the roof panels for layout and cutting. For this reason, I work with the underside of the panel up for labeling, marking, and cutting. To make this system work, I tape the roof plan for the project on vellum or clear reprint paper and print a reverse image (see the illustrations on the facing page). This reverse image enables me to calculate dimensions and mark cuts full scale without having to stand on my head to do it. And while the roof is going up, it's easy to follow the sequence because you are looking at the panel code from inside the structure.

Layout coding for the roof is similar to wall coding. Start with a roof plan and use a double letter code (to differentiate roof sections from wall sections) followed by a number, i.e., AA1, AA2, AA3, BB1, BB2, CC1, CC2, CC3. Each different roof plane will have its own code, and the numbering should be sequenced in the order you will put the panels in.

Gable-roof panels A straight gable roof is the simplest roof to cut. After determining the gable overhang, the layout can begin. For our purposes here, we'll lay out a roof with a total span of 22 ft. and a pitch of 8/12 built with 8¼-in.-thick SIP roof panels. There is a plumb fascia with a 12-in. overhang. Here we will use the plumb-cut ridge method. While there are other ridge detail alternatives that I'll discuss later, the plumb-cut ridge is straightforward and is the accepted industry ridge detail.

1. Begin by finding the panel length. I use a construction calculator to do this, using the following steps: Enter 8-in-12 pitch, enter 11-ft. run to find pitch angle = 33.7 degrees and diagonal = 13 ft. 2⅜ in. Add diagonal of 12-in. overhang = 14⅞₆ in. Total panel length = 14 ft. 5¹⁄₁₆ in. Mark the panel from the bottom because the plumb cut will be into the panel at the bottom and away from the panel at the ridge cut.

2. Make the two cuts across the panel. I use a Skil model 5860 8¼-in. saw with a Prazi attachment (see pp. 60-61) set to the pitch angle, or 33.7 degrees. This saw can handle angles up to 60 degrees, which are needed for lots of roof cuts; I use a guide to keep the shoe running straight (see the bottom photo on p. 94).

3. Next, relieve the foam core back 1½ in. at the ridge and eave with a hot scoop or a hot-wire setup, then install ridge blocking ripped out of 2x stock cut with the same bevel. (I wait to install the subfascia blocking at the eave until the roof is in place.) If this is the first panel in a run, the rake end will need to be blocked in the panel's factory recess, using 2x8 material.

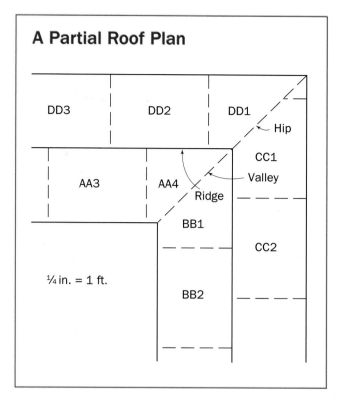

A Partial Roof Plan

DD3   DD2   DD1

Hip

CC1

AA3   AA4   Valley

Ridge

BB1

CC2

¼ in. = 1 ft.

BB2

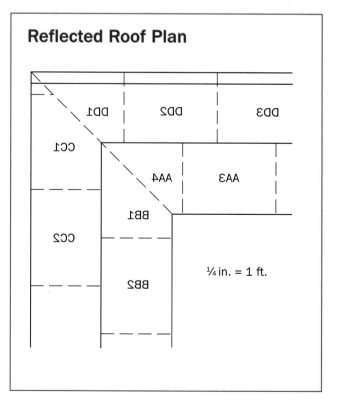

Reflected Roof Plan

DD1   DD2   DD3

CC1

AA4   AA3

BB1

CC2

¼ in. = 1 ft.

BB2

A Section of a Gable-Roof Panel

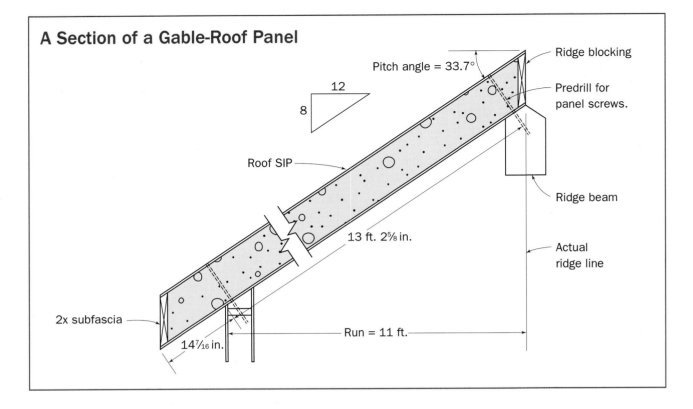

Pitch angle = 33.7°

12
8

Ridge blocking

Predrill for panel screws.

Roof SIP

Ridge beam

13 ft. 2⅝ in.

Actual ridge line

2x subfascia

14⁷⁄₁₆ in.

Run = 11 ft.

When cutting a roof panel at an angle, it is important to use a straightedge guide for accurate cuts.

4. Predrill the ridge end of the panel for the roof screws, since the screws will attach through the ridge blocking into the ridge. A good rule of thumb is to install screws 12 in. o.c. unless wind uplift or seismic conditions dictate another detail. Predrill these locations at the shop, and mark them with a dark circle so they won't be missed in the field.

5. Clearly mark the other locations for roof panel screws that don't need to be predrilled. Along the rake, this distance will be the overhang plus one-half of the wall thickness. At the eave, calculate where the screw needs to enter at perpendicular to drive into the top plate or blocking. When figuring screw lengths, measure so the eave screws are set at least 1½ in. into the plate or beam.

6. For the last piece of the puzzle, install the connecting spline. The type of roof-panel connector depends on the span and the calculated loads of the roof system. The basic joint is the thin spline method using ⅞₆-in. by 4-in.-wide OSB splines on the interior of both the inside and outside facings (see the illustration on

Roof Panel Connections

Thin spline connection

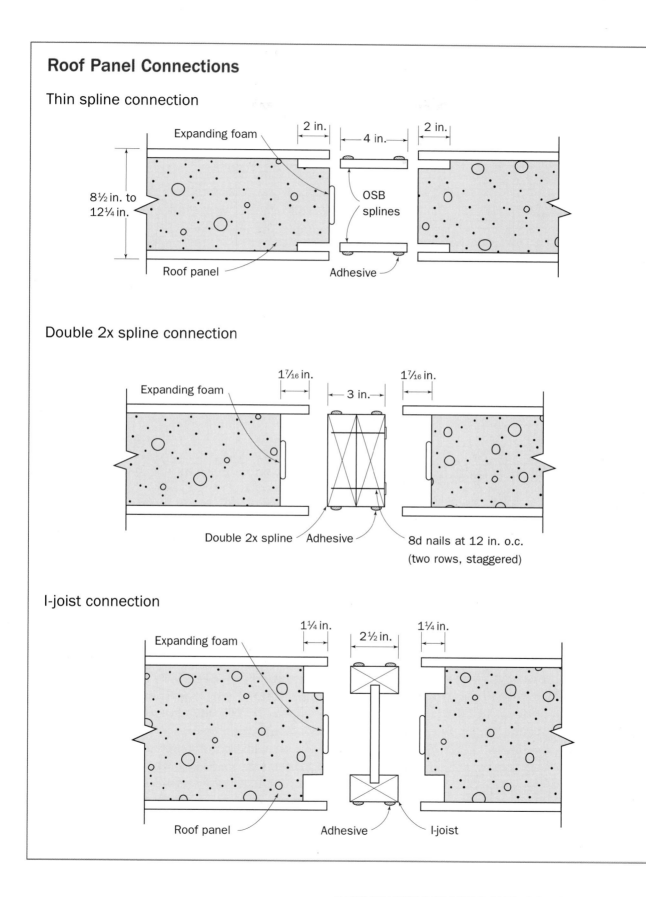

Expanding foam

2 in.

4 in.

2 in.

8½ in. to 12¼ in.

OSB splines

Roof panel

Adhesive

Double 2x spline connection

Expanding foam

1⁷⁄₁₆ in.

3 in.

1⁷⁄₁₆ in.

Double 2x spline   Adhesive

8d nails at 12 in. o.c.
(two rows, staggered)

I-joist connection

Expanding foam

1¼ in.

2½ in.

1¼ in.

Roof panel

Adhesive

I-joist

p. 95). For this type of connection, the splines should be tested for fit but not installed before erection for the same reasons as on the wall panels.

Another spline method is to use either single or double 2x material. I don't use this method any more because a single 2x offers only ¾ in. of wood or less on each side of the joint to try to nail into, so the chance of missing solid nailing with the fasteners is high. The double 2x method is strong and has plenty of nailing surface, but 3 in. of thermal break in the roof every 4 ft. lowers the whole roof R-value considerably, so I try to avoid this approach as well.

Where spans call for the extra support of structural splines, the best option is to use engineered wood I-joists. These splines are straight, light, and very strong. They are also easy to install because they are manufactured to consistent tolerances; if required, I-joists with bigger flanges that offer more load bearing can be used. The manufacturer will supply the panels with the foam core relieved to accept the I-joists, but you may have to fabricate some to fit custom situations. In this case, you should make two templates out of sheet metal to the shape of the I-joist, then clamp them to the ends of the panel. To cut the shape, set a two-handled, resistance-wire tool to the panel length, then have two operators guide the hot wire along the template. When installing I-joists, it's important to use beads of expanding foam on both sides of the web to seal the envelope.

I install roof splines at the time of panel prep on the job site, although they could be shop-installed during panel fabrication in some situations. Especially when there are long soffit overhangs, I wait until just before the panels are airborne before installing splines. While the above procedures may seem like a lot of work for one panel, one person can actually do all the fabrication in 15 to 20 minutes.

Ridge details In addition to the plumb-cut ridge discussed in the previous section, there are other possible ridge details, each with its pros and cons.

For example, a good way to detail a 12/12 pitch roof is with overlapping square-cut panels. This roof detail is simple to prepare on the ground because you just have to add 2x blocking. It's also strong because the screws anchor solidly into the supporting ridge beam (see the top illustration on the facing page).

While this detail is cost-effective for square-cut ridges, it involves more work than any other detail when the pitch is other than 12/12. For example, the center illustration on the facing page shows square-cut factory edges bearing on a double 2x ridge with a factory-supplied foam filler glued into the V between the panels. OSB strips that are 7/16 in. wide are glued on top of the foam, and strapping is installed on 4-ft. centers over this assembly to tie everything together. While this particular ridge detail can work for different pitches and is fast to prep on the ground, it requires more installation time on the roof.

The plumb-cut ridge detail shown in the bottom illustration on the facing page is the most common approach to cutting ridges. It can be used with any pitch, including 12/12, and the prep work done on the ground translates into very little time spent on the roof installing it.

Eave details There are many types of eave overhang and soffit details that can be formed that are compatible with SIPs. Given the outstanding thermal performance of SIPs and the energy-efficient windows now available, eave detailing becomes an issue of style just as much as that of function. It can also be an issue of economics. For example, eave orientation and overhang is an integral part of passive solar design, and the length of this overhang will help determine if it is economical to let the SIPs extend or to stick-build an assembly.

A typical SIP roof system that provides an insulation value of R-30 will be 8½ in. thick. A plumb cut at the eave leaves 10¼ in. of exposure, an unattractive detail. But there are several alternative eave details that will keep the building from looking clunky and top-heavy. These eave details are best left for installation in the field for

Ridge Details

Overlapping square-cut panels for 12/12 roof pitch

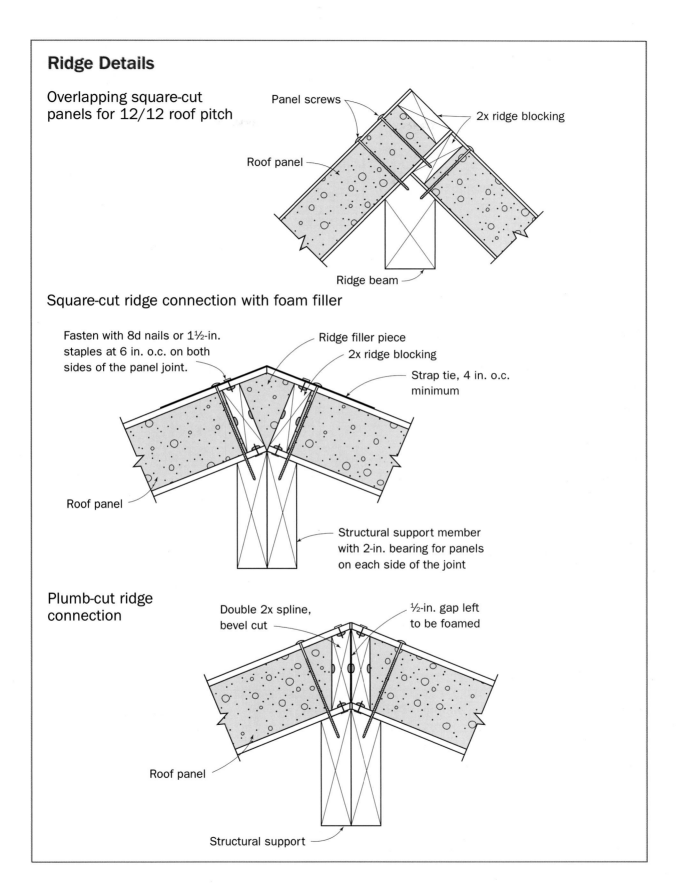

Panel screws

2x ridge blocking

Roof panel

Ridge beam

Square-cut ridge connection with foam filler

Fasten with 8d nails or 1½-in. staples at 6 in. o.c. on both sides of the panel joint.

Ridge filler piece

2x ridge blocking

Strap tie, 4 in. o.c. minimum

Roof panel

Structural support member with 2-in. bearing for panels on each side of the joint

Plumb-cut ridge connection

Double 2x spline, bevel cut

½-in. gap left to be foamed

Roof panel

Structural support

three reasons. First, if there is any trimming to be done for final panel alignment, it's much easier to do this at the outside edges and the 2x blocking would only get in the way. After trimming, the 2x blocking can be installed, spanning several panels and helping to maintain a straight, strong line. Second, some overhang details call for solid or I-joist splines to extend past the wall planes to support the soffit. The 2x blocking would be nailed in after the splines are installed and cut to length. Third, some sort of scaffolding will have to be erected to install soffit, fascia, and trim details so the 2x blocking can easily be installed at this time. For more on installation of eave details, see chapter 7.

Hips and valleys

As with stick-built roofs, laying out a roof with hips and valleys is more complicated than laying out a straight gable roof. When laying out panels for hips or valleys, it is important to visualize each roof plane as it sits parallel to the pitch of the roof. This is because the roof panels are essentially two-dimensional planes with the thickness of the SIP as the third dimension. Once the three measurements of these triangles are established, you need to calculate the bevel cut for the hip/valley to mate this piece to the adjacent panel. And once the panels have been cut, careful attention should be spent on labeling and organizing them so that at the time of erection they can be taken off the stack and installed in the order you want them.

The relationship between the pitch of a roof and the angle of hips or valleys is the same as on stick-built roofs. One way to think about it is that this is like cutting a single conventional hip or valley jack rafter, except that the dimensions are stretched out. But with SIPs, the plumb cut sets the bevel that the hip or valley edge of the panel will be cut to. This hip/valley angle is different from the angle of the common pitch, as any roof cutter knows.

As an example, let's go through the steps used to fabricate a regular valley in an 8/12 roof with a span of 6 ft. Before starting the calculations, it's

important to determine the valley pitch angle, which is different from the common pitch angle. Both have the same rise (8 in.), but the hip run (16.97 in.) is different from the common run (12 in.). For this roof, the pitch angle is 33.69 degrees for the common pitch and 25.24 degrees for the valley pitch. Here are the steps I use to calculate the valley:

1. First I enter into my calculator the pitch (8 in.) and the run (6 ft.), then I generate the diagonal (7 ft. 2½ in.) and the hip/valley length (9 ft. 4⁹⁄₁₆ in.).

2. Using the reverse roof plan that's now labeled with the individual panel sections, I can lay out these two sections. The valley to be cut is the one formed by the intersection of AA4 and BB5.

3. I indicate the ridge and measure the length of the run, 6 ft. from the corner next to a common section of roof panel (point A on the illustration). This new point is the point of the ridge peak (point B). From point A, I measure down the panel the diagonal distance of 7 ft. 2½ in. (point C; this is the length of a

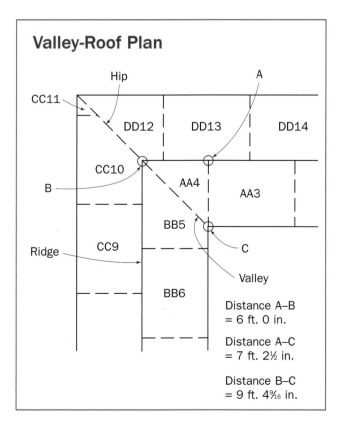

Valley-Roof Plan

Distance A–B = 6 ft. 0 in.

Distance A–C = 7 ft. 2½ in.

Distance B–C = 9 ft. 4⁹⁄₁₆ in.

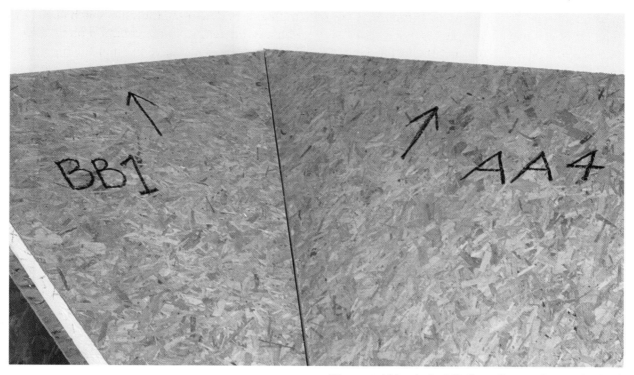

It's a good idea to test-fit the valley sections before shipping them to the job site.

common rafter in stick parlance). Note that I haven't included eave overhang or eave cut here for the sake of simplicity. When these two points are connected, the distance corresponds with the hip/valley length generated in step 1, or 9 ft. 4⁹⁄₁₆ in.

4. Next, I set my saw angle to the valley pitch angle (25.24 degrees). The cut will be made from the ridge down, making the equivalent of a plumb cut on the panel. Remember that when cut from the bottom of the panel, this will be an acute angle for a valley, while for a hip it will be an obtuse angle. After determining the chain offset from the saw shoe and screwing down the MDF straightedge guides, I make the cut.

5. I relieve the foam 1½ in. with the hot-wire setup, and the panel is ready for marking screw locations and installation.

6. Finally, I rip the valley splines from 10-ft.-long (plus the length of the eave overhang) 2x10 stock with the 25.24-degree back bevel and glue and screw them together. This assembly is installed in the field, but it's smart to test-fit the valley pieces before shipping to the job site.

A field hip is assembled with double-beveled hip splines. A hip can sometimes be fabricated without structural support below, but an engineer should review the design for all hips and valleys. (Photo courtesy Sunworks.)

Stick-built infill and panels are combined to help shape a dormer without complicating the roof panel cuts.

The layout and cutting procedures for hips are identical to those for the valley above, with the exception that hip panels are cut at an obtuse angle (from the bottom) with the saw set at the hip/valley angle.

Dormers and skylights

Some builders I know say that it is more cost-effective to stick-build roofs that have some dormers and hips or valleys and then to insulate them with thick blankets of fiberglass or cellulose. But in my opinion, the very best application for SIPs is on the roof, where all of a building's heat tries to exit and where the most amount of time is spent going from the ground to the carpentry task at hand. With some planning and basic roof math, there isn't a roof designed that would not be cost-effective and energy-efficient to fabricate first on the ground out of SIPs.

Dormers of any style can be added to a SIP roof in various ways. A shed dormer that involves two identical sidewalls and a shed roof can most likely be made from one SIP panel. Similarly, a two-piece triangular eyebrow dormer could be overlaid

onto the main roof without having to make the valley cuts just described. In some cases, I build hybrid dormers, using some stick overlay to help shape the dormer without complicating the roof panel cuts.

Of course, dormers for a SIP house can always be stick-built, and they can even be built on the ground and lifted into place. This approach has serious drawbacks, however. Putting a large hole (or holes) in a high-performance SIP roof and then trying to stop the air leakage with conventional framing and insulation materials downgrades the performance of the entire roof. If the plan calls for a cosmetic dormer with no glazing simply to break up a roofline, then it would be cost-effective to stick-build the overlay and keep the SIPs simple. As builders gain more experience designing and building with SIPs, even very complex roof designs will price out favorably with SIPs.

Skylights are a wonderful way to bring lots of light in through the roof without having to go to the trouble of building complicated dormers. Good-quality skylights (I've been installing Velux with good results for 20 years) are available in a

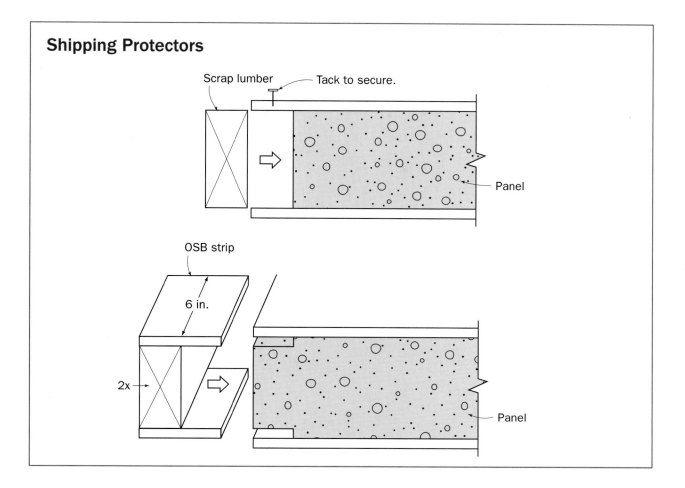

Shipping Protectors

Scrap lumber — Tack to secure.

Panel

OSB strip

6 in.

2x

Panel

number of different configurations with a variety of glazing options. I use the same framing and blocking procedures that I use when installing windows in wall panels. It's easy to plumb or flare the rough opening for other sill and head details. When possible, I try to work the skylight pattern into the roof plan so that the skylights fit into a single panel rather than spanning two separate panels. When it is necessary to span two or more panels, a header that takes into account all the live load possibilities will have to be engineered.

Packing and Shipping

Once all the SIP panels for a project are cut, blocked, and labeled, it's time to set up the site and get ready for the erection. If you've fabricated the panels in a shop, this means that the panels will have to be packed and shipped to the site.

Groups of panels that will be erected together should be sent to the job site in the order in which they will be used. If possible, place a panel with wood on both sides on the bottom and top of the stack to protect the edges. And if the job site is crowded (as it usually is), you may want to deliver smaller groups of panels at a time for installation. I band these groups of panels at the shop and tarp over the banding for shipping and storage. The plastic covers can be held in place by wedging scraps of wood into the facing recess.

The distance to the job site, the storage area at the site, and the weather conditions around the erection window should be taken into consideration when determining how to protect, ship, and store the panels. Once at the site, the panels will need to be placed on sturdy stickers to keep them off the ground (stiff 4x timbers work best) and covered until they are used. I place the

A completed group of fabricated panels is banded for shipment from the Sunworks shop to the job site.

Panels need to be protected from the weather on a job site until they are assembled.

stickers no more than 6 ft. apart and make sure that the panels are at least 3 in. above the ground and sitting absolutely flat. A set of reusable polyethylene tarps sized to fit a big group of panels would be cost-effective, but I've found that readily available rolls of 6-mil plastic also give good protection.

Whatever you cover your panels with, be aware that these enclosures can act as a solar kiln, sucking moisture out of the ground and baking it into the panels. This can raise the moisture content in the facings to high levels and potentially cause some serious edge swelling. During nice weather, it is a good idea to lift up one side of the tent for air circulation.

In the event that some of the panels need modifications during the erection process, the tools needed to cut the panels, relieve the foam, and

apply the adhesives must be on hand. It's a good idea to have the capability to do all the fabrication on the job just in case, regardless of whether the panels are prefabricated by the manufacturer, fabricated in a shop, or fabricated on-site.

A SIP structure will require non-SIP building components, such as floor-system materials and assorted types of plate materials, beams, girders, trusses, roof splines, and lumber for bracing. The materials list for these items is critical for the erection process to be efficient, so it needs to be produced with the same care as the SIP calculations. I like to have this package arrive before the SIPs pack so that the materials can be sorted, labeled, and installed if necessary.

Once all the materials are on-site and the panels are prepped, cut, labeled, and stacked, it's time to install the SIP package.

Chapter 6

STANDING THE WALLS

FOUNDATIONS AND FLOOR SYSTEMS

ERECTING SIP WALLS

Standing the walls on a SIP project is where all the planning and prefabrication of wall sections will really pay off. Once the crew gets all the drills, nailers, staplers, and glue guns rolled out, the assembly will move at a rapid pace. Most custom builders work with 4-ft.-wide wall panels, so once the panels are unloaded and staged around the job site they can be assembled and stood manually. I find that an average-sized house requires a crew of three to five workers.

At the other end of the scale is the production builder who orders huge 8-ft. by 24-ft. wall

The exterior SIP walls of this Southwestern-style home were erected in a single day by the framing crew of Sand Creek Construction, Inc.

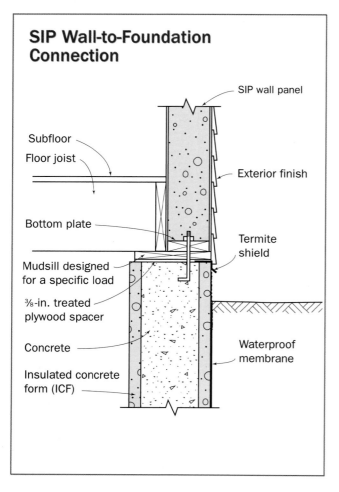

SIP Wall-to-Foundation Connection

- SIP wall panel
- Subfloor
- Floor joist
- Exterior finish
- Bottom plate
- Termite shield
- Mudsill designed for a specific load
- ⅜-in. treated plywood spacer
- Concrete
- Waterproof membrane
- Insulated concrete form (ICF)

sections from the factory with window and door openings precut into the panel and with all the blocking and splines glued and nailed in place. Even in this situation, a smaller than usual crew is required to erect this type of structure, although obviously a crane will be needed to lift the pieces into place.

Before building the walls, you first need to consider the different types of foundations and floor systems that will support the walls.

Foundations and Floor Systems

A SIP structure can be placed on any type of foundation, but it's a good idea for the engineer working on the job to understand that the SIP

shell is somewhat heavier than a stick-framed shell. One other important difference with the SIP system is that the foundation needs to be much closer to square, plumb, and level than is the industry standard. This is because the panels are square and flat, and when the slab or deck is out of level and square you can spend a lot of time trying to adjust the panels to the out-of-level condition. It's worthwhile to emphasize to the concrete subcontractor the importance of a level foundation.

Full basements

When there is a poured concrete basement or a concrete-block basement, the floor system can be installed in the standard platform method, with the walls placed on top of the floor system. Alternatively, some details can be used to better insulate the rim area by bringing the SIP down to the mudsill and bearing the floor inside of the walls (see the illustration at left). To make this detail work, it's important to allow for adequate bearing (at least 1½ in.) of the floor system on the mudsill. For example, if a 6½-in. SIP wall is used over an 8-in. foundation wall, the mudsill would need to be 8 in. wide. Another approach is to hang the floor system from ledgers attached to the SIP wall and not have the floor bear on the foundation at all.

The better-insulated floor-to-wall detail shown in the illustration at left also provides a workable solution when there is an insulated concrete form (ICF) foundation. To achieve a uniform plane for the exterior finish, you need to shift the SIP wall toward the exterior the thickness of the insulating foam of the ICF, typically 2 in. This means that the exterior facing of the SIP will bear on the treated plywood spacer and mudsill, which will partially bear on the EPS foam of the ICF. To compensate for this, most manufacturers require that the mudsill be engineered for the specific load. On the plus side, this makes room for the floor system to bear solidly on the engineered mudsill. The key to these details is that the SIP wall makes a thermal envelope around the building and the floor assemblies remain inside the walls.

Foundation Panels

Atypical stick-built house has myriad air leaks, and it is estimated that 20% to 30% of its heat escapes through the basement walls. That percentage rises to 50% or more when a house is built with SIPs and the rest of the house becomes more airtight. Consequently, many builders are looking for ways to increase the energy efficiency of their basements. To be compatible with the high insulation value of SIPs, many builders are choosing to use insulated concrete forms (ICS) or foam-core panelized foundations for their foundations.

Several SIP manufacturers specifically design and manufacture foundation panels, which typically consist of ½-in. or thicker treated plywood on the exterior, OSB or treated plywood on the interior, and an EPS foam core. For example, Enercept, Inc. (see Resources on p. 181) makes foundation panels in 5⅝-in. and 7⅜-in. core thicknesses. As is typical of many manufacturers, Enercept's foundation panel system includes pressure-treated 2x plates and studs placed within the panel at 16 in. o.c. These panels have a vertical electrical chase next to every stud so that electrical devices can be placed at any height on the wall (there are no horizontal electrical chases in the basic panel).

The axial load test applied to an 8-ft.-tall, 7⅜-in.-thick foundation panel produces a rating of 3,504 plf, which would allow for two full stories to be built above these panels in most cases. Drainage and waterproofing details are important for basements built with foundation panels. These details include an effective foundation drain that starts slightly below the top of the footing, caulking of all exterior joints, and a continuous water-emulsion asphalt coating (or other type of foundation waterproofing) that starts at the footing and extends 6 in. above finish grade. Enercept also requires a below-surface EPS moisture shield rated to resist 30 pcf of hydrostatic pressure to insulate and keep water away from the foundation. The R-30 basement possible with these types of panels is certainly attractive, but the idea of wood foundations has not yet been widely accepted in the industry.

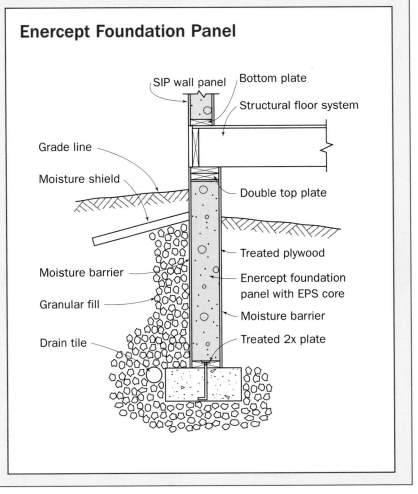

Enercept Foundation Panel

SIP wall panel
Bottom plate
Structural floor system
Grade line
Moisture shield
Double top plate
Treated plywood
Moisture barrier
Enercept foundation panel with EPS core
Granular fill
Moisture barrier
Drain tile
Treated 2x plate

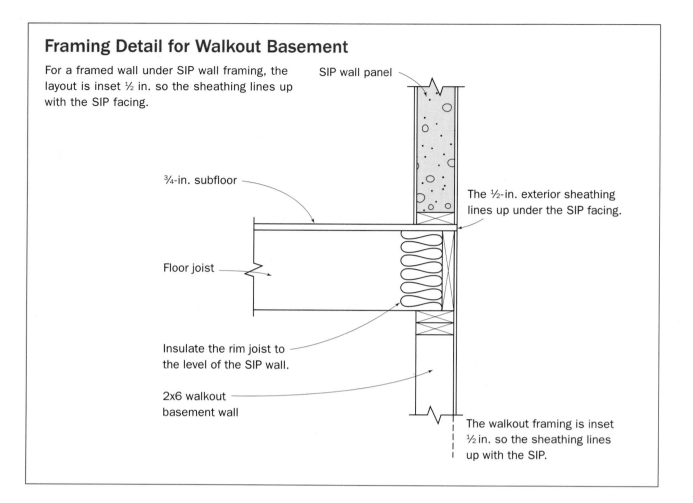

Framing Detail for Walkout Basement

For a framed wall under SIP wall framing, the layout is inset ½ in. so the sheathing lines up with the SIP facing.

SIP wall panel

¾-in. subfloor

The ½-in. exterior sheathing lines up under the SIP facing.

Floor joist

Insulate the rim joist to the level of the SIP wall.

2x6 walkout basement wall

The walkout framing is inset ½ in. so the sheathing lines up with the SIP.

Walkout basements Walkout basements have one or more framed walls that tie into the concrete foundation and support the first floor. In some cases, it makes sense to frame this wall conventionally, for instance, if the site is ready for the first-floor system before the SIPs are delivered to the site. In this case, the framed wall needs to be adjusted for the SIPs above. To do this, set the basement plate ½ in. in from the nominal framing line so the sheathing is in the same plane as the end joist or rim joist. The exterior facing of the first-floor SIP needs to bear fully on the subfloor. Now the SIP facing and the walkout sheathing will be in the same plane. With the framed walkout walls, the floor system can be installed and ready for the SIPs when they arrive.

Slab layout

When a SIP structure is erected on a concrete slab, there are some special details that must be considered for plates and electrical distribution. In addition to the considerations for electrical work (see chapter 8), you need to take three things into account when laying out for the plates: insect protection, moisture to wood contact, and the position of the bottom plate.

A termite shield is probably the least expensive insurance against bugs entering any type of building, regardless of how the building is constructed. The horizontal leg of the shield should be long enough to cover any projection of the foundation and to fit at least halfway under the plate or slab subplate (see the photo on p. 108). Anchor or J-bolts should be at least 10 in. long so they can project through the subplate and

Seismic Connectors

Simpson Strong-Tie (see Resources on p. 183) makes a number of connectors that significantly increase the uplift resistance for foundation-to-wall connections. The PAHD and the HPAHD series are designed to be installed in the formwork before the concrete pour and then to be nailed or screwed to the SIP. The STHD14RJ foundation connector offers a lot of strength and does not need to be precisely positioned because it is screwed or nailed onto the SIPs after the walls are in position.

The basement-wall-to-first-floor-wall connection is a potential weak point in a SIP building because the sheathing cannot be lapped over both walls as in standard framing. Here, a Simpson Strong-Tie CS/CMST/MSCT or other heavy-gauge perforated strap will greatly increase the strength of the connection between walls. These 14-gauge units, which can also be used between first- and second-floor walls, are available in lengths up to 78 in. and can be fastened with nails or screws. They have an allowable load per unit of up to 5,855 lb.

Not all SIP manufacturers specify these connectors in their installation manuals, but to take advantage of the structural properties of SIPs, I strongly recommend working some of this hardware into your project.

Next, knock out the panel sections and relieve all four sides to a depth of 1½ in. with a hot scoop. Apply glue to the insides of the facings all around the rough opening, and apply a bead of expanding foam to the foam core. Install the 2x sill piece, which is cut to the rough opening width plus 3 in., then install the header piece, which is cut to the same length. Finally, hammer in the side jambs, which are cut to the rough opening height.

Once the opening is framed in, nail off all the 2x material from both the inside and outside facings. This is a quick process that offers some real flexibility for builders and designers.

This SIP house, built in a high-wind area in Idaho, uses Simpson Strong-Tie MSTC series straps between floors and STHD series foundation hold-downs to meet uplift requirements. The house features an ICF foundation, 6½-in. SIP walls, and a 10¼-in. SIP roof system. (Photo courtesy Ronnee McGee.)

A Simpson Strong-Tie STHD series hold-down works well with SIPs installed on a slab foundation.

the bottom plate and catch the nut. The holes cut to set the termite shield over the J-bolts can be loose to facilitate accurate layout. Setting the termite shield on a bead of elastomeric caulk will keep the bugs from squeezing under.

Because any wood placed adjacent to concrete should be pressure-treated, the next piece to be installed after the termite shield is a pressure-treated subplate. Some builders use a piece of treated ¾-in. plywood or a 1x treated piece ripped to the outside dimension of the wall panel. For example, a 5½-in. SIP wall panel requires a subplate ripped to 6⁵⁄₁₆ in. so that both facings of the SIP bear fully on the subplate. I've found that it saves time to glue and nail the bottom plate to this subplate before installation so that only one set of holes needs to be drilled for the anchor bolts. These subplate and bottom-plate assemblies should be straight and true for accurate layout. When dimensioning the layout for a slab structure, the subplate is laid out ½ in. to the outside of the bottom plate (the plans will indicate the measurement for the bottom plate). Any corrections to accommodate an out-of-square slab should be taken care of now.

The next step is to snap chalklines and transfer bolt-hole locations to the plate assemblies. Before bolting the plates down, apply a bead of construction adhesive to the top of the termite shield. At the corners, the subplates can butt together, but you need to leave a ⁵⁄₁₆-in. or more gap in one direction or the other when the bottom plates are attached because one SIP wall panel will extend through to the corner. (Which panel bypasses the corner SIP is determined when doing the shop drawings.)

This sequence will be continued around the perimeter of the building. Remember that the use of the subplate will increase the overall height of the wall by ¾ in. (or the thickness of the sub-plate), a factor that needs to be taken into account for second-floor height or stair layout. After the plates are in position and fastened down, mark the location for the wall panels (taken from the shop drawings) on the plates, being sure to include the ⅛-in. expansion gap between panels.

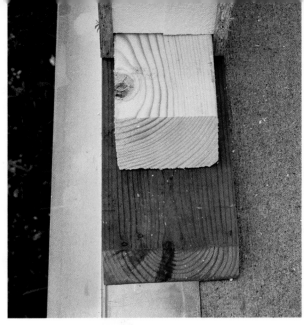

A SIP installation on a concrete slab should include (from bottom) a termite shield, a treated subplate, and a bottom plate positioned so that both facings of the wall panel bear on the subplate. (Photo by Jon Blumb.)

Subfloor layout

I won't take the time here to explain the construction of the floor system or the installation of the subfloor because that subject has been addressed in many framing books, but I will point out a couple of details that are relevant to SIP structures. As mentioned previously, it's very important for the deck to be level and square before installing the wall panels. If necessary, you can shim and grout the mudsills to bring them level. If the deck starts off level and square, the first corner will most likely go together plumb and square when assembled.

When laying out for the bottom plates, make sure that the outer skins of the SIP panels will have full bearing on the subfloor. For a 5½-in. core panel, I snap the plate line 6 in. from the edge of the deck. Before attaching the plate, place a liberal bead of subfloor adhesive or panel adhesive on the deck, which seals one of the biggest potential air leaks in the system. I like to screw the plate down with 4-in. type-W drywall screws to really suck the plate to the deck and make this connection tight. If you're using nails, I recommend a pair of 20d spikes every 16 in. into the rim or joist below. At the corners, you need to

SIP Floor Panels

An alternative to using a conventionally framed floor in a SIP building is to use SIP floor panels. Most SIP manufacturers that make EPS panels promote the use of their thicker (7¼-in., 10¼-in., and 12¼-in.) roof panels in floor applications. Although not many builders are using SIP panels for floors, there are some situations where it's a good idea to think about using them.

SIPs should be considered for use as floors in buildings where a floor is called for over an unconditioned space. This could be an unheated garage or a cantilevered area that extends out from the main living space. Floor panels are also a good choice for remote, off-the-grid buildings, where typically the foundation would be a series of piers rather than a continuous concrete foundation. A SIP floor completes the thermal envelope and prevents air and heat loss through the floor. Obviously, when you can have the entire envelope of the structure insulated to the level that SIPs offer and have the airtight characteristics as well, you have an even greater amount of control over the interior environment.

There are, however, some drawbacks to using SIPs for floors. The main disadvantage is the difficulty in running plumbing (and to a lesser degree wiring) in the floor panels. A penetration through the panel for drains or vents is not difficult to fabricate, but a horizontal chase to run drains, waste, and venting would be hard to justify in terms of the time and energy spent preparing the panel. For electrical distribution, you can order custom chases in almost any configuration, but the difficulty is to go from horizontal to vertical and to be able to fish the wires through quickly and effectively.

Premier Building Systems uses the same load-design charts to calculate loads on roofs and floors. Premier has developed a series of specific details for floor installations that call for the rim material to be continuous from bearing point to bearing point and for solid blocking to be added directly below building point loads (see the illustration below). A floor will typically have more point loads and specific bearing-wall loads than a roof. For this reason, it's important to work with the project engineer to decide how to prepare for the building loads that will come down on a SIP floor panel. As with roof panels (see chapter 7), the loading ability of the floor can be increased by using solid 2x splines (either in single or in double applications) or I-joists in the floor system.

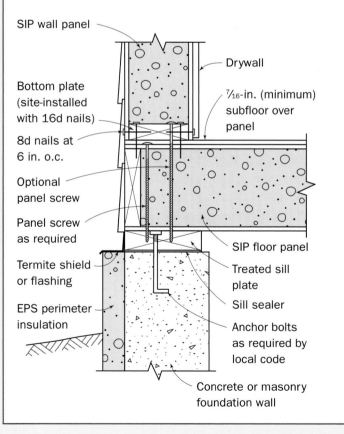

Framing Connections for SIP Floor Panels

- SIP wall panel
- Drywall
- Bottom plate (site-installed with 16d nails)
- 7⁄16-in. (minimum) subfloor over panel
- 8d nails at 6 in. o.c.
- Optional panel screw
- Panel screw as required
- SIP floor panel
- Treated sill plate
- Termite shield or flashing
- Sill sealer
- EPS perimeter insulation
- Anchor bolts as required by local code
- Concrete or masonry foundation wall

Bottom plates should be inset ½ in. from the edge of the subfloor to allow for the exterior facing of the wall panels. Leave a ⁵⁄₁₆-in. gap at the corners to allow the first panel installed to extend through to the outside corner. (Photo by Jon Blumb.)

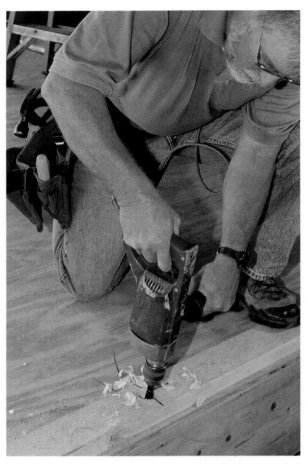

Drill 1¾-in.-dia. holes in the bottom plate that align with the vertical chases in the wall panel.

leave a ⁵⁄₁₆-in. or more gap between plates to allow the first SIP to extend through to the corner before the other SIP is butted up to it (just as you do on the slab layout).

After all of the bottom plates have been set in place, cut the top plates to the same length as the bottom plates. These plates will not overlap and for most applications there is no need for a second (or cap) plate. (You'll need a cap plate only if there are unusual loads on the walls or a heavy point load; the cap plate should be overlapped as in conventional framing.) After cutting, the top plates should be labeled for each wall and stored nearby until they are needed; it's a good idea to predrill the 1¾-in.-dia. holes in the top plates over the vertical electrical chases now, too.

Next, transfer the panel edge locations to the bottom plates, including the ⅛-in. gap between panels, comparing the actual measurements with the shop drawings. Then transfer the locations for the electrical chases to the plate, and drill the holes for the chases. A typical 48-in.-wide SIP has a 1½-in.-dia. chase in the center. Any custom chases that have been ordered from the factory or fabricated at the shop also need to be located and drilled at this time. Using a 1¾-in. self-feed bit, I angle the hole in the plate slightly toward the inside of the building to help the wire pull through. Later, when the electricians loop their circuits from under the floor, they have to spend less time drilling holes because most of the holes they need are already there.

Erecting SIP Walls

With the bottom plates secured, it's finally time to raise the walls. In this section, I'll walk you through two different wall installations: The first is a way of erecting a simple rectangular house with flat-top walls (such as found on a Southwestern-style adobe house), and the second is the method I use on a house with gable-end walls. The main difference is that on the first house most of the walls are installed one panel at a time, whereas on the second house the gable wall is installed on the deck and then raised as a single unit.

Every SIP manufacturer has specific details for connections and installation that need to be followed for their warranties to remain in effect. Therefore, while the wall-erection sequences described here are typical, in some cases certain installation details may vary. Suppliers and other builders tell me that about 90% of the connection details are common throughout the industry, while 10% of them are unique to various panel systems and builders.

Flat-top walls

The best place to start is at an outside corner. First, make sure the bottom plate is free of debris so the panel will sit flush on the deck (I use compressed air to blow off the edges of the plate). Then apply a ¼-in. bead of panel adhesive to both sides of the bottom plate and a slightly larger bead to the top of the plate. A quart-size air-powered caulk gun (see p. 65) makes short work of this task, so I run adhesive along the full length of the plate.

Next, tilt up the first panel, align it with the marks on the bottom plate, and drop it into place over the plate. This first panel should be installed one panel thickness in from the corner so that the last panel will run by it and make the final connection easy. Once the panel is in place, brace it to plumb at the corner and tack along the bottom to hold it against the plate (see the photo at left on p. 112).

Apply liberal beads of panel adhesive to all sides of the bottom plate to ensure an airtight connection.

Tilt up the first corner panel and drop it in place over the bottom plate.

Brace and plumb the first panel. Plumbing each panel as you go helps prevent any out-of-plumb condition from extending along the wall.

With the splines glued into the slots in the standing panel, tilt the second panel into place, align the splines, and mate the two sections together tightly.

The most common connection between wall panels is the thin OSB spline connection (see p. 82). To prepare to install the second panel, apply panel adhesive to the spline slots on both panels, then insert the splines into the slot in the first panel. Apply a bead of expanding foam or adhesive (depending on the manufacturer's recommendations) to the foam core to seal the core-to-core face. Next, tilt the second panel into position, carefully aligning the splines (see the photo at right above). When the two panels are mated, bring them together as tightly as you can to make the structure as energy efficient as possible. (For an average wall, the length will grow approximately ⅛ in. per panel due to normal connection tolerances.)

There are a couple of site-built tools you can use to ensure a tight fit between panels and between the panel and the bottom plate. The first is a beater block made from two scraps of 2x

material and used in conjunction with a sledge-hammer. A narrow 2x scrap, which fits just inside the panel facings, is attached to a 2x scrap that's slightly wider than the panel (see the top left photo on the facing page). To snug up two panels, position the beater block against the bottom corner edge of the panel and strike it with the sledgehammer. The wider 2x scrap spreads out the force of the blows and prevents damage to the facings of the panel.

The other tool is a wall dropper, which is used to encourage a wall panel to slip down over the bottom plate (panels don't always drop down smoothly over the plate when you tilt them up). This tool, which is easy to make from a long 2x and a couple of scraps attached to the end, saves a worker from having to get on a ladder and hammer the wall down to deck level from above.

Once the first two panels are in place and plumbed, it's time to fasten off the connections. I nail all panel-to-bottom plate connections (and all other panel-to-wood connections) with

Use a sledgehammer and a beater block to move a wall section into place after it is tilted up. (Photo by Jon Blumb.)

A site-built "wall dropper" is used to encourage an uncooperative panel to slip down over the bottom plate.

Once the first two panels are standing, fasten off the spline connections between panels and the panel-to-bottom plate connection.

collated 8d nails. The nailing schedule should be specified by the panel manufacturer. At the joints between panels, where the OSB of the facing is being fastened to the OSB spline, I use 1½-in., 14-gauge staples (spaced 4 in. on center). Changing back and forth between nailing and stapling requires some switching around of tools and hoses, but the connections will be stronger.

Subsequent sections are installed in the same manner all around the perimeter of the building. You can use 4-ft.-wide panels throughout or take advantage of jumbo panels on long, straight wall sections. These bigger panels do, of course, require more manpower to raise (unless you have a boom truck or a large forklift on the job site), but they cut down on the number of connections you have to make. If you run into a layout problem as you work around the building, such as a panel that's a little too long, it's easy to cut and scoop the panel to the correct size and continue. A SIP building is a wood building, and making adjustments is easy as you go.

Jumbo SIP panels require a large crew to raise, but they install in the same way as the smaller 4-ft. modules (photos above and right). Instead of using a larger crew to raise jumbo panels a crane can also be used.

Wall sections and headers are assembled on the deck and raised into place as a unit.

Window and door openings There are three ways to handle window and door openings in SIP walls: You can assemble the section on the deck and raise it as a single unit; work with prefabricated panels and assemble them one panel at a time in the normal manner; or cut the openings after the panels have been raised.

To assemble a window or door section on the deck, fasten the two precut trimmer panels to the header panel. The edges of these panels would have been scooped and reinforced with solid 2x blocking during the fabrication process (see p. 85). Nail off the connecting splines (2x studs in this case), flip the assembly over, nail off the other side, and raise the completed section. If the opening is for a window, you'll need to install a precut sill panel once the section is raised (see pp. 85-87).

Cutting a Window in Place

If for any reason you need to install a window or door after the walls have been raised, it's a simple task to cut the unit in. First, mark the rough opening dimensions on the SIP panel, making sure the lines are dark enough to see once the foam starts to fly. The rough opening can be in one panel or extend into two panels. As a safety rule of thumb, if the width of the opening is 5 ft. or more, the load at the header should be engineered.

The perfect tool for cutting the opening is a lightweight chainsaw tool with a stable base plate, as described in chapter 4. Plunge the saw into the panel and make the four cuts. The saw can safely be moved backwards into a corner after a plunge cut before completing the pass.

Next, knock out the panel sections and relieve all four sides to a depth of 1½ in. with a hot scoop (see p. 62). Apply glue to the insides of the facings all around the rough opening, and apply a bead of expanding foam to the foam core. Install the 2x sill piece, which is cut to the rough opening width plus 3 in., then install the header piece, which is cut to the same length. Finally, hammer in the side jambs, which are cut to the rough opening height.

Once the opening is framed in, nail off all the 2x material from both the inside and outside facings. This is a quick process that offers some real flexibility for builders and designers.

A lightweight Poulan electric chainsaw with a stable base plate makes quick work of cutting out a window opening in a SIP wall.

Gluing and nailing the 2x framing pieces into the relieved edges of the panels completes the window preparation.

One way to install a door or window section in a SIP wall is to build it out of precut panels on the deck and then raise it onto the bottom plate as a single assembly. Plumb and brace the wall section, then nail off the bottom plate connection in the normal way.

For smaller window openings, the header can be integrated within a single panel or it can span two panels. The openings in the panels would have been cut during the fabrication phase. Install these panels in the normal way, then add the side trimmers, header, and sill blocking once the panels are raised. Nail off the panel-to-blocking connections all around the opening.

To cut a window or door in place once the walls are standing, see the sidebar on p. 115.

The last panel To complete the perimeter, you need to install the last panel that ties all the wall panels together. As long as you've offset the first panel one panel thickness in from the corner, this last panel should be fairly easy to install. Insert the splines into the second-to-last panel as usual, then slide the last panel over the bottom plate and tight against the standing panel. Once the panel is flush with the outside corner, brace

Window and door openings can be prefabricated in adjoining panels in the shop, then the panels can be installed one at a time in the normal manner.

the corner, check for plumb, and install the long panel screws that will hold this critical connection together. The screws should be at least 1½ in. longer than the thickness of the wall panel (the holes for the screws were predrilled during the fabrication phase).

Once all the perimeter walls are standing and nailed off, the walls can be plumbed and lined (see the sidebar on p. 118). The final step is to install the top plate that ties everything together. If the top plate is composed of several pieces, the plate joints should not break over panel joints; allow at least a 1-ft. overlap. Apply glue to the

Standing the Last Panel

1. Install the OSB splines in the slots of the second-to-last panel.

2. Slide the last panel into place.

3. Plumb and brace the corner.

4. Fasten the last panel to the first panel with screws at least 1½ in. longer than the panel thickness.

Plumbing and Lining the Walls

Normally, I install the whole perimeter of a SIP building before plumbing and lining the walls. Corners raised on top of a flat deck will be so close to plumb that it doesn't take much to tweak them perfectly plumb and brace them, which will pay off later when lining the walls. A completed wall with two plumb corners can also be braced before the rest of the walls are built. The first step is to glue and install the precut top plates.

Once the top plates are in place, I tack 1x scraps onto the wall along the top plate line at both inside corners. Then I stretch a length of mason's twine tightly between them from corner to corner in order to establish a straight plane to measure to. Every 8 ft. (or as often as necessary) I nail a short 2x4 block 1 ft. below the top plate horizontally across a panel joint, then I cut 2x4 braces that are long enough to extend at about a 45-degree angle to the plywood deck and nail

them flat to the top of the blocks. At each brace, I check the gap between the string and the wall with another scrap 1x block; I nail the brace to the deck (into a joist) when the gap between the string and the panel is just a bit more than the thickness of the 1x scrap.

I cut another 2x4 to fit under each diagonal brace and toenail the bottom of the brace to the deck. I push this spring brace against the diagonal brace until the gap between the string and the brace is precisely the thickness of the 1x scrap, indicating that the wall is straight. Next, I nail the spring brace to the diagonal brace, locking the wall into position. This easily adjustable brace system is quick and flexible and will remain in place until the second floor or roof panels are locked in place with long panel screws.

A spring brace system will bring the wall exactly into plumb.

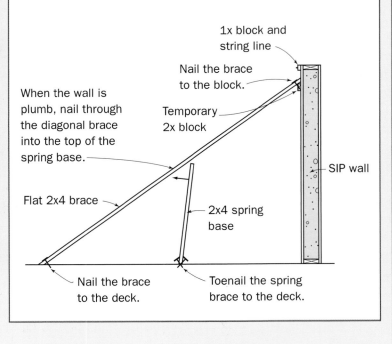

Adjustable Wall Brace

1x block and string line

Nail the brace to the block.

Temporary 2x block

SIP wall

When the wall is plumb, nail through the diagonal brace into the top of the spring base.

Flat 2x4 brace

2x4 spring base

Nail the brace to the deck.

Toenail the spring brace to the deck.

The final step in standing the last panel is to install the top plates that tie the walls together.

insides of the facings, and insert the top plate in the factory-cut recess at the top of the panels. Nail off the top plate from inside and out. The building shell is now ready for installation of a second floor (see pp. 122-124) or a conventional or SIP-built roof (see chapter 7).

Gable-end walls

When a house has gable-end walls, it's best to make these walls extend through to the corners. Therefore, they are the first ones to be set; the eave walls are installed once the two gable ends are up. I build the entire gable wall flat on the deck and then raise it. Normally, the wall can be assembled and raised in a couple of hours, even with windows and siding installed.

A typical gable-end wall is fabricated from 4-ft.-wide panels, with the rakes prefit and cut at the shop. These are heavy, full-length panels, so I like to move them into position either with a big-wheeled forklift or with a wheeled cart (see pp. 69-71). I butt the bottom of the panels against the bottom plate, aligning with the marks for the joints.

On a house with gable-end walls, the entire end wall can be raised as a single unit. (Photo courtesy Thermacore.)

The panels are connected with thin OSB splines as described for flat-top walls. Glue the splines into the first panel, apply glue to the slots of the second panel, and fit the panels together. Continue joining panels for the full width of the

A nylon strap with a ratchet handle is handy for pulling a group of panels tight together on the deck. (Photo courtesy SIPA.)

end wall. If the panels assembled on the deck won't draw tight together, a ratcheting nylon strap can be used to cinch them tight while the splines are stapled off. The beater block pictured on p. 113 can also come in handy for snugging up the panels. Staple off the panel seams using 1½-in., 14-gauge staples at 4 in. o.c. If the gable wall has a ridge beam, a beam pocket has to be fabricated in the panel assembly to bear the load (this detail is installed at the shop, as described on p. 90).

After the last gable wall panel is positioned and the whole wall is stapled off, apply the manufacturer-supplied panel adhesive to the sides and top of the bottom plate and nail off the plates. The wall is now ready to be tilted into place.

Raising the wall To raise a typical gable-end wall safely, you'll need a crew of four workers and the help of two wall jacks. I'm careful to set up the jacks where they'll balance the weight of the wall evenly, that is, the point where there is approximately an equal square footage of wall surface on both sides of the jacks. As both jacks are evenly raised, it will be immediately clear if the wall is balanced; if the middle of the wall lags

behind, you may want to set up closer to the peak. After a little practice, it will be obvious where to set up.

When the top of the wall is about waist high, I set heavy sawhorses under the top plate close to the jacks for safety, then crawl underneath to nail off the top plate (and any beam pockets if they have been installed on the site). The bottom plates hold the base of the wall in position, so I try to nail or staple down as far as is practical before the adhesive starts to set.

Then I raise the wall a little past 45 degrees to start taking weight off the jacks. But before doing this, I nail a 2x4 block across the outside of the beam pocket and run a ½-in.-dia. rope from the peak to a solid point on the deck, such as a stairwell wall or a post. This line is looped 360 degrees around this point, and one of the crew holds the end, letting out a little of the line at a time as the wall is raised. This simple safety procedure prevents the wall from going past 90 degrees. When the wall reaches 90 degrees, it will drop over the plate with a satisfying thud as the wall seats against the subfloor, although sometimes the beater block will be necessary to encourage it into place.

Once the gable-end wall is raised, temporarily brace it to the deck with long 2x4s.

The next step is to temporarily brace the wall to the subfloor with 2x4s, checking that is close to plumb with a level. (I do the final plumbing and lining after all the walls are up; see the sidebar on p. 118.) Once the wall is in position, all of the remaining inside panel joints should be nailed or stapled as well as the SIP-to-bottom plate connection on the inside and outside of the wall.

Eave walls Once the two gable-end walls are in place, you can turn your attention to the eave walls. Unless you're working with jumbo panels and large one-piece wall sections, the accepted procedure is to assemble eave walls one panel at a time. On an eave wall, this method is faster than putting a wall together and then raising it.

The method for installing the eave wall is much the same as that described for a flat-top wall. Before sliding the first eave panel into place against the gable corner, I apply a bead of adhesive down the panel's end stud. Once the panel is in place, I tack it at the bottom to hold it in position. With the two corner panels lined up, I then check the corner for plumb in both directions. This corner is critical and will

determine how smoothly the whole wall—if not the whole main floor—will be assembled, so I make sure to get it plumb, shimming and tweaking as necessary. When I'm happy that the corner is right, I nail off the bottom plate. I check for plumb again, then drive screws at least 1½ in. longer than the thickness of the wall into the corner at the marked locations.

Window and door openings are handled in the same way as that described for flat-top walls. If the building has an angled projection for a bay window, I use a detail developed by Panel Built that increases the structural integrity of the shell and avoids air-infiltration problems. If I am building a 45-degree bay, then I miter-rip the four affected corners to 45 degrees to form the inside and outside corners (see the illustration on p. 122). The key to a tight assembly is to rip the splines at 45 degrees out of 2x material and glue and nail these assemblies together before fitting and raising the pieces. In most cases, 2x6 material will give enough nailing surface to each side of the joint to work.

The last panel on the eave wall can be a little tricky to install because it has to fit inside the gable-end wall (it doesn't run through the corner

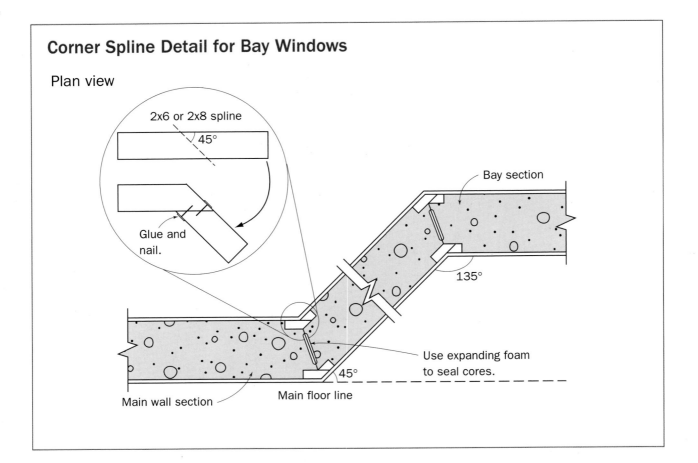

Corner Spline Detail for Bay Windows

Plan view

2x6 or 2x8 spline

45°

Glue and nail.

Bay section

135°

Use expanding foam to seal cores.

45°

Main wall section

Main floor line

as on mating flat-top walls). Careful measurement is needed to ensure that this panel fits exactly to the corner. During shop prefabrication, I don't nail the end stud to this last panel in order to leave room for field adjustments. For example, I may have to trim a panel ½ in. or so, scoop the foam back 1½ in., then glue and nail the stud again before installing this corner. This last panel may have to be lowered down from the top to fit over the splines. A good way to avoid this situation is to start installing panels at a doorway so that the last panel will be a door header and will be simple to install.

Once all four walls are standing, the final step is to install the top plates and plumb and line the walls (see the sidebar on p. 118).

Second floors and second-floor walls

When working on a two-story building, there are a number of ways to set up the second-floor system. Here are three approaches to consider.

In the SIPA-recommended "best practice" approach, the first-floor wall height is taken to the top of the floor frame for the second floor. (see the top illustration on the facing page). After the first-floor top plate is installed, top-hanging joist hangers (Simpson Strong-Tie B, JB, and LB series hangers or similar) for the floor system are hung from the top plate, then the floor joists and bridging are installed. The subfloor is installed all the way to the exterior edge of the SIPs (make sure to take the subfloor to the outside edge of the exterior facing), then the second-floor walls are installed in the same way as the first-floor

SIPA-Recommended Second-Floor Connection

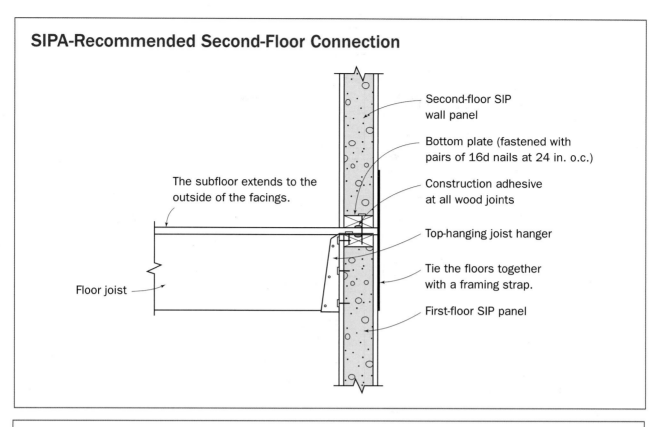

The subfloor extends to the outside of the facings.

Floor joist

Second-floor SIP wall panel

Bottom plate (fastened with pairs of 16d nails at 24 in. o.c.)

Construction adhesive at all wood joints

Top-hanging joist hanger

Tie the floors together with a framing strap.

First-floor SIP panel

Second-Floor Connection with a One-Piece SIP Wall

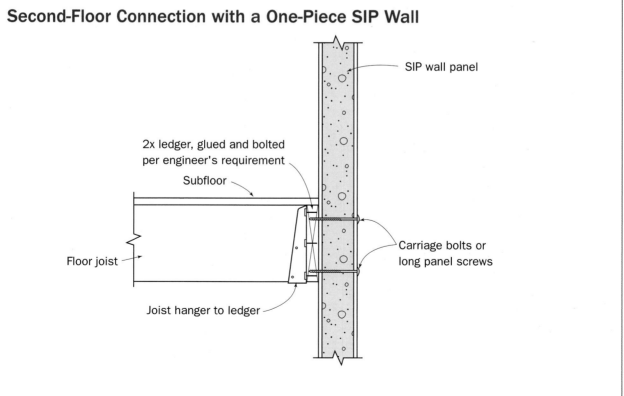

2x ledger, glued and bolted per engineer's requirement

Subfloor

Floor joist

Joist hanger to ledger

SIP wall panel

Carriage bolts or long panel screws

You'll need to hire a boom truck to set the ridge beam in the beam pockets in the gable-end walls. (Photo courtesy Thermacore.)

walls (see pp. 111-119). Steel framing straps should be installed to help hold the two walls together. With this detail, the wall insulation is continuous instead of having potential air leaks around a hard-to-insulate rim joist.

The second option is roughly equivalent to the old style of "balloon framing," a term once used by cynical timber framers who thought the new stick style of building would float away because of the lightness of the frame. Now, modern carpenters shudder when asked to balloon-frame a tall wall: The idea of a high wall of 20-ft. studs conjures up images of having to plane high spots and cut and wedge bows, yet still not ending up with a flat wall. However, a 20-ft.-tall SIP wall will start out flat and stay flat.

The second-floor system is hung from ledgers attached to the SIP wall at the floor framing level (see the bottom illustration on p. 123). This floor-to-wall connection should be one of the project engineer's tasks. The ledgers are attached using a liberal bead of construction adhesive and 3-in. drywall screws (pairs at 24 in. o.c.), then be through-bolted with carriage bolts from the exterior (panel screws 2 in. longer than the thickness of the panel can also be used). Bolt sizes and spacing, which are determined by the manufacturer or engineer, will vary depending on the loads placed on the floor system. This system is fast to install, has no thermal bridge to the exterior, and needs no additional connection between first- and second-floor walls.

The third option is a typical platform floor-to-floor detail. The first-floor SIP wall is built to room height and then the second-floor system is set on top of these walls (this is the same detail as shown in the illustration on p. 106). After the subfloor is installed, the second-floor walls are installed as described previously. This system is well known to framers and has good bearing for the second floor. Special attention should be paid to the insulation in the rim-joist area because the rim joist creates a thermal bridge and there is no insulation to start with. Try to bring the rim up to the insulation levels of the SIP walls by installing sections of rigid foam sealed with expanding foam, then caulk all joints. Steel connectors are recommended between first-floor and second-floor walls.

Once the purlins are in position, nail off the beam pockets securely. (Photo courtesy SIPA.)

Installing beams and purlins

On a gable roof, one of the final things to be done before starting on the roof is to install beams and purlins. Given the transverse loading capabilities of SIPs, a ridge beam can support roof panels with a horizontal span of 16 ft. or more depending on the spline method used and the total loads imposed on the roof. In the house shown in the photo on the facing page, a center ridge beam is bearing on a post at half of the span, and purlins are needed to support the long roof panels.

The beam pockets for the ridge beam and purlins have already been installed in the gable walls (see p. 90), so the first step is to build the center post. You need to take careful measurements at each end of the house to the bottom of the beam pocket and build the center post accordingly. If for any reason the measurements are different, build the post to the taller of the two measurements to keep the beam level and build up the low beam pocket. Use the same approach for the purlins. The supporting posts need to be braced in at least two directions to secure the beam and purlins in place until the roof panels are installed.

There's not much choice other than to get a boom truck on the job to set these beams. I try to have the roof panels ready to set before getting the boom at the site so I can start installing them as soon as the beams are in place. The boom truck picks up the beam with a nylon sling and maneuvers it into position. Once the beams are set in the pockets, toenail them into the 2x material surrounding the pocket, then install lag bolts through the top plates and into the beams.

The midspan purlins are installed in much the same way as the ridge beam. If these purlins are not located at a panel break, you'll need to have the beam pockets engineered for the applied load. The point load needs to be effectively transferred to the panel facings. The panel supplier should have an engineer available to work out this detail.

Chapter 7

INSTALLING THE ROOF

PREPARING
FOR TAKEOFF

PLACING THE PANELS

HIPS AND VALLEYS

One area where the SIP industry is likely to see substantial growth in the near future is in roof applications. The superior insulation values of SIP roof panels are difficult to duplicate with stick-building methods, since 8¼-in. EPS-core panels are rated at about R-32, and 12¼-in. panels are rated at up to R-48. Urethane-core roof panels offer an impressive R-40 of insulation in a thinner 6½-in. profile. Considering that a SIP is a single assembly that includes the interior surface, the insulating core, and the facing for attaching finish roofing, a builder gets a lot of bang for the buck. With the option of prefabrication services and the use of jumbo panels, the erection speed of a SIP roof cannot be equaled by other building systems.

The exceptional transverse-loading capabilities of SIPs enable them to be used for greater spans than conventional building materials (up to 24 ft. in some load situations). This allows designers to spread supporting members farther apart, saving money on materials. This spanning capability is enhanced by the large panels available: 8-ft. by 24-ft. and 8-ft. by 28-ft. sizes are standard now, while 10-ft.-wide jumbo panels may not be far off in the future. When used in conjunction with red-iron steel frames or engineered wood frames, these big panels can be used to enclose large volumes quickly and economically.

SIPs are adaptable to any kind of roof system. Here, a stack of roof panels is ready to be set on a commercial building constructed with I-joists. (Photo courtesy SIPA.)

In light commercial construction applications, the structural capabilities of SIPs allow engineers to simplify the structural elements of a roof by using the spanning capabilities and diaphragmatic resistance of the panels to make a superior hybrid system. The design grid for these large buildings can be increased to a larger module to save material in the shell, while some purlins could be reduced or eliminated in the structural skeleton.

When it comes to comparing the cost and performance of various roofing systems, the larger the roof the bigger advantage the SIP system enjoys. I am going to focus on what is involved in putting up a smaller residential roof, although most of the same tasks and sequences apply to larger-scale applications.

More than any other part of a SIP erection, the placement of the roof is dramatic proof that SIPs go up much faster than any conventional framing system. This is a good opportunity to invite other builders, potential clients, and other interested parties to see the advantages of working with SIPs. In this chapter, I'll first explain how to install a gable roof and conclude with a brief discussion of hip roofs. SIP roof panels are also suitable for use on flat roofs.

Panel Built brings a boom truck in to set the roof panels after the walls have been installed. (Photo courtesy Mic Carmichael.)

Preparing for Takeoff

Preparation and organization are the keys to putting up a roof. You'll need to set up two workstations: one for the ground crew and another for the roof crew. Two workers on the ground and two on the roof can handle most installations.

Stacking Up SIP Roofs against the Competition

While quite a few building companies are comfortable using SIPs for walls, using SIPs for roofs has been slower to catch on. But given the amount of heat that typically escapes out of roof systems, it's worthwhile comparing alternative approaches to roof construction. For most builders, the primary factor that drives the choice of a roofing system is installation cost; insulation value is typically a secondary consideration. But the cheapest roof system isn't necessarily the best system.

Roof-truss systems offer the main economic competition to a SIP roof, and they certainly offer significant advantages over stick-built roofs. Engineered and manufactured from small pieces of lumber, truss roofs go up fast, and it is hard to compete with their installed cost when the space over the ceiling is unused. But when a vaulted or cathedral ceiling is planned, SIP roof systems become more cost competitive. Of course, SIPs can be used over trusses, but often their structural capabilities aren't taken advantage of unless the trusses are wide-span timber-frame trusses.

Truss roofs aren't without their disadvantages. Besides requiring a crane to install them, their webs hog up space that could be used for living area, and they are very difficult to adjust in the field. But the biggest problem with trusses is that they are just plain difficult to insulate effectively. For a cathedral ceiling, a SIP roof system offers a more dramatic interior and much greater insulation values.

Admittedly, cost estimates indicate that a SIP roof package costs more in materials than comparable stick-built or truss roofs. And truss systems cut in on some of the labor savings offered by the SIP approach. But when energy efficiency, speed of erection, and usable interior space are taken into account, SIP roof systems are highly competitive with any other roofing system.

Roof panels spanning 24 ft. installed over wide-span trusses provide a dramatic and well-insulated interior. (Photo courtesy SIPA.)

On roof panels set at a pitch of 7-in-12 or greater, the addition of walkboards makes it easier and safer to move around the roof. (Photo courtesy Advance Foam Plastics.)

For the ground workstation, I build a well-braced temporary staging table out of 2x4s to support each panel as it is readied for installation. I locate the staging table next to the stack of roof panels I am working from so that a panel can be slid onto the table by hand for prep. The roof panels were cut to size and blocked at the ridge during the fabrication stage, but you still need to fasten the connecting splines and set the lifting plates on the panels before they can be installed.

At this point I also install stop blocks on the underside of the first row of panels. These L-shaped 2x scraps are screwed to the bottom corners to help align the rake and eave overhangs and to hold the roof panel in position while the SIPs are being fastened. It's important to get the stop blocks located precisely because it's difficult to move the panels in small increments once they're on the roof. If the roof has a pitch steeper than 7-in-12, I also attach cleats or walkboards on the top side of the panels for safety.

Installing the splines

The basic joint between roof panels is created by using the thin spline method, which employs ⁷⁄₁₆-in. by 4-in.-wide OSB splines. To install the splines, run a bead of adhesive in the spline slots on one edge of the panel, fit the splines in place, and staple off the joint. Apply a bead of expanding foam to the foam core right before liftoff. The other side of the connection will be made on the roof.

OSB splines work fine on standard spans, but for longer spans you'll need to install structural splines to connect the panels. The I-joist spline system is a good one to use for spans more than 12 ft. Engineered I-joists are light, easy to handle, and always straight. Other advantages are that the ⅜-in. web makes a minimal thermal bridge through the roof, and the flanges provide a wide nailing area. As an aid to fitting the panels together on the roof, I make a single pass with a power planer down the top outside flange of the I-joist to create a slight bevel. This will help the sliding panel seat into the fixed one more easily.

To install the I-joist into the panel recesses, apply glue to the inside of the facings, then run a bead of expanding foam along the center of the core so that the roof joint will be airtight. In all of the cases where expanding foam is used in panel connections, you should use a low-expansion, relatively slow-setting foam. These are now

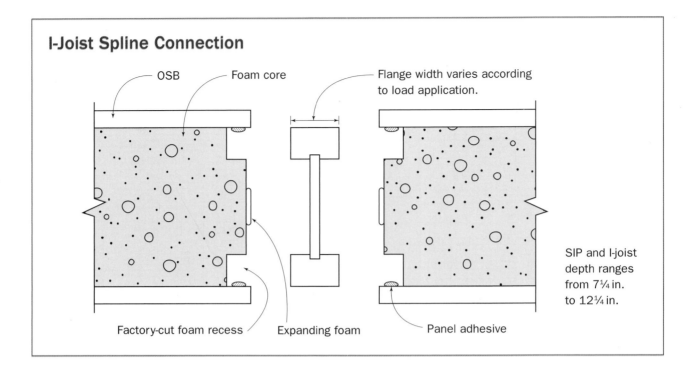

I-Joist Spline Connection

OSB   Foam core

Flange width varies according to load application.

SIP and I-joist depth ranges from 7¼ in. to 12¼ in.

Factory-cut foam recess   Expanding foam   Panel adhesive

sophisticated products, so you can dial in the specific requirement for a task and match a foam to that task. Next, nail off the I-joist on the top and bottom with 8d nails, then apply glue to the top and bottom flange of the exposed half of the spline so it will be ready to nail off as soon as it is in position. Once the splines are fastened to one side of the panel, you're ready to install the lifting plates on top of the panel.

Lifting the panels

There are many approaches to lifting panels with a crane, from looping straps around the panels to using spring-loaded steel lifting eye bolts (see pp. 72-73). Regardless of the method used, quick release of the lifting equipment once the panel is set into place is very important. It is preferable not to have to send a worker up a ladder to undo the interior connection of the lifting plate.

I have used steel fabricated lifting plates with success. They can be fabricated inexpensively (about $50 per pair at my local welding shop), and they can be disconnected by a crew member working from the top of the panel. I attach a lifting plate to a panel with screws that are 2 in.

A welded steel lifting plate is an inexpensive and secure tool for lifting roof panels.

Lifting rings support a long roof panel with a skylight opening. Visible at the right edge of the panel is the connecting I-joist spline. (Photo courtesy Ed Stahl, Sunworks.)

longer than the panel thickness, screwing them all the way through the panel and into 2x12 scraps on the underside of the panel. After the panel is placed in position on the roof, a worker on top unscrews the plate for reuse. One drawback to this method is that the 2x12 blocks then fall to the deck, creating a dangerous situation for workers below.

This type of lifting plate can also be used with panels that have finished materials already applied to the interior facing of the SIP. To do this, the plate is fastened with drywall screws from the top. To determine how many screws it will take to lift a panel, divide the weight of the panel by the pull-out resistance of each screw (at 150 lb. per screw) and multiply the answer by a safety factor of 3. For example, if a panel weighs 500 lb., 500 divided by 150 equals 3.33 screws times 3 equals 10 screws. The plate I use has 18 holes, and I typically put screws in all of the holes, giving me a wide safety margin.

Another simple lifting plate can be fabricated from a 2-in.-wide section of a 5-in.- or 6-in.-dia. pipe with ¾-in. threaded rod welded on. The big eye makes it easy to run wide nylon straps

through the lifting ring. This method requires only one hole in the panel and makes installation quick. However, this type of lifting plate does require a worker underneath to undo it, and it can cause problems with roof panels that have a finished interior surface. Whatever the lifting arrangement, it helps to mount the plates on the panels slightly off-center so that they hang at the approximate angle of the roof pitch.

One final safety item I use is a tag line. I attach one to a bottom corner of each panel before it heads into the air so that someone on the ground can control the panel and keep it from spinning. When the wind is blowing, the operation can quickly become dangerous, resulting in possible damage to the panels, the structure, and to the workers themselves. It doesn't cost much to go the extra mile for safety and control.

Placing the Panels

As well as the framing station on the ground, you'll also need to set up some kind of staging inside the building for the roof crew to work from. I set up scaffold sections on wheels to

Rolling scaffolding on the main floor helps the crew land big roof panels safely.

enable my crew to work up high and move the scaffold sections around to get ready for the sequence of panels to come. Make sure the top crew has a bagful of panel screws at least 1½ in. longer than the panel thickness and a screw gun to crank the screws in. Also up top should be a pneumatic nailer or stapler for connecting the splines (depending on what type of spline system is being used) and a sledgehammer and beating blocks for persuading panels into place.

When the crane arrives on the job site, it should be positioned to do as much of the roof from one point as possible. Giving the operator a good line of sight to the whole job will make his job easier. The lead person should check with the crane operator to go over hand signals. In addition, many of today's operators have lightweight earphone/mike combo units that can be helpful, especially if the crane is out of line of sight.

Once the panel has been prepped and the lifting plates and tag line are fastened, the crane can pick up the first panel. This panel needs to be set accurately because any skewing here will be compounded by each subsequent panel. This is where accurate placement of the stop blocks pays off.

While the first panel is being set on the roof, the ground crew prepares the next one. Once

Ideally, the boom truck should be positioned to set all the panels from one point. (Photo courtesy Mic Carmichael.)

Cranes: A Key to SIP Job Success

When most builders refer to a crane, they usually mean a boom truck. Boom trucks are available with a lifting capacity of around 30 tons, while a hydraulic crane will start at 50 tons and go up from there. Don't underestimate the lifting job at hand. Lifting weight straight up is one thing, but extending that weight over a horizontal distance is a very different thing altogether. It is easy to lift a bowling ball straight up, but try to hold it at arm's length and you will see how weight acts differently when extended.

I regularly use a crane service to help set large beams and roof panels. The service's 28-ton capacity boom truck has a rear-mount turret that offers a 320-degree working arc. Its boom will extend 95 ft. with another 32 ft. of jib length available. With upward of $250,000 invested in one boom truck and hefty insurance premiums, the crane service I use has to keep its machines working. I can hire its 50-ton crane for $150 per hour and its 28-ton boom truck for $100 per hour (with a three-hour minimum), a more than fair price considering the capacity and accuracy of these pieces of equipment.

Here are some important safety guidelines to follow when working with a crane or boom truck:

- Check the clearance from overhead power lines in all directions.
- Insist that everyone wear hardhats when a crane is on the site. Besides the physical protection they offer, wearing a hardhat increases worker awareness that this is a potentially dangerous environment.
- Make sure the whole crew understands the basic hand signals to communicate with the crane operator.
- No one should ever stand or walk underneath a flying panel. This is not just superstition—in this case, gravity is not a friend.
- Keep radios off when working a roof. Everyone needs to be able to hear instructions and warnings.
- Attach a tag line to one of the downside panel corners to add control and make it easier to stabilize the panel.
- Be aware of wind changes and don't hesitate to put off lifting roof panels until the weather is conducive for the task.
- Get organized. The meter is running when a crane is on-site.

The skill of the crane operator can make a big difference in how smoothly a roof installation goes.

Roof-to-Wall Connections

There are several ways to prepare the tops of eave walls for the roof-panel installation if there is a pitch to the roof. The roof panel needs to bear on both facings of the wall panel equally to spread out the loads evenly. The most common detail is to install a 2x spacer beveled to the roof pitch onto the top plate before the roof is installed (see the illustration below). This detail allows electrical wiring to be run along the top plate if a channel is routed into the spacer. After the roof panel is installed, expanding foam is applied to the void behind the spacer through gaps left in the spacer for that purpose. Liberal beads of glue should be applied over and under the spacer to seal this potential air leak.

Another method is to fabricate a top plate to the pitch of the roof and install it in the wall-panel recess made during fabrication (see the top illustration on the facing page). With this method, once the top plate is installed there's nothing else to do except run glue over the top plate. The drawbacks are that special milling of the plate material is required, it is difficult to increase load bearing of the wall with a "cap" plate, and wiring cannot be run along the plate.

Here's the method I prefer, as shown in the bottom illustration on the facing page. First, I install the roof panels onto the top plates with long panel screws every 12 in. (no glue is applied at this stage). Second, wedge blocks are fabricated out of 2x material beveled to the roof pitch, and some of these are tacked in place temporarily. Third, the electrical wiring is run up through the vertical chases to the proper locations. Fourth, the wedges are glued and nailed every 16 in. around the perimeter and, if necessary, trimmed to allow the wiring to pass. These wedges should be hammered in tightly to make sure the roof panel is bearing on both facings. The last step is to inject expanding foam along the gap to seal the joint from any air leakage. This method is fast and flexible, can be used with a cap plate in place, makes adequate bearing for the roof, and works easily with any pitch.

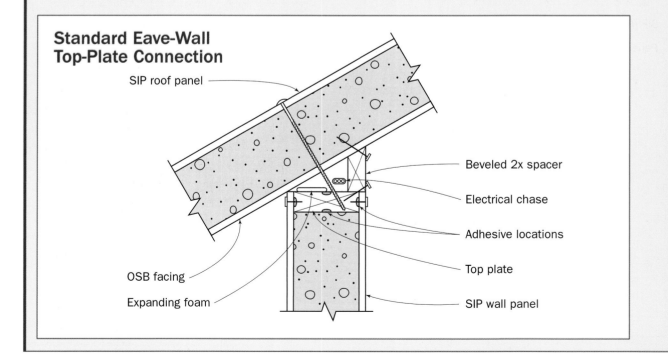

Standard Eave-Wall Top-Plate Connection

SIP roof panel

Beveled 2x spacer

Electrical chase

Adhesive locations

Top plate

SIP wall panel

OSB facing

Expanding foam

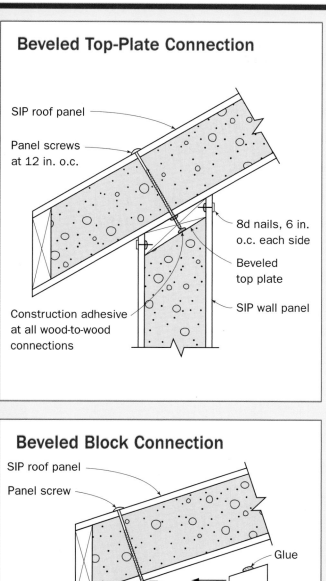

Beveled Top-Plate Connection

SIP roof panel

Panel screws at 12 in. o.c.

8d nails, 6 in. o.c. each side

Beveled top plate

SIP wall panel

Construction adhesive at all wood-to-wood connections

Beveled Block Connection

SIP roof panel

Panel screw

Glue

Wiring

Beveled blocks are installed 16 in. o.c., cut to the roof pitch.

Allow room for wiring, if necessary.

SIP wall panel

three or four big screws are set through the roof panel into the top plate or the ridge beam, the panel is locked in place, the lifting plates are released, and the top crew keeps nailing or stapling and installing screws until the next panel flies in. All of the screw locations have been marked with a magic marker circle around them so they can't be missed. While I typically space my screws 12 in. o.c., different situations may require different engineered solutions. As soon as the next panel is launched, the top crew gets ready to guide it into place, sometimes with the help of a few smacks with the persuader to seat the connection. This sequence continues along the gable and is then reversed on the other side of the ridge.

As well as installing the appropriate long panel screws and fastening the spline connections on the top of the roof, it's important to nail or staple the underside seams of the panels soon after installation. This can be done from the rolling scaffold or a ladder. While the exterior facing of a roof panel is in compression, the interior facing is in tension, so it is worth considering a closer nailing pattern on the interior joints, decreasing the pattern from 6 in. o.c. to 3 in. o.c. Have the engineer spec all the fastener spacings.

Ridge connections in high-wind areas

Once the panels reach the ridge, any of a number of connection details can be used (see the illustration on p. 97). The plumb-cut ridge detail can be easily modified for high-wind situations. When the panel on the first side of the ridge is set in place, I set long screws into the ridge a minimum of 1½ in. Before the other side is set in the same fashion, I gain additional uplift resistance by installing reinforcing angle clips (for example, Simpson Strong-Tie GA or L series clips). Next, I install the other panels to the ridge beam.

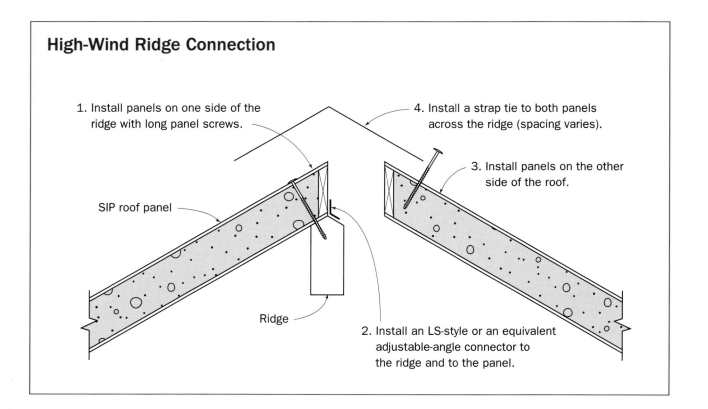

High-Wind Ridge Connection

1. Install panels on one side of the ridge with long panel screws.

4. Install a strap tie to both panels across the ridge (spacing varies).

3. Install panels on the other side of the roof.

SIP roof panel

Ridge

2. Install an LS-style or an equivalent adjustable-angle connector to the ridge and to the panel.

Additional uplift resistance can be gained by using some of the Simpson MSTL, MST, or LSTL series of 12-gauge straps, attaching them over the ridge and fastening them into the splines of the roof panels. While there are many products and approaches to upgrade the seismic and wind resistance of a SIP building, the few hundred dollars spent on the installation of this type of product can be the best and cheapest insurance you can buy.

Placing panels perpendicular to the frame

In situations where the roof structure is a timber frame, steel frame, or engineered wood frame, the panels are often set parallel to the ridge and eave and perpendicular to the rafters or bents. As when installing roof sheathing, once the bottom course is set, gravity becomes your friend and the subsequent panels slide downhill into place.

Setting jumbo panels perpendicular to the frame expands the possibilities for structural support. (Photo courtesy Pacemaker Plastics.)

Sometimes the spans between rafters or bents can be quite long—in some cases more than 20 ft.—in order to take full advantage of the transverse-loading capabilities of SIPs. But it is important to stress that the width of the panels, the thickness of the panels, and the spline system all need to be engineered for each specific application. On shorter spans up to 12 ft., the thin spline method is usually sufficient to take the applied roof load, thus saving money over solid- or I-joist-type splines.

Hips and Valleys

Hip roofs can be fabricated and installed with SIPs as long as support members are provided where the hips and valleys bear. Hips and valleys are elements that need to be carefully calculated and cut during fabrication to ensure a good, tight fit. During the shop-fabrication stage, the hip or valley splines should also have been fabricated. These are two double-beveled pieces that are ripped to the panel core thickness and beveled to the hip/valley angle (see chapter 5 for more details).

Let's assume here that the hip or valley support members have been placed and secured before proceeding with the panel placement. I like to install the hip or valley panels after the closest common panel has been set. The common panel should also have the spline glued and nailed in place so the hip/valley section can slip into position. The hip/valley sections will already have the beveled blocking installed. Starting with the largest triangles at the top, glue and nail each piece at the ridge and the common spline, for

A roof panel with a valley cut is positioned for installation. (Photo courtesy SIPA.)

Careful fabrication of hip or valley panels will ensure a tight fit during installation of the roof. (Photo courtesy SIPA.)

Finishing Off the Eave

The foam core at the eave end of the roof panel is scooped out during the fabrication process (see chapter 5), but I wait to install the blocking, fascia, and soffit until the roof is in place. Here are three overhang details that can be built into a SIP roof.

The thickness of the roof panels can give the roof a heavy, "clunky" look if the panels are left square-cut—and even heavier if a plumb-cut is the finish look. One option is to let the roof panels form the overhang and then fashion a compound fascia, as shown in the illustration at left below.

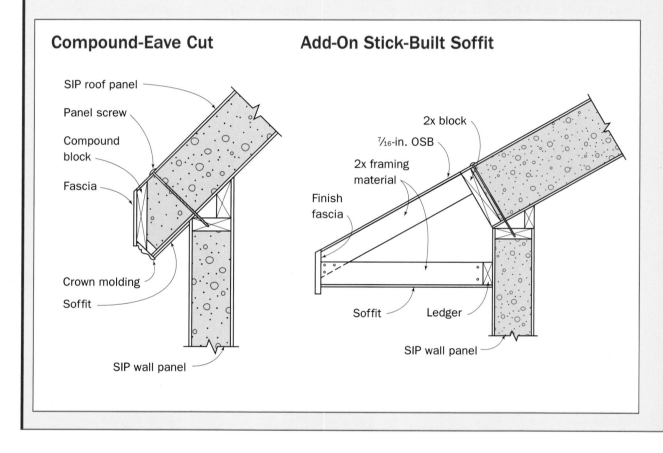

Compound-Eave Cut

SIP roof panel
Panel screw
Compound block
Fascia
Crown molding
Soffit
SIP wall panel

Add-On Stick-Built Soffit

2x block
7/16-in. OSB
2x framing material
Finish fascia
Soffit
Ledger
SIP wall panel

now leaving the hip/valley sitting on the hip/valley support. Starting from the top ensures that any adjustment necessary to the assembly will be made on the smallest triangle at the bottom.

Once all the panels on one side of the hip/valley have been set, you can start from the top of the other side. Because of the complex joint here, you may want to leave a ½-in. or so gap at the hip/valley. Before the second side of the hip/valley is installed, apply expanding foam

to the hip/valley splines to seal the gap. Because the hip/valley sides of the panel sections are sitting on a support member, this connection is really not structural, so it doesn't need to fit as tightly as a spline connection. When each of the last side sections has been positioned, fasten long panel screws into the hip/valley supports to complete the connection.

There is no doubt that fabricating and installing roof panels is a complicated undertaking, especially when hips and valleys are

Although it's tempting to prime and paint the bottom OSB facing of the overhanging roof panel in this situation, adding a soffit board will make for a better-looking finish.

Another approach is to stop the roof panel at the edge of the building and stick-build the fascia and soffit after the roof panels are installed (see the illustration at right on the facing page). Any look can be attained with this method, but it adds time to the installation of the roof. A similar effect can be achieved by letting the I-joist splines extend past the ends of the roof panels. The splines can then serve as the framework to support the soffit. In the illustration below, a level-cut soffit gives a clean, modern finish, but there are many other soffit possibilities as well.

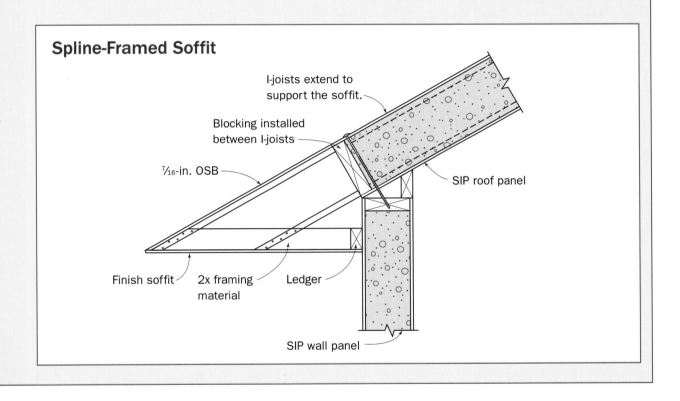

Spline-Framed Soffit

I-joists extend to support the soffit.

Blocking installed between I-joists

$7/16$-in. OSB

SIP roof panel

Finish soffit

2x framing material

Ledger

SIP wall panel

involved. On the other hand, a roof normally doesn't have all the penetrations that a wall does, so typically bigger pieces that are simpler to fabricate are going to be used. This adds up to speed. The reward is in the speed of erection and the strength and energy efficiency that this system adds to a building. The potential for high-volume commercial applications has been barely tapped. The potential for custom panels with finished interior and exterior surfaces is tremendous. Volume demand will be the determining factor here.

There is, in fact, no single "way" to put up a SIP structure. With some planning, coordination, and help from the panel supplier, a builder can come up to speed with this system very quickly, cutting significant time from the erection of the shell, yet still providing a quality product to his customers.

Chapter 8

MECHANICAL SYSTEMS IN SIP BUILDINGS

ELECTRICAL
DISTRIBUTION

PLUMBING
CONSIDERATIONS

WIRING AND PLUMBING
KITCHENS

HVAC SYSTEMS

Two questions that newcomers to SIPs often ask are, "How do you run electrical wiring in SIPs?" and "How do you run plumbing supplies and vents in SIPs?" Besides wanting to know how to install these systems, they're also keen to know if it will cost more to have these mechanical systems installed in a SIP house than in a conventionally framed house. Of course, the stock answer from any contractor worth his or her salt is, "It depends."

Earlier I discussed how to maximize the potential of SIPs by utilizing the size and spanning capabilities of the panels during the design phase. With mechanical systems, too, there are easy ways to include them in a plan and there are hard ways. Contractors who have experience working with SIPs will have good suggestions that can save the client both time and money.

For the most part, SIP buildings require the same set of subcontractors as a conventional house, with the possible exception of the insulating sub. Most of the methods and procedures are the same as in conventional construction, but there are a few specialized details for each trade. Builders shouldn't have to look for subs with SIP experience, but the tendency for any subcontractor asked to bid on unfamiliar specs is to throw a high number at the job to cover the unusual. I try to explain to my subs who are unfamiliar with SIPs that working on this type of house is basically the same as any

A SIP building requires much the same subcontractors as a conventional house. Subcontractors working with SIPs have a short learning curve.

other type of house, except that it will be more comfortable and quieter than the sites they are used to working in.

Electrical Distribution

The subcontractor who will have to adjust his or her approach the most when working on a SIP building will be the electrical contractor. Basically, installing wiring in a SIP building is a lot like running wire in a commercial job, except that the electrician doesn't have to install the conduit because the panels come with factory-cut chases. When the builder erects the shell correctly, he has already drilled most of the required holes in the exterior walls. And while the techniques for installing wire in the exterior walls of a SIP building are different from those for a stick-framed building, exterior walls comprise only part of the overall scope of the job; the rest of the tasks are the same.

Because it's difficult to make changes in SIP wiring once the shell is in place, the electrical distribution plan needs to be thought out and detailed before work begins. Having the electrician involved in this planning stage can

save time and money later on. This is an area where experience can make things easier on the electrician. For instance, if a receptacle outlet (located 14 in. up from the floor), a switch (located 44 in. up from the floor), and an exterior light fixture are all pulled from the same vertical chase, the electrician's life is made easier. Similarly, the erection crew can place some circuit wiring between panel joints during the wall assembly to save the electrician drilling time later. On the other hand, the old builders' saying, "If you can draw it, we can build it," remains true as well. The catch, of course, is the cost.

Wire chases

Most manufacturers offer standard integral wiring chases in their panels, with a standard basic layout as well as several custom options. A typical 4-ft.-wide panel has a 1½-in.-dia. horizontal chase cut into the foam core about 14 in. up from the bottom of the panel and another horizontal chase about 44 in. up from the bottom (see the illustration on p. 75). These locations will accommodate most receptacle circuits and switch locations. In addition, a 1½-in.-dia. vertical chase is typically located in the center of a 4-ft. panel

Working with Subs

For most general contractors, their subcontractors are the key to a successful business. Good ones are hard to find, and I go out of my way to be fair to them to keep them working on my jobs. I have always found that the key is to bring them to a job site that's ready for their specialty and lay out their tasks clearly. This starts with getting their input on their part of the project during the planning stage of the job and working with them so they know where they fit into the schedule and what happens if they don't come in at the scheduled time.

The first time subs are exposed to a SIP project it may take some hand-holding to get them up to speed with an unfamiliar system. I walk them through their tasks and mark out any specific parts (such as the position of holes and chases) with a thick magic marker. The plumber may have to change a few of his routines to keep supplies and vents away from the exterior walls, but each change is relatively minor. A good sub will adapt quickly and really won't take any longer to perform his trade.

The scheduling of subs on a SIP job is complicated by the fact that the shell is erected in such a short time and suddenly the job is ready for them. It doesn't do anyone any good if the shell goes up in five days, but the plumber can't be there for a week and a half. If the speed of assembly is taken advantage of and everyone is ready with his trade in a timely sequence, then some good things occur. For example, the owner can change his higher-interest construction loan into an end loan much sooner and save some interest. Less overall time on a project, of course, means money in the contractor's pocket and the ability to begin new work and make more money. Subs are a vital part of the construction sequence, so it is in your best interest to get them up to speed quickly on the SIP system.

(or two in an 8-ft.-wide panel) so that vertical chases are on 4-ft. centers. This basic grid allows the electrician to run almost all of the wiring for an electrical plan without significant drilling or cutting of the panels.

Besides this standard configuration, factory-installed custom chases can be ordered to virtually any specification to accommodate the most elaborate wiring plan. In addition, there are many custom approaches to getting wiring where you want it. But whichever of the following approaches you use, one key to remember when modifying panels to accept wiring is not to cut through either of the OSB facings around the perimeter of the panel. When the structural shell is complete, this perimeter is under constant load; cutting through this OSB perimeter interrupts the integrity of the system.

Factory-supplied electrical chases make running wire to receptacle and switch boxes an easy task. (Photo by Jon Blumb.)

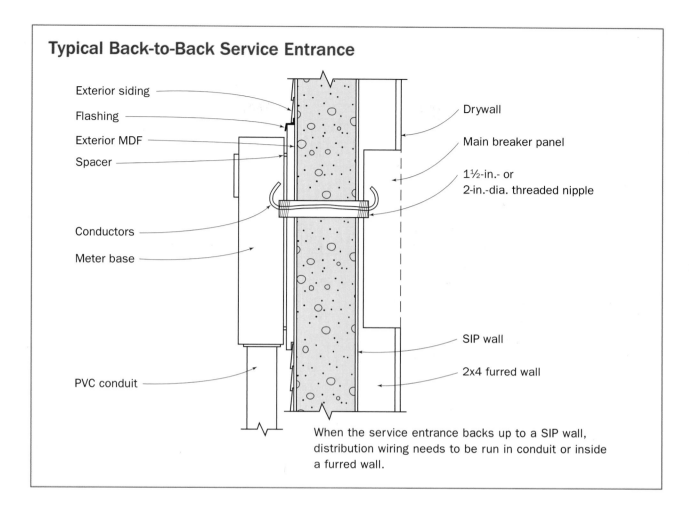

Typical Back-to-Back Service Entrance

Exterior siding
Flashing
Exterior MDF
Spacer

Conductors

Meter base

PVC conduit

Drywall

Main breaker panel

1½-in.- or
2-in.-dia. threaded nipple

SIP wall

2x4 furred wall

When the service entrance backs up to a SIP wall, distribution wiring needs to be run in conduit or inside a furred wall.

Service entrances

Locating the service entrance is sometimes a bit different than with a stick-built structure. Typically, service entrances are brought in either overhead or underground to a meter base that needs to be located on the exterior of the building. From the meter base, power is brought into the main panel, where it is distributed throughout the structure or to other subpanels for distribution. None of these supply cables can be surface-run through any living space, so once inside a SIP structure the cables will have to be inside conduit or inside interior stud walls.

If the main panel is in a basement, the approach is standard practice. But for a slab building or if the main panel is scheduled upstairs, the installation is different and the main panel will have to be located in a mechanical room. There are specific code requirements for clearances from the panel to other objects, as well as in which rooms a panel can be located, so you will have to comply with the building codes that apply to your area.

The main panel may be located back-to-back with the meter base, in which case a 1½-in.- or 2-in.-dia. threaded nipple needs to be installed through the thickness of the panel and tightened to the panel box (see the illustratration above). To waterproof this opening, mount the meter base on a primed, ¾-in.-thick piece of exterior-rated MDF (or equivalent), sized a little larger than the meter base (be sure to install a piece of "Z" flashing over the top of this board). Fix the threaded nipple from the interior and project the nipple through the SIP, carefully caulking the SIP-

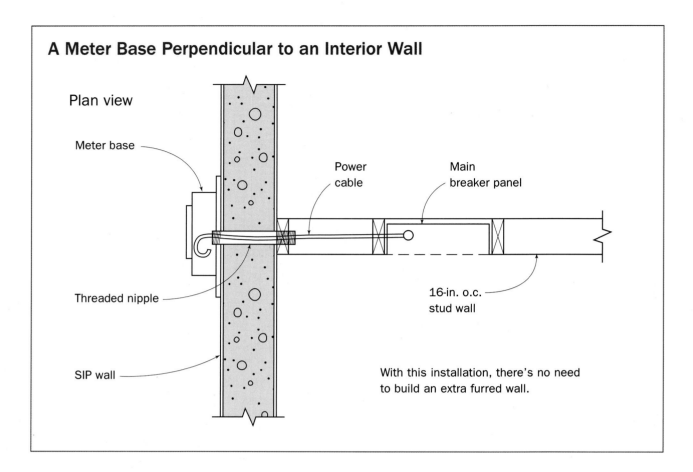

A Meter Base Perpendicular to an Interior Wall

Plan view

Meter base

Power cable

Main breaker panel

Threaded nipple

16-in. o.c. stud wall

SIP wall

With this installation, there's no need to build an extra furred wall.

to-pipe space with a large bead of exterior caulk. Next, mount the meter base with a bead of caulk along the top of the meter base. A better solution is to space the meter base away from the wall with neoprene washers so water can run freely by the panel. On the interior, you'll need to furr out the wall or build a 2x4 wall along the exterior wall on which the main panel will be located. Now the circuit wiring is in a cavity that can be drywalled to meet fire requirements, which will make it code compliant.

Another approach is to back the meter base to the framed wall of a utility room that's perpendicular to the exterior SIP wall. A cable can then be brought from the meter base through the SIP in a steel nipple and pulled through the interior stud wall to the main panel that is mounted there (see the illustration above). From this location, the interior circuit distribution is straightforward.

Outlets and switches

Before the wiring is run, devices need to be located and openings made for the wire runs. If the electrical layout plan calls for some specific custom chases, these should be fabricated before assembly begins, if possible.

One typical switch location is next to an exterior door. Since there won't be many of these, it's a good idea to mark their locations on the set of shop drawings so they will be taken into account at the fabrication stage. I hot-melt a chase groove in the center of the foam core the whole length of the panel, making sure I know which way the door will swing so the switch is on the latch side. Power and switch wiring can then be routed up to the switch-height chase. The location of the switch box will be dictated by the width of the casing to be used and personal preference. Don't install the trimmer stud during

Receptacle boxes are cut into the panel and attached with screws through the mounting ears.

the fabrication phase—the wires need to be run first. It's also important to mark the top and bottom of the chase locations so the top and bottom plates can be drilled during erection.

To prepare for switch boxes, receptacle boxes, and fixture outlet boxes, you need to make openings in the facings of the panels. These can

be cut either with a jigsaw or with a hole saw. You should test-fit the box to be used in the hole before the wiring is run so that you won't have to cut and scrape when wire is in place. The boxes most commonly used in SIP walls are plastic boxes with side mounting brackets that can be screwed to the OSB. Steel boxes with adjustable mounting ears are handy for offsetting the face of the box to accommodate different interior finishes, or extension rings can protect the wires from saws and routers.

If necessary, you can fabricate a custom receptacle location after the panels are up. First, cut the hole for the box, then either cut a slot to within a couple of inches of the bottom plate and drill a hole through the plate to the joist space below or drill a "mouse hole" behind where the baseboard will cover and drill down from there. An alternative is to use surface-mount wiring chases after the panels go up, which add flexibility to the electrical layout and make future changes easy. The simplest way to install surface-mount circuits is with one of the various wire-mold systems that are commonly used in retail work and some light commercial projects. There are complete, quickly installed systems of

Custom baseboard raceways add flexibility to wiring layouts.

connectors and fittings available that can make the job comply with code.

For a custom approach, a baseboard raceway can be fabricated from stock parts, adding a distinctive trim element to the home's interior finish. Add ¾-in. furring strips at the bottom of the interior face of the SIPs to create a chase for the wire runs. Feed the wires along this chase to cut-in boxes in the baseboard, or drill into the vertical chase to install receptacle boxes anywhere in the wall. A shallow, 1½-in.-deep cut-in electrical box mounted in the baseboard will fit between the surface of the baseboard and the panel or drywall. Use this system to feed into stock vertical panel chases or make chases for wall outlets by taking a short piece of ¾-in. soft copper pipe bent to a curve and pushing it up to a cutout in the wall.

One drawback to this built-up baseboard raceway is that the extra thickness of the assembly will project out past standard door casings. In this case, a plinth block could be used or a return to a normal baseboard devised. The top of the base assembly can be a small crown mold or bed mold or a custom base cap.

Lighting circuits

There are some creative ways to run wires to difficult ceiling locations. If there is a cavity over the top wall plate formed when the roof panel sits on a spacer block, this space can be used to distribute wires for ceiling lights and fans. Roof panels typically come with prerouted chases.

To run a switch leg from a wall switch to a light fixture in a roof panel, first locate the ceiling chase, which was marked at the factory. Then take a right-angle drill with a 3½-in.-dia. hole saw and drill up into the center of the chase perpendicular to the roof panel and at the edge of the wall panel. Next, use a framing chisel to pop out the plug so the wire can be fished through the chase to the fixture location. Save the plug, which can be foamed back in place when the wires are run and after the rough-in inspection.

Bring the Romex wire up the wall chase into the open area above the plate, then drill a

Feeding a Ceiling Fixture

1. Use a hole saw to drill out a 3½-in.-dia. plug to gain access to the ceiling-panel chase.

2. Pull the wire up through the vertical chase and run it along the top plate.

3. Use a fish tape to feed the wire to the fixture location.

4. Pull the wire through the knockout before the box is installed.

5. Fill the gap between the wall panel and the roof panel with expanding foam.

1-in.-dia. hole for the fixture halfway into the panel (or until you hit the chase). Use a fish tape to feed the wire through the chase to the fixture location and through a round, ½-in.-deep "pancake" box. I use construction adhesive and four drywall screws to surface-mount this box for all but the heaviest of fixtures. The drywall will be flush with the pancake box after finishing. For heavy fixtures, I drill a hole to the chase for a hex box with a mounting flange using a 4-in.-dia. hole saw. Before the box is installed, pull the wire through the knockout. After the rough electrical inspection, foam in the gap between the ceiling and wall panel.

The Fishing Rod

The fishing rod is a specialty drill bit that's especially useful when wiring a SIP building. Basically a 3-in.-long, ⅜-in.-dia. twist bit mounted on the end of a 4½-ft.-long, ³⁄₁₆-in.-dia. flexible spring steel shaft, this bit can be used to connect chases and cutouts, allowing a fixture or receptacle to be mounted almost anywhere on a panel. A fishing rod can also be used to drill from one panel into another if the panels are connected by using the thin spline method.

To use the tool, aim the fishing rod toward the chase hole, then start the drill with the bit touching the back of the hole, keeping the bit as close to the interior facing as possible. Drill slowly and hook the index finger of your non-drill hand over the drill shaft, pulling the bit down toward the interior facing. Then slowly push the bit along through the foam while drilling at a medium speed. When the bit enters the chase hole, give it a little wiggling room.

The cutting tip of the bit has a ⁵⁄₆₄-in. hole through it, so once it has found the receptacle hole, you can take the bare copper ground wire from 14/2 Romex and twist and tape it to the conductors and over the Romex jacket so the wrap comes to a point at the end of the bit. Now you can fish the wire back to the location hole, cut the ground wire, and install a 3-in. fixture outlet box. Using this method, there are hardly any locations where you would need more than one of these custom holes.

Aim the flexible bit into the chase hole and toward the fixture hole.

Tape Romex wire to the bit and feed it from the chase to the fixture.

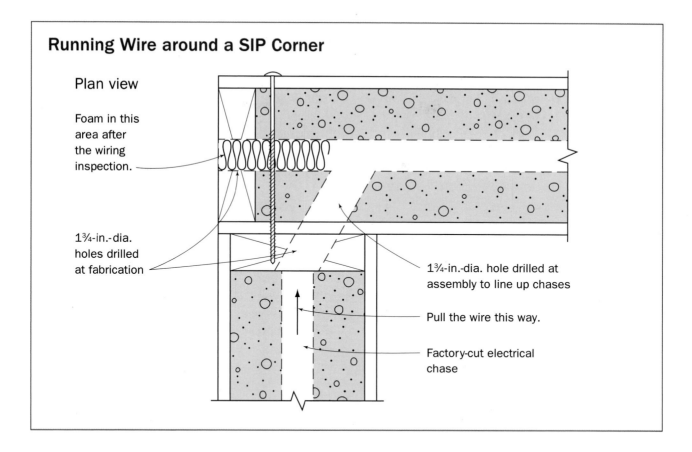

Running Wire around a SIP Corner

Plan view

Foam in this area after the wiring inspection.

1¾-in.-dia. holes drilled at fabrication

1¾-in.-dia. hole drilled at assembly to line up chases

Pull the wire this way.

Factory-cut electrical chase

Custom ceiling-fixture locations can be roughed in in just a few minutes. I mark the location away from the chase and drill two 3-in.-dia. core plugs with a hole saw, one hole at the chase and one at the custom location. After drilling about 3 in. into the core, I pop out the plugs and save them until after the inspection, when they can be glued and foamed back into place. I connect these holes using a long flexible drill bit I call the fishing rod (see the sidebar on the facing page).

I don't know of any detail that allows recessed lighting to be mounted in a SIP roof. If the roof panels are 12¼-in.-thick jumbo panels and 6-in.-tall low-profile cans are scheduled, there might be a way to install them, but my recommendation is either to drop the ceiling if recessed lighting is really desired or to use surface lighting.

Navigating corners

Wiring corners is not much of a concern when a building has a basement or a crawl space because most circuits are looped from below into the vertical chases provided in the panels. But this method cannot be used with slab construction. When the SIP structure is built on a slab, wiring has to be pulled horizontally to feed receptacles and switches, and some way must be found to go around corners.

One common solution is to pull wire up the vertical chase and along the top plate, then drop down in the next chase around the corner, but only certain top-plate details allow this. Another approach involves drilling the corner studs at the same height as the bottom chase of the panels, where the power feeds are run (see the illustration above). The end stud of the panel that butts into the full-length panel needs to have a hole drilled in it at an angle so that the wire will sweep through it and into a connecting hole in the adjacent panel (see the illustration on p. 149). These holes should be drilled during the fabrication stage, before the corner is assembled. While it is unlikely that a switch leg would run around a corner, a similar process would be followed to accommodate this situation.

Remember that wiring needs to be protected from damage by fasteners. Since the stock wiring chases are located in the center of the foam core, they are out of the way of normal fastener penetration (until brought to the surface for a switch or outlet box). But if custom chases are closer to the inside surface, metal nail-protection plates should be installed. Bear in mind, however, that a nail from a pneumatic nailer can penetrate one of these protectors, whereas a 1½-in. drywall screw will penetrate just a little past the combined thicknesses of the drywall and OSB.

Exterior circuits and lighting

For the most part, exterior circuits and lighting are handled the same as interior circuitry. But special care must be used when installing exterior boxes so that water does not penetrate into the SIP (waterproofing is discussed in detail in chapter 9). To minimize the chance of this happening, try to use surface-mounted boxes for outlets, switches, and light fixtures. These units are designed for exterior use and come with durable painted or anodized finishes. Pancake-type boxes can be screwed to the SIP surface with a minimal hole penetrating the exterior. Before the box is mounted, the penetration should be thoroughly caulked with an exterior caulk and the hole from inside shot with expanding foam.

Plumbing Considerations

Plumbers will have to make fewer changes and adaptations than electricians on a SIP job site, but there are a few tricks to be learned. A walk-through with the plumber on the first day can help to head off potential problems, especially if it is his or her first time working with SIPs.

There are a number of ways to make the plumbing more SIP friendly. For example, I might run the supplies and drain/vent to a vanity from a side wall instead of the back if it is located on an exterior wall. I might gang several bathroom vents together and upsize the vent pipe in order to have one less roof penetration. These items sometimes end up costing a little more than the initial bid when working with a plumber new to SIPs. In this case, I usually pay the difference but expect that the plumber will include those changes in the base charges for the stackout in subsequent SIP jobs.

All penetrations to the exterior (here, a plumbing vent through a roof panel) need to be filled with expanding foam. (Photo by Jon Blumb.)

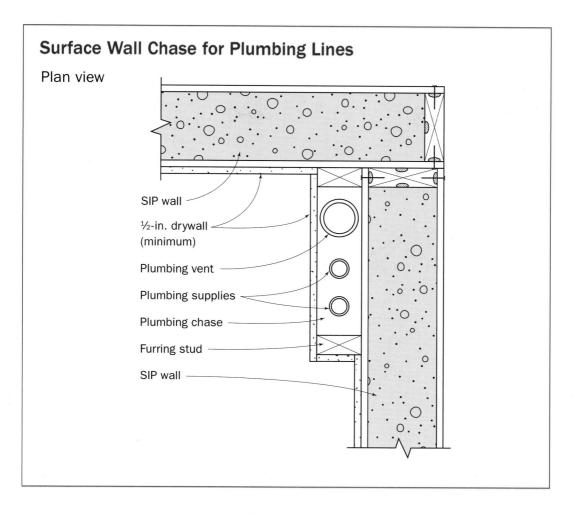

Surface Wall Chase for Plumbing Lines

Plan view

SIP wall

½-in. drywall
(minimum)

Plumbing vent

Plumbing supplies

Plumbing chase

Furring stud

SIP wall

Routing supplies and vents

In colder areas of the country, it is usually sound building advice to keep supply plumbing out of exterior walls as much as possible because of the danger of freezing pipes. This isn't so critical in a SIP building, however, because pipes run in the center of a 5½-in. core SIP wall will still have 3 in. or more of insulation between the pipes and the exterior. Still, it can save some time and headaches if plumbing can be kept away from exterior SIP walls, although in some cases it will be impossible to avoid this situation.

The simplest and most effective way to rout plumbing supplies and vents is to build a chase, the same approach used in masonry construction. But when this isn't feasible, plumbing units that are located against outside walls can have drains and vents installed in various ways. Sometimes this can be accomplished by using a loop vent (see "Wiring and Plumbing Kitchens" on p. 152). In other situations, a combination waste and vent—known as a wet-vented system—is the best solution. In any situation, you or your plumber should be sure that the specific rules applying to venting are followed.

The venting system as a whole can present some problems in SIP construction because a vent system is continuous from the lowest fixture to the roof and it can involve a number of penetrations through the roof. Because I dislike the look of a roof cluttered with random vent pipes, roof ventilators, and various antennae, I like to go over the drain-waste-vent (DWV) plan with my plumber to see if we can reduce the number of roof penetrations. However, the main

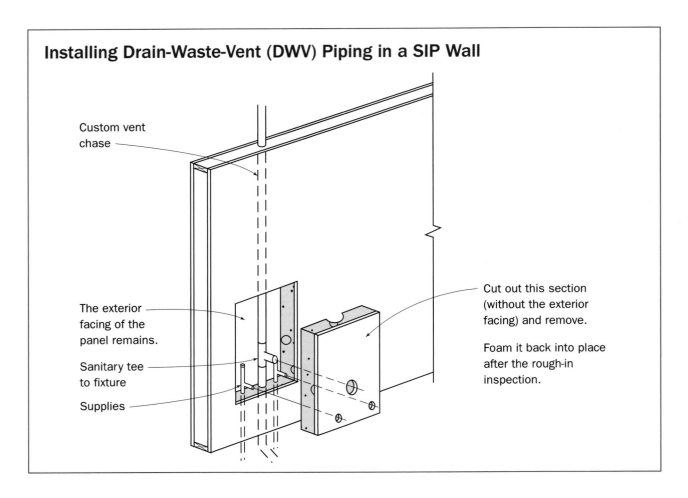

Installing Drain-Waste-Vent (DWV) Piping in a SIP Wall

Custom vent chase

The exterior facing of the panel remains.

Sanitary tee to fixture

Supplies

Cut out this section (without the exterior facing) and remove.

Foam it back into place after the rough-in inspection.

reason to cut down the number of vents is to minimize the potential for air leaks through an excessive number of roof penetrations. These vent penetrations should always be foamed after the pipe is installed.

If I have to create a chase in a SIP, I try to design the chase to be close to the edge of the panel because in the process of slitting the core to reach the vent hole, the panel's integrity is compromised (see "Cutting custom plumbing chases" on p. 89 for a description of the fabrication process). When a panel does have a chase cut into it, it's important to follow up with a solid 2x spline to block the edge and return the strength to the panel. The location for this type of panel modification is important because the strength of the entire system depends on all of the individual sections performing up to specification.

Wiring and Plumbing Kitchens

Kitchens present unique challenges in SIP buildings and require some special detailing to assist electrical and plumbing distribution.

Kitchen wiring

One of the easiest ways to run wiring in a kitchen is in furred-out walls where cabinets are to be installed. This approach has the added benefit of providing a more secure attachment for the cabinets. I've never liked the idea of attaching cabinets to the interior OSB of a SIP panel, although I know plenty of people who do this. So whenever possible, I furr out the kitchen walls where cabinets are to be placed with 2-in. by 2-in. ripped strips glued and screwed to the panels

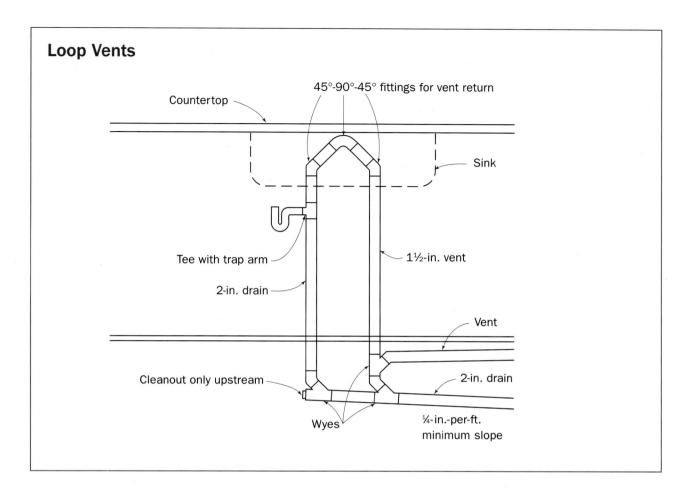

Loop Vents

Countertop

45°-90°-45° fittings for vent return

Sink

1½-in. vent

Tee with trap arm

2-in. drain

Vent

Cleanout only upstream

2-in. drain

Wyes

¼-in.-per-ft. minimum slope

16 in. o.c. before the drywall is attached and before the electrician roughs in the area.

This approach makes it much easier, faster, and less expensive to rough in for receptacles, switch legs, disposals, under-counter lighting, appliance garages, TV cable, phone lines, intercoms, and all the rest of the wiring and devices that go into a modern kitchen. This system works fine for walls that terminate with an inside corner, but if the wall to be furred is continuous to other parts of the building, a neat transition point for the furred wall will have to be detailed.

If cabinets are to be mounted directly to the interior facings of the panels through the drywall, there are still some creative ways to make sure all the wires and pipes can be installed. You could run under-counter or plug-mold wires through ¾-in. routed chases from a counter-height outlet/switch box. These slots in the panel facings won't

be a problem as long as they're not within 2 in. of the edge of a panel. You could also cut a series of 3-in.-dia. holes and use a "fishing-rod" drill bit (see the sidebar on p. 148) to pull wire to the required locations. Of course, this takes more time than working with a furred wall.

Kitchen plumbing

Kitchen plumbing can also present some challenges. Typically the kitchen sink is located in front of a window. An easy solution is to substitute the sill panel section behind the sink base cabinet with a stick-framed area under the window. Water supplies, drains, and electric circuits for a disposal and dishwasher can then be easily installed in this conventionally framed section. After inspection, this area should be carefully insulated with rigid foam cut as close to the utilities as possible and with expanding foam to fill any gaps.

With a little more effort, this work can take place within a SIP panel. You can hot-wire a chase for the vent (see p. 89) and drill the waste line over and tie it into the drain/vent stack without cutting through the perimeter of the panel. In this case, you can cut out a section of the interior skin of the wall panel for the supplies and drain lines, taking care not to cut through the exterior facing of the SIP (see the illustration on p. 152). Use a circular saw to cut through the skin and most of the foam, then use a handsaw to cut next to the outside facing wall before removing the section. This is a time-consuming process, however.

Loop vents are a simple way to avoid venting through a SIP wall (see the illustration on p. 153). They are commonly found in island sink layouts where there is no wall to run a vent through, but they can also be used against an outside wall to avoid the complication of installing vent piping in the SIPs. By code, loop vents must loop at the point closest to the countertop height or 6 in. above the flood line of the fixture and be made up of one 180-degree fitting (or a specified combination of fittings).

HVAC Systems

The standard approach to making a house comfortable is to force several hundred thousand British thermal units (BTUs) through the house to heat it during the cold months and to have tons of cooling capacity for the warmer months. But the almost airtight envelope created by the SIP system offers a unique opportunity to rethink this wasteful approach.

For example, a typical well-built SIP house, with 5½-in. EPS core walls, a 7¼-in. EPS core roof, a passive solar design, an ICF basement, and argon-filled low-E glazed windows, would allow as few as 1.0 air changes per hour (ACH) compared with the average of 20 to 30 ACH for stick-built houses. A measure of air leakage through the exterior envelope of a building, ACH is the best indicator of a building's airtightness and energy efficiency as it gains or loses heat to the outside environment. The fact that SIP buildings are typically many times as tight as conventional stick-built houses adds up to significantly lower heating and cooling requirements, lower initial installation costs, and much lower operating costs over the lifetime of the building.

In the Midwest, where my company builds, the temperature can fluctuate 60 degrees or more in a

A tightly built house, such as this SIP demonstration house constructed by the Center for Housing Innovation at the University of Oregon, lets very little heat escape. Warm colors (reds and oranges) show heat escaping from the envelope. Blues and greens show the cool exterior surface of a SIPs house because the heat remains inside. (Photo courtesy University of Oregon.)

single day. Because of this potential temperature swing, systems such as radiant heating are thought to be marginally effective because their slow, even heat delivery cannot keep up with drastic meteorological changes. But a well-insulated, airtight building can retain a given temperature for an extended period of time, regardless of outside air temperature, thus placing a smaller demand on the heating or cooling system. As the required size of these systems decreases, the options for the type and configuration of the system increase. While a comprehensive treatment of existing and future heating and cooling systems is impossible here, I hope to spark some critical thinking about how current approaches are applied and outline some innovative solutions.

What are the HVAC options?

Heating and cooling systems in buildings can get their energy from many sources. The most common fuels are natural gas, propane, other condensed gases, petroleum-based fuels, as well as electrical resistance heat units. To a lesser extent, air-source or ground-source electric heat pumps are used. In addition, there are the so-called "alternative systems" such as the various types of pellet fuel technologies, geothermal sources, solar-powered systems, fuel cells, and many more. Heating and cooling strategies can be divided into general categories of active and passive and subdivided into ducted systems and radiant approaches.

Ducted systems An HVAC system that relies on ducting for the supply and return of forced air is the norm in most parts of this country. This system consists of some type of furnace to produce hot air, a compressor or chiller to produce cool air, and an air handler to distribute the conditioned air. A major advantage of ducted systems is that they offer rapid disbursement of air throughout a building, in addition to being familiar to installers. The return side of the system can also be easily tied into heat-recovery ventilators (HRVs) to maintain fresh air quality.

Disadvantages of ducted systems are the noise of the turbulent air moving through the system and the drafts that they create.

In a SIP building, the actual installation of supplies and returns varies little from a standard layout, keeping in mind that supplies and registers should not be placed in exterior walls. Floor or ceiling outlets will work well without disturbing the integrity of the SIP exterior envelope. Your HVAC contractor will be able to determine the best locations for convection airflow and proper distribution. Often, for example, a supply register is placed under a window to take advantage of the convection caused by the temperature differential at the window. Instead of a wall register under the window, I place the supply grille in the floor under the window. Because floor registers are a little more visible than wall registers, I upgrade my grilles, and, if the floor is hardwood, I use wood grilles so they will blend.

One of the advantages of SIP buildings is the ability to create vaulted spaces easily. Vaulted spaces add to the feeling of volume in a room, and the dramatic spaces created can be a big selling point for new homes. The tight qualities of a SIP house will mean that warm air will tend to be trapped at the high side of the vaults, so I like to mount the cold-air returns with a dampered grille high up on a wall of a vaulted room. A more flexible approach is to have one grille high and one low in the same chase and have them both dampered. This way, hot air can be returned to the cooling unit from the top grille and recirculated in the summer, while in the winter the hot air can be left to condition the room and the cooler, lower air can be returned to the HVAC system to be warmed from the lower grille.

Sizing the HVAC system is the key to its success. All manufacturers make software programs available to their dealers to help installers size the system, but if your HVAC contractor uses this service, make sure the software takes into account the ACH factor of SIP construction and the higher R-values of the walls and roof. Most residential HVAC contractors use a

Radiant floor heat is an excellent choice for a SIP home because the even, gentle heat is kept constant by the SIP envelope. (Photo courtesy Ed Stahl.)

basic rule-of-thumb formula calculated per square foot of living space and cubic feet per minute per square foot of airflow. In the Midwest, cooling capacity drives most system designs, so contractors often throw an extra ½ ton to 1 ton of cooling capacity in a house to make sure that the system can meet the anticipated comfort requirements of the occupants. But besides costing more for the equipment and the ducting, it takes more energy to run these oversized systems. In addition, the added fan horsepower increases the static pressure within the system, causing significant energy loss through the leaks within the ducts and unnatural air movement in the house. Smooth wall ducting and tight joints will lessen system inefficiencies caused by turbulence and make a significant difference in the system's performance.

Radiant systems Radiant systems differ from ducted systems in that they rely on pumped liquids rather than forced air to transfer heat. One type of radiant heating system circulates hot water through a network of distribution pipes and fin-tube-style baseboard radiators to warm the living space. In another variation, hot water runs through loops of tubing placed directly beneath the finish floor or embedded in a concrete slab.

This type of heating system is quieter than forced-air systems, has generally lower maintenance costs, and is considered to be more comfortable because the air is not dried out and the temperatures are more constant. One drawback is that radiant systems take a comparably longer time to change interior temperatures, while a bigger drawback for many clients is the lack of compatible cooling equipment. In the Midwest, when potential radiant customers hear that they will have to have a ducted A/C system to meet their cooling needs, the costs of the dual systems generally leave the radiant heat on the cutting-room floor.

Indoor air quality

Unlike some engineered wood products, SIPs are relatively benign as far as off-gassing of harmful chemicals. However, because of the airtight nature of a SIP building, you'll have to deal with interior pollutants from such items as carpets, furniture, and paints as well as appliance fumes, radon, and

Heat-Recovery Ventilators

More and more SIP builders are installing heat-recovery ventilators (HRVs) as a standard piece of equipment. The simplest HRVs are air-to-air heat exchangers designed to extract energy from the exhaust airstream and add it to the fresh intake airstream. Basically, incoming fresh air and exhausting stale air pass by each other via a series of thin metal tubes or plates. As the temperatures of the two airflows try to equalize, heat from one is transferred to the other.

HRVs provide balanced ventilation with maximum energy recovery during both heating and cooling seasons. Currently, most building codes only require bathroom fans, but in some locations (Minnesota, for example) a balanced air-exchange system is required in a new home.

On the downside, HRVs are expensive, around $2,000 to integrate into the HVAC system. They also need to be regularly maintained by changing the filters. To me, however, they are an indispensable component of a healthy house. Not only do they greatly increase the energy efficiency of the heating and cooling cycles by preconditioning the fresh air, but they also help control humidity levels, thwarting the growth of many kinds of bacteria, fungi, and other molds.

excess humidity. Most of these air pollutants can be controlled by mechanical ventilation. The goal is to exhaust the stale indoor air and replace it with fresh outside air while controlling the humidity. This can be accomplished by using simple solutions such as ventilating windows and exhaust-only systems to sophisticated air cleaners and air-to-air heat exchangers. Humidity stabilization and air temperature stabilization are best controlled by a heat recovery ventilator (see the sidebar above).

Besides being important to the health of the homeowner, indoor air quality (IAQ) has a practical importance for builders, many of whom are being asked to provide warranties on their new homes that are in effect for as long as five to ten years. The occupants and the occupations that go on in a house produce a tremendous amount of moisture, which will find areas to migrate to and begin to destroy the house. In fact, it isn't at all uncommon to find five-year-old houses with expensive moisture-related problems. The money and effort spent installing a well-designed, efficient whole-house ventilation system in an airtight SIP house is well worth it, not only in terms of IAQ but also as a hedge against expensive repairs and possible litigation down the road.

Green building strategies are still a hard sell in this economy, in part because the life expectancy of the buildings being constructed today is so short. This isn't to say that the buildings will fail (although most houses aren't built for the long term) but rather that most owners usually don't expect to occupy houses for very long. These owners, I've found, are reluctant to pay for long-term items that they don't feel they will benefit from. But a niche group of home buyers (what I call "last home" buyers) are open to green building ideas. These home buyers are done with the corporate shuffle, and their kids are grown and gone. They want a low-maintenance, sensible home, perhaps one with some accessible features. This is a very aware set of consumers, and chances are good that they already know about SIPs.

Chapter 9

FINISH MATERIALS FOR SIPs

EXTERIOR FINISHES

INTERIOR FINISHES

From the outside, a SIP building looks just like its stick-built counterparts. But if homes had large LED displays on their roofs showing their energy consumption, it would be easy to find a SIP house: It would be the one with half the consumption of its neighbors. If it were in a row of houses when a hurricane hit, it would probably be the only one left standing. It would be the last one on the block to have the snow melt off the roof (because the heat stays in the house), and it would be the one without all the ugly roof vents. But for the most part, a SIP house looks like most of the other houses around because the same materials that clad the exteriors of "standard" houses will work on a SIP house.

Although a SIP house may look the same as a conventional house, as an engineered system it offers much higher performance both structurally and from an insulation standpoint. Because the strength is formed by the integration of the facings and the core, special attention has to be given to keeping moisture away from the panels. A failure with waterproofing and flashing details can have serious consequences and cause potential structural damage. In this chapter, I'll look at approaches to exterior and interior finishes, paying particular attention to how they can be weatherproofed and how they can meet various fire codes.

A small, energy-efficient SIP home looks no different from the outside than its stick-built neighbors. (Photo by Jon Blumb.)

Exterior Finishes

After a SIP building shell has been erected, what type of exterior finishes are appropriate? Chances are good that extra thought and money has already been spent on solar orientation and siting, clad low-E windows, and an energy-efficient heating/cooling system; after all, this is a house that is built to last. Now you will want to protect it with the best-quality (but also reasonably priced) roofing, siding, and trim materials. While this book can't be a comprehensive guide to roofing and siding materials and practices, I can look at the differences between a SIP house and "standard practices" and examine the pros and cons of some of these choices, as well as look ahead at what we can expect from the SIP industry in the future.

Roofing choices

When clients ask me what type of roof they should put on their SIP house, I explain to them how I look at roofing choices. When the initial installed cost of a roofing material is divided by the expected life of the roof, different types of roof systems with seemingly huge differences in price actually end up costing about the same per year over the lifetime of the roof. So, really, the question is one of commitment: Is this the family homestead built for generations, or is it a high-quality spec house that needs to be competitive in the marketplace?

I'm not advocating a copper roof on every house, but the roof should be in keeping with the style and presentation of the property. Builders have to make decisions based on marketplace realities, and sometimes a builder will choose to have a big, half-round window above the

Hot Roofs, Cold Roofs

Is a hot roof or a cold roof more appropriate for a SIP building? A cold roof is formed by creating an air space between the finish materials and the sheathing, usually by installing furring strips and a second layer of sheathing. This air space allows heat that builds up as the roofing absorbs solar radiation to dissipate from the underside. While there are some ongoing studies trying to determine if a cold roof can extend the service life of composition shingles, I don't know of any completed studies that confirm the increased life span of roofing materials under these conditions.

This air space can also prevent heat buildup on the interior of the building. In fact, some SIP manufacturers offer panels with ventilated slots under the exterior facings that make them perform like a cold roof. These panels are not structurally rated SIPs, but they can be used over a structural framework. A builder working in one of this country's hot climates who wants to roof with a dark-colored asphalt composition shingle might consider a cold roof. However, this cold SIP-roof configuration will be a hard sell when the expense of the furring and second layer of sheathing is added to a roof that already is more expensive than a stick-framed roof.

A typical SIP building uses the exterior roof facing as the sheathing, with roofing materials installed on top of felt paper or membrane placed over the sheathing. Theoretically, this is a hot roof, but with SIPs this configuration is more of a neutral roof. The high R-values of the 7¼-in., 9¼-in., and 11¼-in. core SIPs will prevent heat radiation from penetrating to the interior. Realistically, a builder could upgrade to a concrete tile or metal roof for the same amount of money spent trying to ventilate a SIP roof. There are also some drawbacks to a cold roof if a metal roof is the finish surface. For example, temperature changes can cause condensation to occur under the metal, so extra care has to be taken with roof flashing details so as not to trap moisture inside the envelope.

---

grand front door rather than to pay for an upgraded roof.

In terms of installation, roofing a SIP building is no different from roofing a stick-framed building. The OSB exterior facing of the SIP is the same as the sheathing you will find on almost every roof in this country.

Asphalt composition shingles Asphalt composition shingles are the number-one roofing material used in residential construction in the United States, but some questions have been raised concerning the compatibility of SIPs and these shingles. Since EPS foam begins to soften at around 165°F and melts at about 200°F, it isn't recommended to subject EPS to prolonged exposures of 150°F to 175°F. In a hot climate on a hot day, a roof with dark shingles can reach a surface temperature of close to 150°F.

Does this push the material limits of EPS and make composition shingles incompatible with SIPs? In 1996, the Asphalt Roofing Manufacturers Association (ARMA) cautioned against using asphalt shingles over any unvented roof (see the sidebar above), reasoning that heat dissipation from below might be reduced in the case of an exterior fire. Another concern is that prolonged exposure to these high temperatures would also shorten the life span of the shingles, although no ongoing study about shingle durability has been completed to back up this claim.

It has been pointed out that if exposure to heat were a real problem, it would have shown up long ago because EPS has long been an insulating

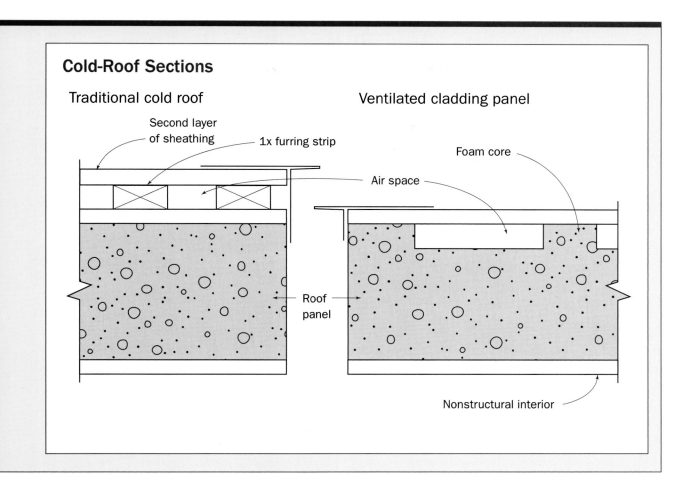

Cold-Roof Sections

Traditional cold roof

- Second layer of sheathing
- 1x furring strip
- Roof panel

Ventilated cladding panel

- Foam core
- Air space
- Roof panel
- Nonstructural interior

material on commercial flat roofs, and there have been no published reports of failures caused by EPS in these applications. It has been suggested that the safety factor applied to the design parameters for EPS are very conservative and that these hot conditions really don't push the material's limits.

Another reason ARMA is reluctant to warrant composition shingles over SIPs is the fact that the exterior facing on the vast majority of SIPs is 7/16-in. OSB, while some of the shingle manufacturers insist on a minimum of 1/2-in. sheathing under their shingles. But this requirement is based on dated information. Not long ago, the standard for roof and wall sheathing was 1/2-in. CDX plywood. Manufacturers didn't want their shingles applied over thinner 3/8-in. plywood

because of the possibility that the sheathing would flex and cause the shingles to loosen and blow off the roof.

The reality is that 7/16-in. OSB has been thoroughly tested to perform as a shingle underlayment and has been rated as an equal to plywood for this job. It has, in fact, become the standard for roof sheathing in almost all applications. What this actually means is that a large percentage of the asphalt shingles installed in this country are not technically under warranty. Of course, shingle companies want to continue to sell their shingles, so you aren't likely to see warranties removed from all the builders who use OSB roof sheathing, whether the OSB is part of a SIP or is nailed directly to roof rafters.

Currently, there are several companies that specifically warrant their products for use over SIPs, including Malarcky Co., Elk Mfg. Co., and Certainteed shingles. SIPA has recommended that its members specify shingles from these cooperative companies while the rest of the industry catches up. As the SIP industry gains strength and momentum, the other players will come around, and the issue of sheathing thickness will cease to be a problem.

Other roofing materials I haven't come across any data that suggest there might be problems associated with SIPs when metal roofs or clay or concrete tiles are installed. Of course, the added weight of tile or slate roofing material needs to be added into the dead-load calculations when figuring SIP spans. Due to the problem of long-term creep (see the sidebar on p. 31), it is important to calculate roof-panel spans carefully. In the case where the spans are approaching the design limits of the roof panels, it would be a good idea to shorten the span or increase the thickness of the panel.

Wood shingle and shake manufacturers have no reservations about their products being applied over SIPs. These roofing materials are considered a premium roof covering and will find many applications in the upgraded SIP building packages.

Flashing a SIP roof

The proper flashing of eaves, rakes, chimneys, valleys, skylights, and vent penetrations is of vital importance to the moisture integrity of a roof, regardless of the type of finish roofing. For the most part, flashing a SIP roof is no different from flashing a standard roof: You just have to detail the flashing so that water flows off the panel.

One detail that's often mishandled is the corner where the eave flashing intersects the rake flashing. For this application, I like to use T-shaped metal drip edge (known as "A-style" in my neck of the woods) because it gives some

Flashing a SIP Roof

1. Install the eave flashing over the eave panel and fascia.

overhang and extra protection to the roof. First, I nail the drip edge directly to the top of the eave panel or overhang sheathing and over the finish fascia, placing the fastener as high up on the drip edge as possible. Then I install 15-lb. felt paper to the edge of the eave, extending over the rake edge by 1 in. so that it will protect the edge of the SIP. (As an option to felt paper, many builders today use a self-sticking, waterproof bitumen membrane as an ice dam at the eave or as the underlayment over the whole roof; this is the material shown in the photos on these two pages.)

2. Apply self-sticking bitumen membrane (shown here) or 15-lb. felt paper over the eave flashing and down onto the rake fascia.

3. Cut and bend the rake flashing before installing it over the rake fascia. Finish by wrapping the cut edge of the rake flashing over the end of the eave flashing.

Next, I prepare the rake flashing by cutting and bending the vertical fin at 90 degrees so it will wrap around the corner by about 1 in. When installed, the overhang of the rake flashing goes over the building paper and tucks over the overhang of the eave flashing.

Exterior siding options

The variety of available siding choices is vast and will be dictated as much by the style of the building as the customer's budget. Sidings all start with a SIP shell, and the preparation for them is basically the same.

Preparation For the SIP industry to thrive and grow while gaining and keeping the confidence of the public, a standardized set of industry-wide water-shedding details needs to be developed. SIPA has taken steps in that direction, initiating in 1999 a committee of architects, fabricators,

To waterproof the head of a door opening, fold and install a strip of felt paper in the sequence shown.

builders, and erectors to develop a standardized set of installation procedures that would include water-shedding details. While all of the manufacturers I've spoken with are happy to provide cut sheets or full-installation manuals for the erection of their particular panel systems, none of them specifically mention the importance of keeping moisture away from the exterior facing of a SIP. This may seem like an obvious necessity that any builder worth his salt knows, but it isn't necessarily the case.

The standard practice is to wrap the sheathed frame of a house with a house-wrap material before installing the siding. But I don't use house wraps on my SIP buildings because these products are essentially air barriers that are designed to allow moisture to migrate from the interior of a building to the exterior. A SIP building doesn't need an air barrier. The shell has far fewer joints, all of which have been glued, foamed, and nailed or screwed together. It is already tightly sealed against air infiltration and exfiltration. Besides, house wraps let moisture in as well as out, and what we don't want is moisture trapped underneath the siding and next to the exterior facing of the SIPs. No moisture will migrate from the interior through the panels themselves, so why go to all the trouble of wrapping a house with a product that will allow outside moisture in?

Instead of house wrap, I use 15-lb. black asphalt-impregnated felt paper in standard 36-in.-wide rolls. Felt paper is economical, manageable, readily available, and, most important, waterproof. The first thing I tell a new crew member when installing felt paper is to think like a drop of water: The material above always laps over the material below. I start about ½ in. below the mudsill so that when the first course of siding is installed 1 in. below the mudsill, the paper won't show. The paper needs to be pulled taut so that there aren't any wrinkles or folds, and I take care to keep the courses parallel to each other. Although ⅜-in. staples hold well, I also like to add some plastic-cap roofing nails around the corners for extra wind resistance.

Flashing door and window openings When I come to a door opening, I run the bottom course of paper right over it. Then I slit the felt paper at 45 degrees from the bottom corners and fold the bottom over the subfloor and staple it in place. Next, I install a sheet-metal or vinyl prefabricated sill pan to keep moisture away from the subfloor and framing. The pan is set on a liberal bead of elastomeric caulk and nailed through tabs into the side jambs. Finally, I fold the felt paper over the tabs on the jamb sill, wrap it around the side jambs, and staple it off.

At the top of the door opening, it's important to overlap the paper to keep water out. First, cut out a couple of 5-in. by 12-in. strips of felt paper

Flashing a Window

1. After cutting out the rough opening in the felt paper, run a bead of caulk all around the opening.

2. Install the window, then apply strips of self-adhesive flexible flashing over the nailing. Install the bottom strip first and then the sides.

to use as flashing corners. Fold the strips in half and staple one end to the underside of the header. Wrap the felt paper down over these strips, then fold and staple the paper over the side jambs, tucking it under the bottom half of the corner strips. Now staple the strips to the side jambs. Finally, apply a dollop of caulk to seal the small gap at the outside corner, and the opening is ready for installing the door.

Watertight windows can be accomplished by using consistent installation practices and some new flashing products available in the marketplace. Some builders staple a series of reinforced-mesh flashing strips around a window opening, but I prefer to staple 15-lb. felt over the walls first to protect the SIPs and then install the windows. To do this, cut the felt paper flush with the rough opening or let it wrap around the

3. Install the top strip of flexible flashing last.

4. After installing the wood trim, nail a strip of metal flashing over the head trim.

opening a little. Next, shoot a thick bead of caulk within 1 in. of the edge and set the window in place. Once the window is squared, leveled, and nailed in place, I install a self-adhesive flexible flashing called Moistop E-Z Seal made by Fortifiber Corporation (see Resources on p. 182) to the bottom first, then the sides and finally the top. This tough, reinforced fiberglass membrane has 3 in. of self-adhesive and sticks over the nailing flange of the window, keeping all moisture out.

When I install wood trim around a window, I use a metal head flashing, bending the ends of the head flashing down over the end grain of the head trim. I cut a slit in the building paper at the

5. Finish by applying a strip of flashing membrane over the head flashing.

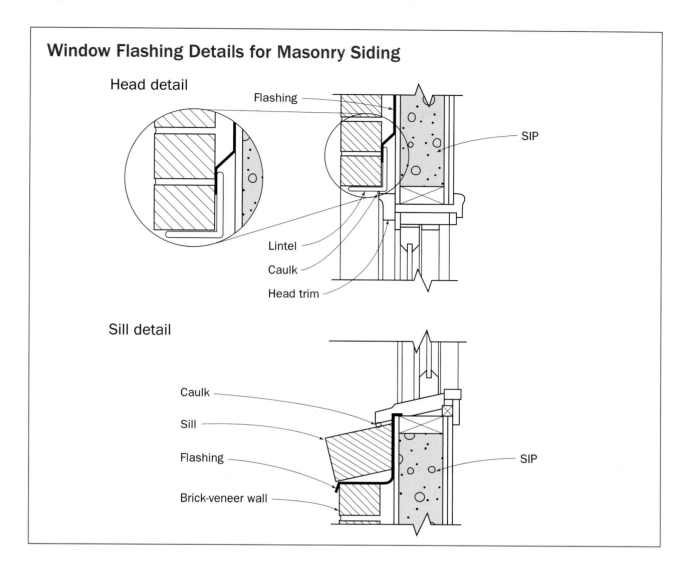

Window Flashing Details for Masonry Siding

Head detail

Flashing

SIP

Lintel

Caulk

Head trim

Sill detail

Caulk

Sill

Flashing

Brick-veneer wall

SIP

head of the window and slip the vertical leg of the head flashing before nailing it. For a final waterproofing detail, I apply a strip of Fortiflash Waterproof Flashing Membrane (also made by Fortifiber) over the metal flashing. These products take the guesswork out of window and door flashing and are inexpensive insurance against any callbacks.

Other penetrations need to be as carefully detailed as window and door openings. Outside combustion air ducts, dryer vents, air-to-air heat exchanger inlets and outlets, condensate drains, and furnace vents all need to have more than just

a bead of caulk around the pipe. A metal hood can be fabricated for uncommon duct sizes, while special inlet and outlet caps are available from companies that specialize in custom sheet metal. Before the caps or hoods are installed, it is important to put a bead of elastomeric caulk around the pipe or duct after making sure that it is properly flashed, and the inside of the penetrations should be shot with an expanding foam.

Masonry exteriors Stone and brick are excellent siding choices for a SIP building. The inert nature

Stucco siding, shown here on the first floor of a remodeled house, is highly compatible with the SIP building system. Two coats of cement stucco are applied, followed by a top coat of a synthetic elastomeric stucco to ensure a long-lasting finish.

of the SIP panels prevents the building from suffering any shrinkage that could distort walls and cause joint cracks in the masonry. Besides requiring very little maintenance, masonry protects the SIPs from impact damage. For brick and stone, a concrete ledge needs to be included in the foundation design.

The attachment of the masonry to the SIP wall is no different than to a standard framed wall, although I recommend that the corrugated masonry ties be screwed to the panel instead of nailed for added pullout resistance. The critical flashing area in a masonry siding detail is at the window sills. It takes a careful sequence of material installation to ensure watertightness here (see the illustration on p. 167). It is far too

common to rely on a little mortar or a bead of caulk to seal these gaps.

Stucco finishes Stucco finishes are highly compatible with the SIP system. The inert panels give a very stable substrate on which the stucco can be applied. Traditional three-coat stucco starts with a base, or scratch, coat that is applied over metal lath. It is raked while fresh to provide adhesion for the second, or brown, coat that levels the first coat and prepares it for final finish. A cement-based finish coat about ⅛ in. thick is then applied. The finish either has color in it or it can be painted afterward. The total thickness of this finish ranges from ¾ in. to 1 in., partly to compensate for the irregularity of the substrate and the need to level the brown coat before finishing.

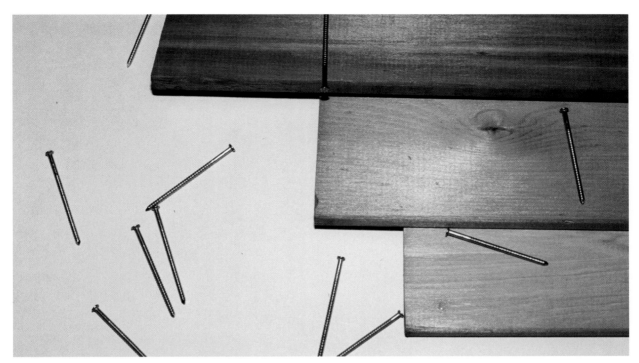

Kiln-dried redwood siding can be a long-lasting siding on SIP buildings if attached with stainless-steel "slim jim" siding nails.

In the Midwest, plasterers apply stucco over expanded metal lath, while on the West Coast, they apply it over a self-furring type of stucco wire. Either system involves spacing the metal lath away from the building paper in order to fully embed the metal lath with the scratch coat material to avoid corrosion. At the same time the metal is installed, corner bead, control joints, and drip screeds are applied to limit the size of the stucco panels to help control expansion and contraction and to act as grounds for leveling the stucco. These panels usually are limited to approximately 100 sq. ft., although their shapes can be altered to fit architectural considerations.

Because of the flat, straight walls typical of SIP houses, my plasterers start with a ½-in.-thick scratch coat. Sometimes if the weather is cool and moist enough they can double back with the leveling coat at the same time, attaining a total thickness for the two coats of about ½ in. to ⅝ in. After the scratch/brown coats have cured well (about a week should be sufficient), they then apply an elastomeric acrylic top coat with integral color, basically the finish coat of an exterior insulation and finish (EIFS) system. This type of finish makes available a wider range of colors than cement stucco, and the elastomeric qualities of the coating help the material bridge the hairline cracks that will inevitably occur as stucco cures. This synthetic stucco finish system gives my clients the best possible application of this type of finish.

Lap siding SIP manufacturers will tell you that any exterior finish is compatible with their panels. While this is essentially true, when I look at best choices I put lap sidings lower on the scale. As a carpenter, I know the solid feeling that comes when the final hammer blow sets the siding nail head flush with the surface of the siding because the nail is going into a stud wall. I don't get that feeling with SIPs because I'm nailing into OSB only.

Cementboard lap siding needs to be double nailed to meet the manufacturer's 50-year warranty.

If you insist on using lap siding, there are some details that will help make for a good installation. First, using quality, kiln-dried siding is essential to resist the warping or twisting that can cause some distortion and fastener pullout. In addition, some siding makers recommend that the nailing pattern be shortened to 8 in. o.c. for installation over SIPs. This is a good idea, and I also recommend that "slim jim" siding nails be used. These are 2-in.-long stainless-steel ring shank nails with a small head (see the photo on p. 169). Longer nails are unnecessary because once the point of the siding nail is driven through the exterior facing of the SIP, the connection becomes weaker every millimeter it penetrates. Another piece of insurance when attaching wood siding is to use a cap corner detail to provide a solid nail base at the corners. Make sure the cap blocking is wider than the corner boards (if they are going to be used).

Cementboard lap siding, an alternative to wood lap siding, is catching on fast in the marketplace. These cement and wood fiber products are stable, are available preprimed, and some come with a 50-year warranty (which really got my attention). I have attached this siding onto stud walls with good success using collated galvanized siding nails, but I don't feel comfortable using this approach with SIPs.

James Hardie Co., which makes a cement fiber product sold as Hardie Plank, specifies a double-nailing fastening schedule at 8 in. o.c. for use with SIPs. This means the installer nails through the lower edge of the top siding piece into the upper edge of the siding below. According to a representative at Hardie, this double nailing is necessary because of the weight of the plank material and to ensure a good connection. This is a rather unsightly detail compared with the blind nailing that is typical for this type of siding installation, but you need to follow the company's specs to get its 50-year warranty.

Other siding materials One of the most compatible siding materials to use with SIPs is cedar sidewall shingles. Besides being beautiful and durable, they can be fastened to the SIP facing without any special detailing. I prefer to use a ½-in. crown pneumatic stapler to install the shingles and use 1½-in.-long staples. As an underlayment, 15-lb. felt paper should be used.

Vinyl siding is an economical and compatible material to use with SIPs. It won't warp or twist, so it can be installed with typical short nails or with screws for added pullout resistance. I haven't had much experience installing vinyl siding, but one concern I do have is the long-term effects of ultraviolet (UV) light on the material.

There are some siding materials that should be avoided. I won't use innerseal-type lap siding materials or products such as Masonite or hardboard. The same goes for T-111 textured siding. The siding decision should be based on durability of materials, and these choices simply don't offer a long enough service life to be considered for a high-quality, well-built house.

Interior Finishes

When you first walk into a SIP building after the shell has been erected, the first thing you notice is that there are no studs, insulation batts, pipes, or wires showing. The interior is a continuous surface of the interior OSB facing. Unfortunately, you can't just paint this surface because all model building codes require a fire-resistant surface on interior walls.

The standard finish for interior walls of SIP buildings (as for framed buildings) is gypsum wallboard or drywall. In most residential construction, ½-in. drywall meets the 15-minute fire-resistance requirements. Light commercial applications require a higher fire resistance,

typically 30 minutes to one hour. These requirements can be met with one or two layers of ⅝-in. type X or type C drywall. In addition, SIPs offer a few more options when it comes to ceiling finishes.

Wall finishes

It would be tempting in a SIP building to put a paint finish right over the interior facing because it is a continuous, solid surface. But this would be a mistake for several reasons. First, the rough surface of the OSB doesn't take paint very well. Even several coats of a heavy-bodied primer would leave a very rough surface and an aesthetically unacceptable finish. And although some people might be able to live with this rough finish, the walls would not meet code-established 15-minute fire-resistance requirements.

Standard procedure is to apply drywall to the walls. Even if wood paneling or wainscoting is scheduled, the first step should be to install drywall and to fire-tape the joints. Because there's a solid surface behind the drywall, ½-in. drywall is more than adequate to absorb impacts to the wall. When drywall is added to standard SIPs, the assembly becomes ½ in. thicker than standard door and window jambs. This is because SIPs are manufactured with the cores cut to match dimensional lumber (i.e., 3½ in. thick, 5½ in. thick, 7¼ in. thick, 9¼ in. thick, 11¼ in. thick). Custom jamb widths can certainly be ordered, but most manufacturers add an upcharge for jamb extensions. This adds an extra expense that isn't being incurred in conventionally framed houses yet produces the same end result. Fortunately, there may be a method that can solve some of these problems effectively while offering a higher level of finish than standard drywall: veneer plaster.

In the future, I hope to see some fire-resistance testing done on a SIP with a single thickness of gypsum veneer plaster applied directly to the interior OSB facing. This material would likely meet code requirements for fire resistance while

Preapplied ceiling finishes are available from several SIP manufacturers, such as this Insul-Lam cladding panel over tongue and groove from Premier. (Photo courtesy Premier Industries.)

"Blazeguard" finish, a hard, gypsum-like coating available in a smooth and textured version, meets residential fire-resistance requirements and simplifies the finishing of ceilings, especially high vaults. (Photo by Jon Blumb.)

solving some of the wall-thickness problems just mentioned. Briefly, here is how the system is applied.

The doors and windows are trimmed out without any jamb extensions and nailed right into the interior facing of the SIP. Next, corner bead is installed, and the joints are taped with mesh tape. A base, or scrim, coat is applied using an all-purpose structural plaster, such as United States Gypsum's Structolight (see Resources on p. 183). The next day the finish plaster veneer can be applied. This surface is allowed to cure and is then sealed with a coat of shellac. A more durable clear urethane finish can be applied over this to complete the wall surface. This is a method that I'd really like to try soon, but liability will persuade me to wait until it is approved by building codes.

Preapplied ceiling finishes

Many SIP manufacturers offer factory-applied interior finishes to their products. In some cases, drywall, plywood, and even some finish lumber can be laminated directly to the foam core (these, of course, would not be rated as structural panels and could only be used as cladding over a structural framework). Most of these same finishes can also be laminated over the interior OSB facing, in which case the panel can be used as a structural element.

Often a fabricator/installer will apply the finish material, such as tongue-and-groove cedar and pine, finish plywoods, and drywall, at the shop to precut roof panels. There are some problems with this approach. The mechanical problem of lifting a panel without drilling through the finished interior facing can be worked out by using side clamps or lifting plates that are screwed to the top facing only. Extra handling care can keep panels from being damaged. But the problem of installing a complete vapor barrier under roof panels is hard to solve when they have a finish applied to them.

A complete vapor barrier under the roof panels is highly recommended as inexpensive insurance against moisture-related problems. This moisture is generated inside the building and it wants out, particularly through any seam available to it in the ceiling plane. A vapor barrier helps to contain this moisture so it can be mechanically vented. The idea of preapplied ceiling finishes is an attractive one, but it's important to make sure that moisture ventilation is adequately dealt with in the design phase before considering this option.

Afterword

FROM A BUILDER'S PERSPECTIVE

When I began research for this book, I expected to find some sort of Achilles' heel with the SIP system. Frankly, in spite of my company's positive experience with panels, it really seemed too good to be true. If the SIP system is so good and has been around for more than 50 years, I wanted to know why isn't everyone using panels. But over the last year as I've crisscrossed the country and talked with manufacturers, suppliers, architects, fabricators, and builders, I've concluded that SIPs are the real deal. They are overachievers in the building materials field, and I'm convinced that SIPs will be the building material of choice for professionals in residential and light commercial applications within a relatively short period of time.

Look at the competition: Traditional stick-and-fiberglass construction has had its day and has left millions of leaky homes to suffer the consequences when much higher energy rates become a reality. Light-gauge steel construction, in spite of millions of dollars of promotion, hasn't really made a dent in the industry. Why? Because it is still a bunch of sticks, with all the stick-related problems, as well as being slow and expensive to put together. It's difficult to see how the thermal transfer problems associated with steel framing will ever be solved without covering the whole building with a foam blanket. And even then, the system still isn't as strong as a SIP system. While insulated concrete form (ICF) systems are energy efficient and super strong, they have the problem of foam being on the exterior, which is subject to insects and impacts. Aboveground, they are more expensive than SIPs, and I've yet to see an ICF roof.

ICFs can be grouped with low-E argon-filled windows, high-efficiency HVAC systems, and many other energy-efficient components that can significantly increase the performance of the building. But unless the shell of the building is the tightest, best-insulated system available, the extra money spent on all these add-on pieces isn't getting the best return. SIPs should be the key component for the shell of a good building. There simply isn't anything in the marketplace that will give the owner as big an increase in strength, energy efficiency, and overall performance as SIPs.

What is most striking is that using SIPs today doesn't cost more than the competition—without even taking into account the thousands of dollars saved on fuel bills over the life of the building. Stable costs and lower labor costs make the choice to use panels a simple one. You will get more than your money's worth from panels. To emphasize this, I want to revisit a couple of performance features that show just how well SIPs hold up.

Engineered for the Real World

The transverse and axial loading capabilities of panels were discussed in chapter 2 in terms of pounds per foot, spans, and load ratings. But what do these terms mean when you are about to design and build a building? They mean you can eliminate some of the structural framework because SIPs can support more weight and span farther than conventional materials. By eliminating some posts and purlins and spreading out the grid support, you can save money on material and labor to install these items, and the building will be put together stronger.

Let's take a SIP roof on a steel-frame commercial building, for example. You can set the main frames at 24 ft. on center and the purlins on 8-ft. centers. Using 8-ft. by 24-ft. jumbo panels staggered 12 ft., you don't need any other pieces or diagonal braces.

It is clear that the structural capabilities of SIPs have enlarged the traditional support grid. Designers and engineers haven't yet fully explored this larger module, but I think some really exciting buildings will be the result as they realize the potential that SIPs offer.

No other feature of panels has impressed me as much as their ability to resist racking forces. We need only look at some recent natural disasters to see what this means. In the 1993 earthquake in Kobe, Japan, SIP houses were left undamaged amid general destruction. Hurricanes in the southeastern United States destroyed large sections of communities, while SIP buildings came through unscathed. A tornado ripped through a Georgia suburb, wrecking conventionally framed houses but causing only superficial damage to a SIP home in the middle of the destruction. A 130-mph Michigan storm blew five mature trees down on top of a SIP home and caused no structural damage. SIP houses don't creak or groan in high winds, and drywall callbacks for cracks are almost unheard of. You cannot build a stronger, safer home.

Open to Debate

As also mentioned in chapter 2, there are a couple of debatable areas connected with SIPs: fire resistance and insect resistance.

To see how a SIP building really performs in a fire, the Winfield, Illinois, fire department recently conducted a field test. In the study, the furniture in a 12-ft. by 14-ft. by 8-ft. furnished room built with 5½-in.-core R-Control panels was set on fire, and the door and windows were then shut. The fire brought the interior temperature of the room close to 2,000°F, then it quickly dropped in intensity without affecting the structural integrity of the room. No delamination between the foam and the OSB facings was found, and apparently the fire resistance of drywall was dramatically increased by the OSB facing underneath it. The fire department's conclusion was that a tight SIP structure will quickly starve a fire for oxygen and that there is no air in the wall cavities to feed the flames.

When actually exposed to flames, both EPS and urethane foams will burn. But in a panel configuration, flames have a difficult time finding any foam to light on fire. And, as we saw in chapter 2, burning foams have a relatively low toxicity compared with many other materials typically found in a burning building, making a SIP building inherently safer even in a fire.

Termite and carpenter ant intrusion in SIP buildings can become a serious problem for individual building owners and the industry as a whole. EPS, XPS, and urethane foams are all equally susceptible to invasion by these determined pests. While these foams are nonnutritive, the insects are attracted to them because they offer easy entry and a place to nest. Because there are reports of intrusion from all areas of the country, manufacturers need to inform their customers more clearly of the danger and work out details to prevent entry.

The insect problem has so alarmed some code officials that in 1996 the Southern Building Code Congress International (SBCCI) outlawed the use of foam in ground contact except under certain conditions.

Besides carefully detailing a barrier system to prevent insect entry, there are some products that can make a difference in the war against bugs. Extensive testing has proven that AFM Corporation's patented borate-treated EPS foam, called Perform Guard, is effective in killing pests that try to bore into it. A fine, stainless-steel mesh has recently come on the market that is shown to be 100% effective for preventing ant and termite infestation. The mesh is designed to be imbedded in the base coating for EIFS systems.

The Bottom Line Is Green

From the postwar housing boom of the 1950s to the stock-market-fueled boom of the 1990s, speed and cost have been the driving forces in the building industry. Forests have been cleared across the landscape to make lumber for housing developments, while builders and home buyers have been hoodwinked into thinking that spun fiberglass (which allows air and moisture to pass easily through it) is a good insulator. But with energy—in the form of oil, gas, and electricity—dirt cheap, who cares? Our entire economy is dependent on inexpensive energy, and it isn't likely that any time soon one of our politicians will say, "We need to increase the price of gasoline about 100% to cover the cost of its production and to clean up the pollution caused by its manufacture."

The fact is, though, we are digging a deep hole for ourselves from an energy standpoint. Energy-efficient, green building technologies are at the leading edge of a growing movement to take care of the planet and encourage a sustainable economy. According to David M. Nemtzow, president of the Alliance to Save Energy, the energy used to operate the average home produces an estimated 22,000 lb. of carbon dioxide annually. Many lawmakers with some foresight and vision see this area as one of national economic security. In 2000, the International Residential Code (IRC) has started to replace the existing building codes. The IRC contains prescriptive energy-efficiency requirements for single-family detached homes and townhomes.

With a situation anywhere close to the energy crisis of the 1970s, legislation for the housing industry will quickly be put in place that is similar to what happened to the auto industry. The message will be, "Change the way you build houses and make them much more energy efficient." Stick-and-fiberglass technology simply will not be able to keep up with required changes. Builders who embrace energy-efficient, green technologies now will be ready to lead the way to a stronger, more sustainable economy. In fact, there are already some very proactive government-sponsored programs available to energy-wise builders, product manufacturers, and consumers who are willing to spend a little more money to invest in energy-efficient technologies.

The Fuzzy Crystal Ball

If I were any good at predicting the future, I would have put a lot more money in the stock market 10 years ago. I didn't, so it looks as though I will be

Energy Star Builder Program

Builders of energy-efficient homes have long sought a means to distinguish their homes, which cost more to build, from the average product in the marketplace. Now builders have found an ally in the form of the U.S. Department of Energy (DOE) and the U.S. Environmental Protection Agency (EPA), who are working together to promote the Energy Star Homes Program. This program has been developed to help make energy-efficient homes cost competitive in the marketplace, giving incentive to home buyers to make smart decisions that will pay dividends throughout the life of the building.

To qualify for this program, a home has to be 30% more efficient than homes built to the national Model Energy Code. This measurement is based on the Home Energy Rating System (HERS) that has been developed by the DOE and the HERS Council. The 30% energy reduction is equivalent to a HERS rating of at least 86 on a scale of 100. The rating is attained by having a certified HERS rater compare your home with a reference model that is the same size and shape. The building is then tested for tightness and a rating is calculated. Although this service costs a few hundred dollars, the rater can help a builder find where the inefficiencies are and help make the next building better.

The program offers builders a way to distinguish their work in the marketplace by providing them with a brand-name label and preferred mortgage financing. Besides the fee for the HERS rating, the program costs the builder nothing to join and can be a big help with marketing and financing. A yellow sticker similar to that found on modern appliances is attached to the electric service panel to identify the house as an Energy Star Home to consumers, who can compare these numbers as they shop for homes.

This increased level of energy efficiency can be reached by the builder's choice of many different approaches and technologies (typically a combination of advanced insulation, tight construction, high-performance windows, and HVAC systems). A standard SIP house is so tight and well insulated that it will easily meet these standards, and many SIP builders are raising the bar for energy efficiency to much higher levels. A conscientious SIP builder can put up some big HERS numbers and really get the attention of informed consumers. In addition to saving tens of thousands of dollars over the life of the mortgage, Energy Star SIP homes will be positioned for higher resale with years of low utility bills.

working for a long time to come. Even so, I am going out on a limb to make a few predictions about the evolving SIP industry.

Structural insulated panels are poised to change the way we think about what energy performance should be in a building. SIPs can create a building envelope that puts the occupants in control of their environment as never before possible. Panels have reset the bar for building performance to a level that is significantly higher than the current standards. Industry-wide, the current explosive growth rates will continue as word of mouth and increased visibility make SIPs a household word.

Increased demand and production will cause a shakeup for SIP manufacturers. Some big players are poised to emerge and throw some serious weight at the marketing end of the business. Some little guys will get gobbled up, and some others will start up with some better ideas about how to build panels. Both of these trends will be good for the industry.

Service will become better, and precutting panels will lower installed costs and enable builders to give their clients a precise, premium product in a shorter amount of time than ever before. Manufacturers or third-party operators will provide panel delivery services that will include an onboard boom system that

Light commercial construction

The application of SIPs to commercial construction, where the emphasis is on the bottom line, has been barely tapped to date. But smart designers and builders are realizing that at the design end the larger design module that SIPs offer and the shear strength of these big panels mean that wood and steel framework can be more efficiently designed. Owners/operators of light commercial buildings can see the long-term cost savings of this system, since it starts paying back big dividends immediately and continues over the life of the building. As more factory-applied exterior finishes are developed that make the panels even more competitive in the marketplace and as businesses realize that they can be up and running much faster than with conventional systems, I see a real boom in this major area of construction.

Customer choices

At present, most manufacturers offer a bread-and-butter SIP typically composed of $\frac{7}{16}$-in. OSB facings with an EPS core. While this is a tough panel suitable for many applications, I'm reminded of the old saying at the Ford Motor Company when the Model T came out: "It's available in any color you want as long as it's black." This limited choice of panel configurations is due strictly to the current relatively low demand for SIPs and the costs associated with testing each panel configuration before its approval.

As the demand for panels increases, manufacturers will offer more custom-panel configurations. Panels are now accepted as a tried-and-true building material all over the country, so codes will allow more diversity in panel facings. Currently, panels mainly take the place of framing, insulation, and sheathing tasks. When you add exterior finish and interior finish to the factory panel, you have one component that comprises a truly integrated system. Let's make a visit to a SIP builder's office in the not-too-distant future and see what is available.

You'll sit down while the builder loads the CD of your completed house plans into the computer and begins a fly-through of the house so you can see a bird's-eye view of the exterior massing and rooflines. Then the scene shifts to the interior to see each different room from many angles. At the end of the visual trip, the builder brings up a panel spec sheet so you can order the type of panel you want to build with. First choice will be exterior facing: You can choose cementboard for a site-applied stucco finish or a preapplied synthetic stucco that will only require seams to be sealed on the job. Other choices include preapplied fiber-cement panels or a prefinished wood siding panel. You could also stick with the basic OSB and have a custom-applied wood siding added in the field.

Next, you'll decide on the core thickness for the walls and roof, and, depending on the climate where the building is situated, you can have a choice of foam types and densities. The final panel choice is the interior facing. Your choices may include factory-applied Blaze Guard coating for the walls and a tongue-and-groove cedar ceiling attached to the roof panels over a factory-applied heat-reflective vapor barrier. Wall panels for the bathroom might have cementboard skins for direct tile installation.

After you sign the contract and leave the office, the builder orders the precut panels with the indicated finishes and arranges for the panels to show up on the job site in three weeks on a flatbed truck with a knuckle boom to place the panels in a couple of days with his experienced field crew.

This isn't my imagination. All these possibilities are available right now and can be ready to go for builders and homeowners with just a few phone calls. Looking to the future, I will continue to provide building services for clients and I also plan to offer a service as a SIP broker to connect clients to manufacturers and builders who can provide goods and services anywhere. (See Resources on pp. 179-183 for the most complete directory available of SIP manufacturers, designers, and builders.) The most rewarding part of the research and writing of this book has been meeting the dedicated network of professionals. These "panelheads" are what the industry is all about. I am proud to count myself among them and hope you will let these experts help you with your next building project.

Resources

Architects

The following architects have experience designing SIP buildings:

Chaleff & Rogers Architects
1514 Montauk Hwy.
Water Mill, NY 11976
(516) 726-4477
Fax (516) 726-4478

Coriolis
123 W. 8th St.
Lawrence, KS 66044
(785) 841-1906

Kiss + Cathcart Architects
150 Nassau St.
New York, NY 10038
(212) 513-1711
Fax (212) 513-7267

Krogsgard Architects
2328 Villere St.
Mandeville, LA 70448
(504) 626-7204
Fax (504) 674-0517

Scanada Consultants
446 Reynolds St.
Oakville, ONT, Canada
(905) 842-3633
Fax (905) 842-3638

Scholz Design, Inc.
3131 Executive Pkwy.
Toledo, OH 43606
(419) 531-1601
Fax (419) 534-6364

Fredrick Stoenner
563-D Idaho Maryland Rd.
Grass Valley, CA 95945
(530) 274-9418
Fax (530) 477-1218

Van Der Ryn Architects
245 Gate Five Rd.
Sausalito, CA 94965
(415) 332-5806
Fax (415) 332-5808

David Wright Associates, AIA
563B Idaho Maryland Rd.
Grass Valley, CA 95945
(916) 477-5057
Fax (916) 477-1218

Builders

The following builders have experience working with SIPs:

ACSYS Inc.
1907 E. Overbluff Rd.
Spokane, WA 99203
(509) 532-8849
Fax (509) 532-8843

Amerimax Building Products, Inc.
1140 All Pro Dr.
Elkhart, IN 46514
(219) 262-2468
Fax (219) 266-0009

Angel Design & Development
31 Albert St.
Rugby, Warwickshire, England
01-44-788-573
Fax 01-44-788-577

Armstrong World Industries
P.O. Box 3511
Lancaster, PA 17604
(717) 396-5154
Fax (717) 396-5811
www.armstrong.com

Bailey International
25 Bellam Blvd., Suite 130
San Rafael, CA 94901
(415) 459-0309

Blue Heron Timber Works
305 Orchard Valley Dr.
Harriman, TN 37748
(423) 435-1371
Fax (423) 435-4616

W. A. Brown & Son
2001 S. Main St.
Salisbury, NC 28144
(704) 636-5131
Fax (704) 637-0919
www.wabrown.com

CASE-LIM Housing Systems
1863 Kalorama NW
Washington, DC 20009
(202) 232-6220
Fax (202) 232-7891

Clingan & Associates, Architects
P.O. Box 198
Ridgeland, MS 39157
(601) 981-9305
Fax (601) 981-3713

Jim Crowley Builders
10586 Salcido Ln.
Grass Valley, CA 95949
(530) 268-1242

Ferrier Builders, Inc.
1977 Live Oak Cir.
Azle, TX 76020-4317
(817) 237-6628
Fax (817) 237-5758

Foamed Polystyrene Alliance
1801 K St. NW, Suite 600K
Washington, DC 20006
(202) 974-5226
Fax (202) 296-7354
www.socplas.org

Hart Housing Group, Inc.
1025 E. Waterford
Wakarusa, IN 46573
(219) 862-4461
Fax (219) 862-4559

Hindman Manufacturing Co., Inc.
P.O. Box 1290
Salem, IL 62881
(618) 548-2800
Fax (618) 548-2890
www.americana.com

Morley Inc. Builders
700 Mississippi St.
Lawrence, KS 66044
(785) 843-7007
Fax (785) 843-7007
Specializes in the design, fabrication, and erection of SIP structures throughout the Midwest.

North Woods
P.O. Box 1166
Burlington, VT 05402-1166
(802) 644-2400
Fax (802) 644-2509
www.nwjoinery.com

PortesLaforge Doors Ltd.
P.O. Box 1688
Grand Falls, NB, Canada
(506) 473-4034
Fax (506) 473-4283
www.sn2000.nb.ca/comp/1

Premium Building Contractors, LLC
6065 North S.R. 19
Etna Green, IN 46524
371-0207
Fax (219) 858-2593

Sand Creek Construction
15850 N. 35th Ave. #6
Phoenix, AZ 85053
(602) 298-8777
Fax (602) 298-8778

Shepard Construction Group LLC
5201 N. 199th Ave.
Litchfield Park, AZ 85340
(623) 853-1033
Fax (623) 853-1034

Shirey Contracting/Enercept
1042 W. Lake Sammamish Rd.
Bellevue, WA 98008
(425) 747-3001
Fax (425) 643-3954
www.shireycontracting.com
*Distributor for Enercept SIPs in the
Pacific Northwest; provides full construction services for both residential
and commercial buildings.*

Structural Insulated Panels, Inc.
881 E. Reidhead #1
Show Low, AZ 85901
(520) 587-7271
Fax (520) 532-7271

Structural Thermal Building Systems,
LTD
P.O. Box 3365
Terre Haute, IN 47803-0365
(812) 460-1362
Fax (812) 877-8440

Sunlight Homes
9911 Glendale NE
Albuquerque, NM 87122
(505) 865-5888
Fax (505) 865-5777
www.sunlighthomes.com

The Sunworks Co.
563-D Idaho Maryland Rd.
Grass Valley, CA 95945
(530) 273-1934
Fax (530) 273-3618
www.oro.net/~sunworks

Unified Homes Consulting Firm, Inc.
7647 Widrig Rd.
Cleveland, NY 13042
(315) 675-8010
Fax (315) 675-8050
www.unifiedhomes.com

Valley Truss & Metal LTD
P.O. Box 720
Kensington, PEI, Canada
(902) 836-3661
Fax (902) 836-3671

Whitaker Design & Construction
500 Lindo Dr.
Mesquite, TX 75149
(972) 285-4759
Fax (972) 285-4759

Fabricators

Better Building Systems, Inc.
563-A Idaho Maryland Rd.
Grass Valley, CA 95945
(530) 477-8017
Fax (530) 477-1218
www.betterbuilding.com
*Specializes in the design, engineering,
prefabrication, and construction of
R-Control SIP structural systems.*

Monache Enterprises/SIPs
245 N. Hockett
Porterville, CA 93257
(559) 783-9107
Fax (559) 783-9109

Panel Built
111A New Mohawk Rd.
Nevada City, CA 95959
(530) 265-8827
Fax (530) 265-8847
*Fabricator/distributor of R-Control
SIPs, serving California and the
Western states.*

PanelPros Inc.
P.O. Box 689
Keene, NH 03431
(603) 352-8007
Fax (603) 352-7475
www.panelpros.com
*Fabricator/distributor of Insulspan
SIPs.*

Thermal Shell Homes
P.O. Box 572721
Houston, TX 77257
(800) 220-1746
Fax (713) 529-8951

Information

Alden B. Dow Archives
315 Post Rd.
Midland, MI 48640
(517) 839-2744
Fax (517) 839-2611
*Information on early development of
structural panels.*

Antarctic Support Associates
61 Inverness Dr.
Englewood, CO 80112
(303) 790-8913
Fax (303) 790-9130

Building Systems Magazine
10640 W. Girard Ave.
Lakewood, CO 80227
(303) 985-3564
Fax (303) 763-2802
*Trade magazine serving the systems-
built housing industry.*

Energy Studies in Buildings
Laboratory
Dept. of Architecture
University of Oregon
260 Onyx Bridge
Eugene, OR 97403
(541) 346-5647
Fax (541) 346-3626
darkwing.uoregon.edu/~esbl/

Environmental Building News
122 Birge St., Suite 30
Brattleboro, VT 05301
(802) 257-7300
Fax (802) 257-7304
www.ebuild.com
*Newsletter on environmentally respon-
sible design and construction.*

Florida Solar Energy Center
1679 Clearlake Rd.
Cocoa, FL 32922
(407) 638-1000
Fax (407) 638-1439

National Renewable Energy
Laboratory
1617 Cole Blvd.
Golden, CO 80401-3393
www.nrel.gov
*U.S. Department of Energy laboratory
for renewable energy and energy-
efficient research, development, and
deployment.*

Natural Resources Defense Council
71 Stevenson St.
San Francisco, CA 94105
(415) 777-0220
Fax (415) 495-5996
www.nrdc.org

Oak Ridge National Laboratory
P.O. Box 2008
Oak Ridge, TN 37830-6070
(423) 576-8176

Manufacturers

***There are more than 100
manufacturers of SIPs in the
United States; some of the leading
companies include:***

Advance Foam Plastics, Inc.
5250 N. Sherman St.
Denver, CO 80216
(303) 297-3844
Fax (303) 292-2613
www.advancefoam.com
*EPS foam products, including
R-Control panels and ICFs.*

Allied Foam Products, Inc.
P.O. Box 2861
Gainesville, GA 30503
(800) 533-2613
Fax (770) 532-8123
www.alliedfoamprod.com
R-Control panels.

Apache Products Co.
P.O. Box 160
Union, MS 39365-0160
(601) 774-8285
Fax (601) 774-5777
www.apacheproducts.com

Big Sky Insulations, Inc.
15 Arden Dr.
Belgrade, MT 59714
(406) 388-4146
Fax (406) 388-7223

Enercept, Inc.
3100 9th Ave. SE
Watertown, SD 57201
(605) 882-2222
Fax (605) 882-2753
www.enercept.com
EPS panels

Extreme Panel Technologies
P.O. Box 435
Cotton, MN 56229
(507) 423-5530
Fax (507) 423-5531
www.extremepanel.com
EPS panels

FischerSips Inc.
1843 Northwestern Pkwy.
Louisville, KY 40203
(800) 792-7477
Fax (502) 778-5587
www.fischersips.com
EPS panels; Samson Homes

Foam Laminates of Vermont
P.O. Box 102
Hinesburg, VT 05461
(802) 453-3727
Fax (802) 453-2339
www.foamlaminates.com
*Structural and nonstructural wall and
roof panels; supports the timber-
frame industry.*

Insulated Building Systems
326 McGhee Rd.
Winchester, VA 20166
(540) 662-0882
Fax (540) 662-9104
www.rcontrolibs.com
*R-Control panels with PerformGuard
termite-resistant foam cores.*

Insulspan/GLI
9012 E. U.S. 223
Blissfield, MI 49228
(517) 486-4355
Fax (517) 486-2493
www.riverbendtf.com
EPS panels.

Insulspan/Idaho
1004 McKinley Ave.
Kellogg, ID 83837
(208) 784-7373
Fax (208) 786-1500
www.insulspan.com
EPS panels.

Insulspan Southeast
806 Washington St.
Greenville, MS 38701
(800) 454-3270
Fax (601) 335-5656
EPS panels.

K. C. Panels
2110 E. 14th St.
Tucson, AZ 85719
(520) 629-0118
Prefabricated urethane panels.

Korwall Industries
326 N. Bowen Rd.
Arlington, TX 76012
(817) 277-6741
EPS panels.

Lamit Industries
P.O. Box 3002
Newark, OH 43058-3002
(740) 345-9691
Fax (740) 349-9305

Murus Industries
Rt. 549
Mansfield, PA 16933
(570) 549-2100
Fax (570) 549-2101
www.murus.com
*EPS panels, cam-lock isocyanurate
panels.*

Pacemaker Plastics Co., Inc.
126 New Pace Rd.
Newcomerstown, OH 43832
(740) 498-4181
Fax (740) 498-4184
www.pacemakerplastics.com
EPS panels.

W. H. Porter Company
4240 N. 136th Ave.
Holland, MI 49424
(616) 399-1963
Fax (616) 399-9123
www.portersips.com
EPS panels.

W. H. Porter Company
711 Airdustrial Way SW
Turnwater, WA 98502
(360) 704-3359
Fax (360) 704-3362
www.portersips.com
EPS panels.

Premier Building Systems
4609 70th Ave. E.
Fife, WA 98424
(800) 275-7086
Fax (253) 926-3992
www.pbspanels.com
EPS panel systems.

Premier Building Systems–
Mid-America
RR 1, Box 101
Mead, NE 68041
(402) 624-6611
Fax (402) 624-2325
www.pbspanels.com
EPS panel systems.

Premier Building Systems–Phoenix
3434 W. Papago St.
Phoenix, AZ 85009
(800) 240-6691
Fax (602) 269-6999
www.pbspanels.com
EPS panel systems.

Schmucker Manufacturing Company
417 E. 4th St.
Derry, PA 15627
(724) 694-8082
Fax (724) 694-9876
EPS panels.

South & Sons Panels Inc.
140 Industrial Dr.
Franklin, OH 45005
(800) 874-4088
Fax (513) 746-9706

Stress Panel Mfg., Inc.
104 S. Industrial Dr.
Arma, KS 66712
(316) 347-8200
Fax (316) 347-8202

Superior Wood Systems Inc.
1301 Garfield, P.O. Box 1208
Superior, MI 54880
(800) 375-9992

Team Industries, Inc.
4580 Airwest Dr.
Grand Rapids, MI 49512
(800) 356-5548
Fax (616) 698-0605
www.teamindustries.com
*R-Control panels with PerformGuard
insect-resistant foam cores.*

Therma Foam, Inc.
P.O. Box 161128
Ft. Worth, TX 76161
(817) 624-7204
Fax (817) 624-7264
www.r-control.com

Thermal Foams, Inc.
2101 Kenmore Ave.
Buffalo, NY 14207
(716) 874-6474
Fax (716) 874-8180
www.thermalfoams.com
*R-Control panels with PerformGuard
insect-resistant foam cores; ICFs*

Thermapan Industries, Inc.
2514 Hwy. #20 E.
Fonthill, ONT, Canada
LOS 1EO,
(905) 892-0888
Fax (905) 892-3494
www.thermapan.com
EPS panels.

Thermocore Panel Systems
60 James Baldwin Dr.
Martinsville, IN 46151
(765) 349-8312
Fax (765) 349-1483
www.thermocore.com
Prefabricated urethane panels.

Vermont Stresskin Panel
184 John Putman Memorial
Cambridge, VT 05444
(802) 644-8885
Fax (802) 644-8797
www.stresskin.com
Stresskin panel wall and roof systems
to enclose timber- and steel-frame
structures.

Winter Panel Corporation
74 Glen Ome Dr.
BrattlebW. H. Porter Inc.
711 Airdustrial Way SW
Turnwater, WA 98502
(360) 704-3359
Fax (360) 704-3362
www.portersips.com
EPS panels.

Organizations

APA–The Engineered Wood
Association
P.O. Box 11700
Tacoma, WA 98411-0700
(253) 565-6600
Fax (253) 565-7265
www.apawood.org
Formerly American Plywood
Association; nonprofit trade associa-
tion representing manufacturers of
plywood, oriented strand board,
structural composite panels, glulam,
and wood I-joists.

EPS Molders Association
2128 Epsy Ct., Suite 4
Crofton, MD 21114
(410) 451-8341
Fax (410) 451-8343
www.epsmolders.org

The Society of the Plastics Industry
1801 K St. NW, Suite 600K
Washington, DC 20006
(202) 974-5364
Fax (202) 822-8481
www.socplas.org

Structural Board Association
45 Sheppard Ave. E., Suite 412
Willowdale, ONT, Canada
(416) 730-9090
Fax (416) 730-9013
www.sba-osb.com

Structural Insulated Panel
Association
3413 A 56th St. NW
Gig Harbor, WA 98335
(253) 858-7472
Fax (253) 858-0272
www.sips.org

Suppliers

AFM R-Control Building Systems
24000 W. Hwy. 7, #201
Excelsior, MN 55331
(612) 474-0809
Fax (612) 474-2074
www.r-control.com
Group of manufacturers formed to
develop, test, manufacture, and
market consistent R-Control brand
name EPS products.

Ashland Chemical
5200 Blazer Pkwy.
Columbus, OH 43017
(614) 790-3625
Fax (614) 790-3206
www.ashland.com
Manufacturer of adhesives used in
laminating SIPs.

BASF Corporation
3000 Continental Dr. N.
Mount Olive, NJ 07828-1234
(800) 526-1072
Fax (973) 426-3904
www.basf.com
Manufacturer of styrene beads.

CI Professional Services, Inc.
P.O. Box 2059
Folsom, CA 95763-2059
(916) 988-8841
Fax (916) 989-6939
Third-party testing of materials.

DiversiFoam Products
9091 County Rd. 50
Rockford, MN 55373
(612) 477-5854
Fax (612) 477-5863
www.diversifoam.com
Extruded and expanded polystyrene
foam products.

Energy Federation Incorporated
14 Tech Cir.
Natick, MA 01760
(508) 653-4299
Fax (508) 655-3811
www.efi.org

Fomo Products, Inc.
P.O. Box 1078
Norton, OH 44203
Urethane foam and adhesives.

Fortifiber Corporation
300 Industrial Dr.
Fernley, NV 89408
(775) 575-5557
Fax (775) 575-4995
Flashing products.

Georgia-Pacific Corporation
133 Peachtree St. NE
Atlanta, GA 30348-4706
(404) 652-4706
Fax (404) 230-5624
Engineered wood products.

Greco Manufacturing Inc.
835 Terra Coop
Buchanan, MI 49107
(616) 695-3350

Huber Corporation
10925 David Taylor Dr.
Charlotte, NC 28262
(800) 933-9220
Fax (704) 547-9228
www.huberwood.com
Engineered wood products for SIPs.

Huntsman Chemical Company
5100 Bainbridge Blvd.
Chesapeake, VA 23320
(757) 494-2522
Fax (757) 494-2769
www.huntsman.com
Adhesives and chemicals for the SIP
industry.

Johns Manville Intl. Inc.
10100 W. Ute Ave.
Littleton, CO 80127
(303) 978-5579
Fax (303) 978-5082

NOVA Chemicals Inc.
400 Frankfort Rd.
Monaca, PA 15061-2298
(724) 770-5537
Fax (724) 770-2489
www.novachem.com
Manufacturer of EPS beads.

Olympic Fasteners
P.O. Box 508
Agawam, MA 01001
(800) 633-3800
Fax (413) 786-1760
Long panel screws.

Owens Corning
Technology Center, 137 East Ave.
Tallmadge, OH 44278
(330) 633-6735
Fax (330) 633-4939
www.owenscorning.com

Polyfoam Packers Corporation
431 Allied Dr.
Nashville, TN 37211
(615) 832-6222
Fax (615) 832-1983
www.polyfoam.com

Polyfoam Packers Corporation
2320 Foster Ave.
Wheelin, IL 60090
(847) 398-0110
Fax (847) 398-8052
www.polyfoam.com

Reichhold Chemicals, Inc.
P.O. Box 13582
Reasearch Triangle Park, NC
27709-3582
(800) 213-4805
Fax (919) 990-7886
www.reichhold.com

Rohm & Haas
100 N. Riverside Dr.
Chicago, IL 60606
(312) 807-3136
Fax (815) 338-2653
*Adhesives and chemicals for SIP
industry.*

Simpson Strong-Tie Co., Inc.
4875 Long Shadowy Dr.
Coeur d'Alene, ID 83814
(800) 925-5099
Fax (208) 676-1903
Connectors and hold-downs.

Tolko Industries
P.O. Box 39
Vernon, BC, Canada
(250) 549-5318
Fax (250) 545-5133
www.tolko.com
Engineered wood products.

Trus Joist MacMillan
501 E. 45th St.
Boise, ID 83714
(208) 376-7506
Fax (208) 373-2938
www.tjm.com
Engineered wood products.

United States Gypsum Co.
125 S. Franklin St.
Chicago, IL 60606
(312) 606-4428
Fax (312) 606-4476
www.usg.com
Drywall and plaster products.

Weyerhaeuser Company
2568-A Riva Rd.
Annapolis, MD 21401
(410) 224-4751
Fax (410) 266-6990
www.weyerhaeuser.com
OSB and plywood panels.

Testing Agencies

***The following are third-party
testing agencies for the SIP
industry:***

PFS Corp.
2402 Daniels St.
Madison, WI 53718
(608) 221-3361
Fax (608) 221-2084
www.pfs-teco.com

RADCO
3220 E. 59th St., Suite 33
Long Beach, CA 90805
(562) 272-7231
Fax (562) 529-7513
www.RADCOinc.com

TECO
2402 Daniels St.
Madison, WI 53718
(608) 221-3361
Fax (608) 221-0180
www.pfs-teco.com

Tools

Black Bros. Co.
501 Ninth Ave.
Mendota, IL 61342-0410
(815) 539-7451
Fax (815) 538-2451
www.blackbros.com
*Panel presses and machinery used to
manufacture SIPs.*

Calculated Industries
4840 Hytech Dr.
Carson City, NV 89706
(702) 885-4975
Hand-held calculators.

Demand Products Inc.
1055 Nine North Dr.
Alpharetta, GA 30004
(770) 772-7448
Fax (888) 534-838X
Hot Rod foam-shaping tools.

Kahnetics LLC
1000 Luskin Rd.
Apex, NC 27502
(800) 447-6326
Pneumatic caulk guns.

L & H Manufacturing Co.
410 6th St. SE
Mandan, ND 58554
Resistance foam-shaping tools.

Little Samson, Inc.
P.O. Box 96
Plains, MT 59859
(800) 973-5438
Small cranes and lifting devices.

Muskegon Power Tool
2357 Whitehall Rd.
Muskegon, MI 49445
(800) 635-5465
Fax (616) 766-3846
Linear Link chainsaw.

Prazi U.S.A.
P.O. Box 1165
Plymouth, MA 02362
(800) 262-0211
Fax (508) 746-8655
www.praziusa.com
Beam saw attachment.

Windlock Corporation
1055 Leisczs Bridge Rd.
Leesport, PA 19533
(877) 468-5643
Fax (610) 926-5997
www.hotknife.com
Foam-shaping and cutting tools.

*For further information on SIPs, a
comprehensive directory of industry
professionals, and links to related sites,
visit the author's website at
www.sipsmart.com.*

Index

A

ACH: *See* Air changes per hour.
Additions:
    process for, 57
    requirements for, 56
Adhesives, characteristics of, 26–27
Air, quality of, 156–57
Air changes per hour (ACH), comparisons of, 155
Air conditioning. *See* HVAC systems.
Architects, education of, 41–43

B

Basements:
    foundation panels for, 105
    heat loss from, 105
    walk-out, 106
    See also Slabs
Boom trucks: *See* Cranes.
Brick veneer, corner detail for, 83
Building, efficiency of, 46
Building codes, acceptance by, 8

C

Cabinetry, methods for, 152–53
Caulk,
    adhesive, for EPS, 68
    guns for, 65
Ceilings:
    finish materials for, 172–73
    moisture-proofing, 173
Commercial buildings, advantages of, 50–52
Cranes:
    preparing for, 132
    safety guidelines with, 133
Cutting:
    jigs for, 68–69
    templates for, 68–69

D

Design:
    CAD, advantage of, 39–41, 43
    engineered, 43–44
    flexibility of, 47
    for on-site fabrication, 77
    possibilities of, 48
    See also Drawings
Doors:
    flashing, 164–67
    headers for, 85–87
    openings for,
        assembling, 114–15
        in-place cutting, 107, 116
        prefabricating, 114, 116
    rough openings for, 84, 85
    sills for, 85–87
Dormers, adding, 100
Drawings:
    of elevations, 78
    floor-plan, 77–78
    and lumber stream, 78–79

E

Earthquakes, resistance to, 175
Electricity: *See* Wiring.
Energy efficiency:
    government program citing, 177
    possibilities for, 48, 50
    subdivision of, 54
    tested, on-site, 44–46
Energy Star Homes Program, discussed, 177

F

Fabrication:
    ordered vs. on-site, 75–77
    subcontracted, 76
    of roof panels, 90–101
    of wall panels, 78–90
Facings:
    oriented-strand board (OSB), 21–22
    secondary, 23
Finishes:
    exterior, 159–71
    interior, 171–73
    See also Roofing; Siding

Fire resistance, tested, 35–37, 175–76
Flashing, for door and window openings, 164–67
Floors:
    panels for, 109
    second-story, 122–24
    sub-, layout for, 108–110
Foam:
    kits for, 68
    termite-resistant, 176
Foundations:
    panels for, 104–105
    trueness of, need for, 104
Framing:
    steel, and SIPs, 51–52
    timber, 52, 53

G

Geodesic domes, possibilities for, 52–53

H

Headers, factory vs. fabricating, 86–87
Heat exchangers:
    importance of, 157
    need for, 45
Heating systems: *See* HVAC systems.
High-end projects, advantages of, 49–50
Hold-downs: *See* Metal connectors.
House wraps, redundancy of, 164
Hurricanes, resistance to, 175
HVAC systems:
    ducted, 155
    radiant, 156
    sizing, and ACH factor, 155–56
    for tight envelopes, 154–55

I

Insect resistance, discussed, 36, 176
Insulated concrete form systems, compared, 174–75